Genders in Production

Genders in Production

Making Workers in
Mexico's Global Factories

Leslie Salzinger

UNIVERSITY OF CALIFORNIA PRESS

Berkeley / Los Angeles / London

University of California Press
Berkeley and Los Angeles, California

University of California Press, Ltd.
London, England

© 2003 by the Regents of the University of California

Grateful acknowledgment is made for reuse of material from previous
publications by the author: "From High Heels to Swathed Bodies:
Gendered Meanings under Production in Mexico's Export-Processing
Industry," in *Feminist Studies,* vol. 23, no. 3 (Fall 1997): 549–574, by
permission of the publisher, Feminist Studies, Inc., and "Manufacturing
Sexual Subjects: 'Harassment,' Desire and Discipline on a Maquiladora
Shopfloor," in *Ethnography,* vol. 1, no. 1 (July 2000): 67–92, reprinted
by permission of Sage Publications Ltd. (© 2000 Sage Publications Ltd).

Library of Congress Cataloging-in-Publication Data

Salzinger, Leslie
   Genders in production : making workers in Mexico's global factories /
Leslie Salzinger.
      p.   cm.
Includes bibliographical references and index.
   ISBN 0-520-22494-9 (Cloth : alk. paper) — ISBN 0-520-23539-8 (Paper :
alk. paper)
   1. Women offshore assembly industry workers—Mexico—Ciudad
Juárez—Case studies.   2. Sex role in the work environment—Mexico—
Ciudad Juárez—Case studies.   3. Working class women—Mexico—
Ciudad Juárez—Case studies.   I. Title.
   HD6073.0332 M486   2003
   306.3'615'097216—dc21

                                                          2002013908

Manufactured in the United States of America

12 11 10 09 08 07 06 05 04 03
10 9 8 7 6 5 4 3 2 1

For Tova,
with all my love

Contents

Acknowledgments

This project has been with me for the better part of a decade. In the process, I have been inspired, helped, and supported by a shifting host of friends and colleagues. It is my great pleasure to name them from the beginning.

My first debts go back to the early nineties, when I had the good fortune to grapple with feminist theory in the company of friends. Deborah Little, Ann Ferguson, Deborah Gerson, Teri Pohl, and I struggled to capture the nature, meaning, and experience of gender, and to confront the tricky and profound links between politics, emotions, and intellectual work. Despite the time and distance accumulated since those conversations, this work remains my attempt to answer some of the questions we first formulated together.

Michael Burawoy—chair, colleague, friend, inspiration . . . Michael first introduced me to ethnography—a practice which has transformed my ways of living and seeing both inside and outside the academy. And once having started me off on my journey, he was a dependable companion—responding to long letters from the field and endless drafts with generous, insightful, and clarifying commentary. Working with students myself now, I am only the more impressed. On my committee, Peter Evans's expressive confidence and easy, intense engagement made thinking through problems the pleasure it should be. My thanks too to Kristin Luker and Dick Walker for readings and conversation.

The project has had many institutional homes and supports. The research was supported by the Fulbright-Hays Doctoral Research Abroad fellowship, by the OAS Regular Training Program fellowship, and by the Woodrow Wilson Dissertation Award in Women's Studies. Writing was supported by several fellowships from the UC Berkeley Department of Sociology and by the Center for U.S.-Mexican Studies at UCSD. During my research, I was affiliated with the Colegio de la Frontera Norte (COLEF) of Ciudad Juárez. They provided more than a mere affiliation. While I was in Juárez, COLEF was often community and company as well. They also gave me access to the Centro de Orientación de la Mujer Obrera (COMO) archives on their premises, on which most of Chapter 3 is based. Martín Camps also provided invaluable research assistance for that chapter, working in other newspaper archives in the city. Following my research, I spent a year at the congenial Center for U.S.-Mexican Studies at UCSD. The manuscript's final revisions were done at the University of Chicago, where the crackling intellectual atmosphere helpfully pushed me into new intellectual worlds. I am deeply grateful to all.

At every stage, I have been blessed by incredible friendships. In Ciudad Juárez, Marta Silvia Montañez welcomed me with open arms into her life and extended family. Her insights into the life of the maquilas—intellectual, political, and personal—are reflected on every page of the manuscript. For political/intellectual conversation and ongoing companionship, I am indebted to Pablo Vila, Eduardo Barrera, Wilivaldo Delgadillo, Cipriano Jurado, Jesús Montenegro, Patricia Mendoza, and Beatríz Vera. In El Paso, Debbie Nathan and Barbara Ferry provided much-needed doses of politics, humor, skepticism, and interest, reminding me that the work had real-world antecedents and consequences. In El Paso, Pablo, Juanchi, and Paloma Vila were my family. Such relationships go beyond thanks.

In San Diego, Jeff Rubin and Steve Epstein read, commented, and brainstormed with me, becoming the friends and colleagues they remain today. Continuing in Berkeley, Julian Gowan and Jackie Orr made intellectual work possible. Always eager to engage personally, politically, and intellectually, able to help me find my way back to the reasons for writing, they both remain partners and inspirations. Beth Sauerhaft, friend on two coasts and over many lives, reminded me of the importance of thinking with integrity inside and outside the academy alike.

As I began rewriting the introduction to this book, I was able to take stock of how much I had learned, in formal and informal settings alike, at the University of Chicago. My deepest thanks for both friendship and intellectual inspiration to Leora Auslander, Susan Gal, Lisa Wedeen, Nadia Abu El-Haj, Saskia Sassen, Bill Sewell, Moishe Postone, and

Norma Field. I am particularly grateful to Susan Gal for the great gift of reading and commenting on the final manuscript.

Eric Hirsch kept me company when writing got lonely—exploring prairies, reading drafts, reminding me of a life beyond the academy. Fortunately for me, his capacity to take inchoate ideas and turn them into schematic outlines is unparalleled. The marks of that skill are on every chapter of the book. For all this, thank you only grazes the surface. Suzy Salzinger and John Antrobus offered my daughter and me a home, company, and "real dinners" during the book's final revisions. We were very lucky.

Many people commented on many versions of the material presented here, often on short notice, often in writing. My deepest gratitude to Michael Burawoy, Susan Gal, John Lie, Jackie Orr, Deborah Little, Eric Hirsch, Ava Baron, Peter Evans, Leslie Sklair, Debbie Nathan, Julian Gowan, Jeff Rubin, Steve Epstein, Suzy Salzinger, Pablo Vila, Josh Gamson, Deborah Gerson, Leora Auslander, Richard Walker, and Kristin Luker, as well as two anonymous reviewers for the University of California Press. My thanks also to members of workshops at Berkeley, Madison, UCLA, and the University of Chicago, and to Jennifer Pierce's graduate seminar, where audiences and readers perceptively engaged my work. Throughout a very long process, Naomi Schneider, my editor at UC Press, kept the faith—making tactful and perceptive suggestions without pushing, and chatting about life in the interstices. Debbie Nathan and Sue Carter both provided thoughtful and engaged responses above and beyond the duty of "copy editor." Sue Heinemann shepherded the book through the production process with great equanimity. Again, many thanks.

Finally, I am immensely grateful to the many people who spoke with me in Ciudad Juárez. Managers at the plants discussed here gave me extraordinary access. I am only sorry that confidentiality requirements keep me from naming them. I am deeply indebted to them for their willingness to discuss the intricacies of their work, and to answer my sometimes interminable questions. To the young women and men I worked beside, gossiped with, confided in, and listened to on these shop floors, my debts are of a different sort. From distant locations, we formed intense links. It was within those connections that I formed this account of the moment-by-moment creation of gendered subjectivities. I only hope I have done their experiences something close to justice.

The book is dedicated to my daughter, Tova, with the wild but tenacious hope that in understanding something of how gender works, she will inhabit a less constraining world.

Ways of Seeing

On a cold, dark morning in the winter of 1992 I stand blankly in front of my closet. Subject to my subject, I am once again rooted to the spot, wondering what to wear. My goal is to be at Panoptimex,[1] my factory fieldsite, in an hour, and things are not looking good. Back in Berkeley, my loose, layered clothes performed a legible, if expressly conflicted, femininity. Here the same clothes speak a different language—dowdy and desexualized to the point of unintelligibility.

Panoptimex is a global factory located in Ciudad Juárez, on Mexico's northern border. Owned by one of the hundreds of transnational corporations that have come to this desert outpost to produce goods for the U.S. market, the plant is a glowing example of the corporate fruits of globalization. It is also a socialist-feminist nightmare made flesh. A pristine TV assembler full of young women, it is a profoundly objectifying space—both sexually and otherwise.

My new fashion self-consciousness and the young, sexualized women who fill the shop floor are both at the fulcrum of a fundamental economic process—the creation of "cheap labor" for transnational production. Although the young women working in global assembly are generally understood as intrinsically "cheap, docile, and dextrous"—as original instances of a natural femininity—time spent on transnational shop floors suggests otherwise. Panoptimex, like all effective arenas of production, makes not only TVs but workers. The bedecked young women who surround me on the shop floor are reproductions of a global fantasy, generated by the shop floor itself. These willing, supplementary earners, objects of managers' multiple desires, are in fact management's unconscious creation. They are formed by the fantasy of a naturally productive femininity even as it purports to describe them.

Transnational capital's dream of productive femininity is not always invoked as successfully as it is in Panoptimex, but in global production, it is always at work. In the three other factories I studied, gendered discourses elicit dramatically different subjects: assertive, "nontraditional" women in one; masculinized producers in a second; embattled, would-be men in a third. The image of productive femininity sets the parameters through which workers are identified and assessed on shop floors around the world, but its consequences are multiple. Against its gendered injunctions, different shop floors generate different workers. Tracing this process, we will follow the category of productive femininity into Ciudad Juárez, where it shapes a labor market, and then further onto these four contrasting shop floors, where it constitutes equally varied gendered subjects. In the process, we can begin to grasp gender's centrality in global production and weigh its consequences for people and profits.

The ever more frenetic and far-flung search for the ideal assembly worker—malleable, "trainable," undemanding—is reshaping the contemporary world. Understanding that capital makes rather than finds such workers, and that gender is implicated in that process, gives us new tools for thinking about how we might challenge the terms under which global production takes place. Thus, starting from the feminist injunction that the personal is political, we add the economic, making visible the connections between the production of subjects and the production of commodities.

It would be unbearably ironic to embark on such an investigation without placing oneself within the panorama. Thus, as observer and analyst, both in the field and in my writing, I attempt to define my position and to keep that position apparent.[2] This is not because the book is about me. It is not. Rather, in clarifying my location, I give the reader the chance to understand the social/intellectual vantage point from which this story is told. My account aims to be what Haraway felicitously named "situated knowledge"[3]—knowledge created from a self-conscious and explicit political and theoretical perspective.

This commitment means that the book is written in at least two registers. Its bulk, measured in words and pages, is description and story, filtered through my own personal, political, and theoretical commitments and habits of attention. Here my aim is to bring the reader with me into the social world of the plants, to make obvious the way that gendered selves come to matter in global production. In these descriptive sections, theory is mostly embedded in the narrative, not pulled out for autonomous treatment. In contrast, Chapters 2 and 8 are primarily analytic and theoretical, exposing the structure that undergirds the narrative chapters.

My fieldwork, which involved immersion in one of the many local universes of global production, began in late 1991 and ended in the summer of 1993. I located myself in northern Mexico, where I did fieldwork for sixteen months along the border in Ciudad Juárez and for two months in a small agricultural city to its south. During that time, I worked in a group of transnationally owned export-processing plants known as *maquilas*.[4] I interviewed managers, workers, job seekers, company lawyers, and industry representatives. I toured shop floors and read newspapers. I searched archives for records of the industry from its inception through the early nineties.[5] I spent a summer watching for organized resistance.[6] Most important, however, I worked as an ethnographer. For a feminist investigating transnational economic processes, ethnography was an obvious choice. The use of the embodied, emotional, thoughtful self as a research "instrument" is well suited to the enterprise of making connections between the purportedly public and private, between economics and gender, between the production of workers and that of their products.[7] Thus, I immersed myself in the habits and taken-for-granteds of four shop floors, observing and sometimes participating in the meaningful practices and practiced meanings of daily production.[8]

Throughout those journeys, I kept myself attentive to gender and to specificity. That is, I attended to the economic and political causes and consequences of the emergence of gendered subjects in production, and within that context I kept an eye open for difference, for variation, for idiosyncrasy. These attentional practices are motivated in equal parts politically, theoretically, and empirically. Much of the following chapter is devoted to accounting for their prominence in the analysis.

Readers have my points of departure laid out in Chapter 2, but the people I studied had little context for a "sociologist." Despite my many attempts to account for myself, they never had access to the social world within which I was intelligible, either to myself or others. The confusion this engendered merged into disquiet as my repeated oscillations between participant and observer raised questions of membership, judgment, and power. These responses emerged with particular force in Panoptimex, where labor control was already expressed and enforced through multiple hierarchies of watching and watched. A telling pair of incidents revolved around the figure of my car—a tiny, ancient Ford Fiesta with a smashed-up front. Early in my period in the plant, the American personnel manager invited me to attend his negotiations with the union, held in an elite local club. As we emerged together from its dim recesses into the harsh Juárez daylight, my car stood directly before us, an eyesore in a parking lot full of shiny sedans with tinted windows. "*That's* yours?" I reluctantly admitted it was. "Oh, you bought it here." He offered the explanation laughing—a gleeful American co-conspirator. My abashed admission that it was *really* mine, that I had actually brought it with me across the border, stopped him in his tracks. For several days he was noticeably less forthcoming, until eventually I seemed to blend back into expat togetherness. Nonetheless, the query made momentarily visible always hovered in the background of our conversations: Was I "us" or "them"? And if them, which "them" was that?

A couple of months later, a supervisor with understandably different concerns from those of his boss hesitantly asked about a story circulating among his colleagues. Rumor had it, he said, that my car had an incredible motor camouflaged beneath its battered exterior. Was that true? I hastened to reassure him of its authentic ricketyness. Nonetheless, the question suggested both the depths of distrust and the effort being expended in placing me. Perhaps the friendly, underdressed, Spanish-speaking woman who looked as young as a worker was actually another watchful gringo whose sharp eyes spelled trouble. What power lurked beneath the disarming exterior?

These confusions were not my "subjects'" alone. Over the course of a day's fieldwork, I found myself identifying in vertiginous succession with worker and manager, woman and man, Mexican and American. When I worked on the line, a single error was enough to throw me from analyst of supervisory tactics to crushed, inept worker. Chatting intimately with a woman in the next work station, an insinuating, hungrily curious, "but in the United States, the women are very *liberated*,[9] aren't they?" catapulted me from engrossed confidant back into recognition of my otherness. Complacent flirtation and feminist refusal took unpredictable turns. Managerial interviews were journeys into the empathy that flows from deep listening. Later, typing fieldnotes in the evening, I found myself broiling as I assessed the damaging consequences for workers of these so-understandable perspectives.

These constant shifts were confusing, but they were also productive, of power and knowledge alike. Once at home, writing, I was indeed

evaluator and judge. I was creating a portrait whose parameters its subjects would ultimately not control, often written through the lens of a
politics they did not share. What's more, it was precisely the dizzying
and constant shifts from watched to watcher, from participant to observer, that made it possible for me to tell this story at all. These movements and contextual truths were unsettling for everyone concerned,
but they were not something to fix. On the contrary, such movements
across identifications and social terrain and from intimate to analyst and
back again are the inherently problematic meat of ethnographic work.[10]
It was precisely this set of processes that revealed the social world I
sought to describe. Later, as I moved from one plant to another, once
even between plants competing for status and resources within a single
corporation, these issues became still more complex. Nonetheless, they
remained productive, every oscillation in my local role or social experience a new clue to the gendered configuration of production in a given
factory.

In every factory, gender has a distinctive architecture, structured and
bounded by managers' ongoing, sometimes contradictory, efforts to
constitute productive workers. These attempts are incarnated in the
most mundane, repetitive, and trivial of linguistic and bodily practices.
Their repercussions are reflected in the texture of shop-floor life—in
mood, conversation, relationship, gesture, style. As I located myself
within this field, the practice of participant observation became one of
honing attention, of learning to watch others, to watch myself watch
others, to watch myself in action and reaction. Thus, I saw supervisory
pressures and social dynamics from without, but I also learned their
contours through watching my own responses, experiencing them from
within the social world of the factory and from within myself.

Panoptimex was my entry point into the industry. The head of personnel approved my presence casually, if brusquely, refusing my request
to work but otherwise imposing few restrictions. Nonetheless, as the
weeks went by, I felt increasingly uncomfortable. Returning exhausted
in the late afternoons, I would find my room strewn with discarded
clothes—too baggy, too shabby, too loose. Weekends I bought lipsticks, pale attempts to blend with the fiery, two-tone oranges and reds
in the plant and still recognize myself. Despite my best efforts to pass,
the women of Panoptimex kept offering unsolicited beauty tips.
Guided by my own discomfort, I began to notice the centrality of the
visual in the plant—the primacy of appearance as a rhetoric through
which production was grasped as well as beauty. My role as she-who-

needs-fashion-advice made evident the process through which an apparently preexisting femininity was actually created through managerial strategies of shop-floor control.

The second plant I entered was Anarchomex, a mixed-gender Juárez auto parts plant. The shop floors could not have been more different. It was dark, noisy, and chaotic in Anarchomex, and supervisors appeared on the line only to yell. Over my first incompetent weeks, I found myself constantly entangled with two young men just down the line. Sometimes they snapped, mocked, and complained at my falling behind. Sometimes they came by to help, speeding me up immeasurably and making errors throughout, to the line technician's immeasurable irritation. Sometimes they worked ahead, interfering with my tenuous rhythm so they could finish early and take a flirting break—either with me or other women. To the amusement of my colleagues at a local research institute, I became obsessed with speed, coming in after work not with astute sociological observations, but with endless talk about keeping up. Again, my social discomfort proved to be a rich lode of information, as it propelled me to recognize male workers' ongoing struggle to redefine and claim a legitimate masculinity—and the disastrous consequences of this struggle for production quality. Here, it was not women but gendered meanings that were on the line.

From Anarchomex I moved to Particimex, a subsidiary of the same corporation which owned Anarchomex, using virtually the same technical process. Nonetheless, once again the plants felt remarkably different. Particimex was located in a small city south of Juárez, where desperate managers had moved in search of the legendarily pre-controlled women they could no longer rely on in the larger city to the north. And in Santa María, they indeed found daughters and wives home schooled in obedient gestures. Nonetheless, to my eye, on the shop floor these women did not appear docile. To the contrary, I found myself constantly taken aback by the contrasts between what happened inside and outside the plant. Accounts of evenings spent with my co-workers, who waited interminably to be asked to dance, sat jarringly in my fieldnotes next to stories of their take-charge attitudes at work. Disconcerted by these contradictory experiences, I began to notice the emphatic, persistent managerial description of Particimex workers as *not*–"traditional Mexican women." Labor control practices in Particimex addressed women workers in direct and explicit contrast to common transnational images of third-world femininity. It was this process that evoked women workers' remarkable shop-floor assertiveness. By the time I left Particimex, I had begun to grasp the possible magnitude of variation in the content of femininity across space and time.

Andromex, a mixed-gender Juárez hospital garments plant, was my last—and initially my most daunting—fieldsite. Gender seemed invisible, femininity absent. One day, shortly after I began work at the smock folders' table, we returned from lunch to find my completed work missing. I was slow; there wasn't much to steal. It was public knowledge that the maquila wasn't paying me. Nonetheless, indignation over my loss consumed the work group for the rest of the day and re-erupted periodically throughout my tenure in the plant. My coworkers speculated over who was responsible, ruminated on how they'd managed to get away with it, and excoriated those responsible as immoral. Wondering over this obsessive accounting, I came to realize that the apparent absence of femininity was not something to debunk, it was an anomaly for analysis. The indignation, the ongoing fomentation of conflict, were central here. These shop-floor practices responded to a framework that located them within the implicitly masculinized category of breadwinner/producer. Femininity was not elaborated here because women and men alike were addressed within masculinized categories, leading to the intense shop-floor competition over productivity. For the first time, over meager piles of smocks, I began to consider the place of masculinity in transnational production.

Analysis is its own fieldsite. Over time, my fieldnotes became an independent object, and incidents widely separated by time and space were thrown into close proximity. Although I was struck by the idiosyncrasies of each plant during fieldwork, it was, ironically, only during my later search for general patterns that I came to appreciate not only the powerful impact that gendered ways of seeing had on the industry as a whole, but the enormous and highly contingent range of gendered subjects who actually emerged within industry bounds. The book tells these intertwined stories, emphasizing the combination of gender's persistent presence and unique configuration in each plant.

It is tempting to speak about transnational production as a process that develops without people, or conversely, to assume that it is composed of the accrued actions of many preset individuals. The reality is more complex and more interesting—and it became visible to me only as I placed my socially susceptible self on the line and noticed what happened. Once located in the distinctive crosscurrents of a particular shop floor, my own embodied self-consciousness showed the marks of its pressures and eddies. In the process, "femininity's" generative rather than descriptive character became apparent, and it became possible to trace the impact of gendered meanings on who workers are and ultimately on commodity production itself. Thus, through ethnography, I was able to enter the gendered heart of global production, where the subjects who produce are themselves produced. In consciously situating my idiosyncratic, theorizing self in that space, I became capable of telling meaningful stories about the world beyond.

2

Producing Women

Femininity on the Line

The image of a nubile young woman bent over a motherboard haunts contemporary global production. It provides a structure of expectations within which hiring and supervision occur in export-processing factories around the globe. This image is important not because it reflects reality, but because it constitutes reality—functioning as a template against which workers are imagined and imagine themselves. In this process, the image evokes a wide variety of subjectivities. It is through these subjectivities that workers produce, or resist producing, on shop floors throughout the world. Habits of being "womanly," structures of feeling "manly"—we rarely think of these when confronted by the wave of commodities and profits that roll from third world to first. However, immersing ourselves in the social worlds from which these objects emerge, we can see how local femininities and masculinities shape the course of production. The pages that follow explore this process—investigating the role of gendered meanings in constituting subjects in global factories and exploring the ramifications of that process for transnational production itself.

Globalization has many components, but a central impetus for the process as a whole is capital's increased capacity to move in search of better—cheaper, more malleable, more highly skilled—workers. Insofar as these assessments are made in terms of gender, gender becomes a central feature of the process.[1] Furthermore, the inextricable connections between hiring and labor control mean that the criteria by which workers are initially defined as hireable continue to function on the shop floor, as workers are addressed in production via the categories through

9

which they were hired. Thus, gender operates throughout global production, framing decisions about technology, hiring, and labor control. In the process, these gendered meanings and practices name, describe, and thus create workers' shop-floor subjectivities, with consequences for both resistance and productivity.

Gender's significance—both its specific meaning and its level of importance—varies widely across social arenas.[2] In contemporary transnational managerial frameworks,[3] "femininity" has become closely linked to productivity, and "masculinity" to sloth and disruption. Thus, the icon of the "docile and dextrous" woman worker has emerged as a standard against which all potential workers are assessed in these industries. Of course, managerial images of preestablished feminine productivity do not accurately describe shop-floor realities. Anyone who has spent time observing capitalist production knows the impossibility of simply hiring shop-floor acquiescence—feminine or otherwise.[4] Docility, no matter who exhibits it, is produced on the shop floor, not acquired ready-made. The notion of an "always-already"[5] docile, dextrous, and cheap woman, that is, of a potential worker whose productive femininity requires not creation but recognition, is thus a transnationally produced fantasy. Nonetheless, it is a fantasy with consequences, for it is precisely within these gendered discourses that decisions about production are made and that shop-floor subjects—whether productive or resistant—are constituted.[6]

The global nature of corporate rhetoric lends remarkable staying power to its claims—even when those claims are contradicted by local experiences. As a result, the mirage of guaranteed feminine productivity operates throughout the variegated field of transnational production, shaping hiring, labor control, and overall assessments of what is possible on global shop floors. Even when specific shop-floor assumptions about femininity and masculinity bypass the question of productivity or ignore gender entirely, they do so within the parameters of the overarching discourse. It is the hegemonic nature of the idea of productive femininity, rather than its precise reincarnation in diverse production contexts, which makes it so empirically important and analytically interesting.

Local variations of this transnationally produced icon are due mainly to the way such images enter functioning social arenas. Every shop floor is a discrete, if multiply linked, social universe, structured through the intersection of a unique set of imperatives and understandings. The transnationally generated "fact" of women's docility is "cited,"[7] filtered, and transformed within each of these contexts, to widely varied effect. Managers' other commitments, intentions, tactics, and limitations interact with gendered paradigms, producing shop floors that differ in what is taken for granted. The result is a set of sui generis femininities and masculinities. It is these gendered subjects who are ultimately responsible for producing the widgets, profits, and losses of transnational production.

These processes are clearly in evidence in the maquiladora industry located on Mexico's northern border. Export-processing plants were first established in the 1960s, in self-conscious imitation of the export-processing plants then emerging in East Asia.[8] This development model made a reserve army of docile and dextrous young women its centerpiece.[9] Thus, the feminine image of the ideal worker framed maquila industry development from the outset, leading to young women's widespread recruitment by management and their male peers' equally generalized depreciation. Ultimately, and somewhat ironically, this paradigm forced maquila managers to deal with unruly women as well as young men of all sorts, as the supply of young women willing to work for low wages fell dramatically in the boom of the 1980s, and their purportedly natural docility proved fragile in the face of a tight labor market. In reluctant response to these developments, some managers imported women from outside border cities, some moved production further south, and most hired men into the industry's feminized job descriptions. By the early nineties, the image of the Young Woman Worker was as present as ever in the maquila industry, but was operating in a highly diverse set of shop floors populated by a wide variety of workers.

As a consequence of this history, maquila shop floors are a fertile arena in which to investigate how gender really operates in global production. Maquila jobs are indeed "feminized," but this does not mean they are occupied solely by women. To the contrary, feminization here emerges as a discursive process which operates on both female and male bodies, producing a pool of "maquila-grade" labor.[10] Inside the plants, a more diverse set of gendered meaning structures generate productive (or resistant) local subjects. These factory-level discourses interact with, but do not necessarily reproduce, the larger narrative of worker femininity. Thus, the shop floor is an important site in the feminization of transnational production, and ethnographic immersion in an individual plant's daily routines and emotions is an apt method of catching this gendering in action.

Engendering the Global

As young women increasingly emerged as the workers of choice in global industries in the seventies and eighties, discussion of the phenomenon flourished. Even theorists for whom gender was not a fundamental variable acknowledged the distinct impact of the new organization of production on women and men.[11] Perhaps more important, the image of third-world girls snatching jobs from first-world (male) breadwinners became a set piece in political rhetoric and a magnet for first-world public anxieties. Within this context, feminist social scientists and activists began to analyze the gendering of global production more systematically, arguing that the process was as problematic for those being drawn into production as for those being expelled.[12]

Among the earliest and most influential analyses of these processes was a body of writing by leftists and socialist-feminists which came to be loosely tagged in the eighties as the "new international division of labor" literature.[13] Folker Fröbel and his colleagues had first identified these processes in the late seventies,[14] noting women's overwhelming representation in export-processing workforces, but not discussing it. It remained for others to elaborate and theorize this observation. In 1983 Annette Fuentes and Barbara Ehrenreich published an influential pamphlet, *Women in the Global Factory,* which focused directly on the reasons for this predominance. Along with others investigating this shifting economy, these writers argued that transnational capital's ability to extract high levels of surplus value was contingent upon its access to cheap, docile, and dextrous women workers. That is, young women were not merely useful to global production, they were intrinsic to its operation. It was in filling production lines with exploitable workers that transnational factories guaranteed the high profit margins required by late capitalism. In this formulation, capitalism was understood to have an essentially parasitic relationship to a preexisting and entrenched household patriarchy. By piggybacking on family structures which enabled women's cheapness, enforced their docility, and trained their nimble fingers, capitalists made shop-floor management unnecessary. Effectively, femininity enabled global corporate profits.

These analysts argued that gender subordination lay at the heart of global production's skyrocketing third-world profits. That claim had two implications: first, that labor control processes are fundamentally shaped around the gender of those hired; and second, that gender's importance increases as the search for cheap labor accelerates in response to technical advances. The first of these claims has been extensively theorized in the last decade, as feminist analysts of work have begun to demonstrate that production overall is structured through gendered assumptions.[15] Most recently, a few ethnographers of transnational production have begun to follow this thread into global factories, providing analyses that show the centrality of gender in particular sites and tracing the consequences of this fact.[16] As a result, in thinking through these questions today, we have far better theory and data than were available to earlier scholars.

Nonetheless, despite exhaustive quantitative evidence, increasingly sophisticated conceptual tools for linking gender and other social structures, and compelling ethnographic evidence, the work of the analysts who defined the new international division of labor has generated surprisingly few echoes in the major works of the "globalization theorists" which have emerged in the last decade. Although a flourishing literature on consumption, citizenship, and transnational identities[17] has begun to conceptualize gender as central to globalization, such considerations are strikingly absent in analyses of transnational production.[18]

Assessing the role of gender in global production thus requires that we return to these earlier theorists and more precisely assess their contributions and distortions. These authors, and the many activists and nonacademic writers who joined them,[19] recognized women's overwhelming presence in transnational production as an integral element in the system. That breakthrough remains pivotal to any serious analysis of global production. Nonetheless, their analysis of this fact was limited. Because these scholars focused on labor markets and hiring processes, stopping their research at the factory gates, they were able to show the correlation between gender and job, but not the processes through which such correlations were established. Thus, their theories about the mechanisms through which gender operates in production were essentially speculative. This book intends to remedy that omission by entering the shop floor and watching gender at work. Before entering that arena, though, we need to grind our lens.[20] We will begin by considering closely the claims of these authors, identifying what enabled them to see and what obscured their vision.

Made to Order?

Theorists who first described the new international division of labor began from the classically feminist insight that women's work fuels global production, and that this matters not just for "women," but for production itself. In keeping with much of the feminist writing of the period, however,[21] their capacity to conceptualize the process through which gender comes to matter was impeded by their tendency to take the category of "woman" for granted. That is, they failed to question the notion that women workers necessarily would exhibit a predictable and consistent constellation of "feminine" traits. Instead, while denying femininity's biological roots, they accepted its inevitable and static nature. Locating its origins firmly in the patriarchal family, they wrote as if these early experiences had consequences as straitening and predictable as biology itself.[22] Thus, they decried capital's invidious use of women's intrinsic exploitability, without checking to see if such exploitability was indeed available for the asking. Certainly they did not try to account for its local emergence.

The data they used to investigate these questions, primarily quantitative data showing women's preponderance in assembly jobs and managers' accounts of their own decision making,[23] contributed to the static nature of their vision of gender at work. In the sixties and seventies, as producers took flight from demanding workforces in the rich countries to scour the globe for cheaper and more malleable labor, they were transfixed by the hope and promise of hiring for shop-floor control. Good workers, they believed, could be found ready-made.[24] In response to this emergent demand, local promoters' accounts lauded the innate pliancy and nimble fingers of "their" women workers and emphasized the possibilities inherent in their employment. Companies responding to local advertising echoed promoters' claims. In this infinite loop, the trope of the always-already docile woman worker increasingly achieved the status of natural fact, as managerial data and accounts reflected their social origins. However, managers' capacity to produce profitably did not rely on any actual knowledge of their workers' gendered subjectivities, still less on any insight into their own constitutive assumptions about third-world women. In fact, traits managers described as homegrown were frequently characteristics they had effectively created themselves. Thus, although these narratives, and the demographics of the workforces such frameworks produced, provided important information about managers' own gendered beliefs, they were of little value in understanding the social processes which produced quiescent women workers.

These authors' strategic reliance on quantitative data and managerial narratives made possible their identification of the links between the superexploitation of young women and burgeoning transnational profits, but it also had analytic costs. Distracted by outrage at women's overrepresentation in low-paying jobs and managerial boasts about their utilization of young, third-world women's externally enforced pliancy, theorists took employers' claims about their female workers at face value. Focused on contesting attributions of causality (social, not natural) and moral tone (exploitable, not productive), they left unchallenged the basic assertion of women's preset docility. As a result, they overestimated the importance of hiring at the expense of analyzing shop-floor management, thereby underestimating both the constitutive power of labor control practices and the malleability of the gendered self.

In looking at assembly lines filled with women and saying, "this is not an accident," these authors illuminated a fundamental, and too-often overlooked, aspect of contemporary production. However, their commonsense essentialism—that is, the basic assumption that gendered meanings and the subjectivities they evoke are fixed—led them to misunderstand the connection they identified. In arguing that capital is dependent on its access to women, they confused cause with consequence. Docile and dextrous women are produced in production relations, they do not autonomously enable them. On maquila shop floors, it is the insistent invocation of femininity, rather than its consistent enactment, which is most striking. Assuming gender's essential rigidity makes this process impossible to perceive. These analysts' failure to interrogate the illusion of gendered fixity thus impeded their capacity to recognize the ongoing and variegated constitution of feminine and masculine subjectivities within production relations. In turn, this led them to misunderstand the mechanisms through which gender plays a crucial role in global production.

I am arguing here that gender is indeed a fundamental element of global production, but not in the way these authors claim. Femininity is a trope—a structure of meaning through which workers, potential and actual, are addressed and understood, and around which production itself is designed. The notion of "productive femininity" thus crystallizes through a process of repetitive citation by transnational managers, and the imperative to hire such workers operates as a creative force, shaping both workers and the technical structure within which they work. In this context, hiring and labor control processes emerge as messages which address potential workers within specific understandings of who they are and what the work requires. Insofar as these rhetorics and practices resonate with those hired, they shape shop-floor subjectivities. Insofar as they fail in that project, they lead to shop-floor chaos. Thus, gendered subjectivity intervenes at all levels of the process, from managerial decision making to worker compliance or resistance, but it is never fixed. Contrary to managerial hopes and feminist fears, docile labor cannot simply be bought; it is produced, or not, in the meaningful practices and rhetorics of shop-floor life. It is in the daily routines of the shop floor that gender shapes possibilities, profits, and transnational production.

These contrasting visions of the role of gender in global production have their roots in more fundamental differences in how we understand the self. I am arguing here that the self is always in (re)construction, a process that occurs within and in terms of the local arenas through which it moves. This claim has important ramifications for how we see both work and gender.

Making Subjects

The profound personal experience of consistent and continuous self-hood makes arguments about women's fixed nature appear unproblematic. The same experience makes it seem correspondingly unlikely that the much-fabled "femininity" of assembly workers is produced on the shop floor. On the other hand, in practice, supervision always involves shaping others—providing a hands-on (if not necessarily self-conscious) experience of the malleability of worker selfhood for managers themselves. It should come as no surprise, therefore, that the literature on labor control is full of contradictions on the question of worker subjectivity. These are particularly evident in the writing of Frederick Taylor, the crusading manager who fathered "scientific management" in the early years of the twentieth century. Arguing fervently against the system of labor control through "(personal) initiative and (managerial) incentive" that he saw implemented by his predecessors,[25] Taylor advocated keeping workers from making any decisions at all as the route to increased productivity.

Harry Braverman's pathbreaking early seventies analysis of the capitalist labor process made Taylor its antihero. Taking Taylor at face value, he claimed that since scientific management operated by separating conception from execution,[26] it made worker agency irrelevant to the success or failure of the capitalist labor process, and thus to its analysis as well.[27] Nonetheless, a close reading of Taylor reveals a managerial strategy directed more at converting subject into object than at bypassing him *[sic]* entirely. This focus is most evident in the many anecdotes which sprinkle Taylor's work.

In an extended narrative, quoted in full by Braverman, Taylor describes training a man he calls "Schmidt" to load pig iron at four times the customary speed. He gleefully recounts organizing Schmidt's every move, thus converting him from working subject to worked object. Taylor prefaces the training by asking Schmidt what sort of man he is ("Are you a high-priced man?").[28] The structure of this query is noteworthy. Substantively, it asks about something Schmidt does. However, formally it is presented as a question about what Schmidt is. By framing the question as if referring to an inherent characteristic of the man, as if indexing something that were already true, rather than a new, external suggestion, Taylor creates the very subject he ostensibly recognizes, giving him a power over Schmidt that goes beyond that of controlling his behavior to that of defining Schmidt's self.[29] In fact, Schmidt recognizes this, commenting (in Taylor's own orthography), "Did I vant $1.85 a day? Vas dot a high-priced man? Vell yes, I vas a high-priced man."[30] In accepting the offer he can't refuse, Schmidt actually becomes the "high-priced man" of Taylor's fantasy of control. Only once this is achieved does Taylor's scripting, and thus Braverman's "deskilling," become possible.

In this story of addressing, and so constituting, Schmidt as a worker—and one of a particular sort—the birth of a subject is made visible, for it is through being studied and commanded that Schmidt is empowered to work at all. Here, we can see how the worker to be managed emerges in the act of "management"—a subject in all its mutually contingent meanings: object of narrative and knowledge; vassal; agent.[31]

It is no accident that one of the classic origin stories of modern management takes this form. Braverman's analysis notwithstanding, "interpellation," the process whereby a subject is created through recognizing her- or himself in another's naming,[32] is a primary mechanism of workplace control. It has become commonplace to observe that workers' selves are in play in contemporary workplaces, particularly in the service industry.[33] However, even time spent in "traditional" workplaces, whether as sociologist or worker, suggests the profound ways in which selves are made at work, and the centrality of this process to managerial control.[34]

Taylor's narrative demonstrates the process of interpellation in its most straightforward form—that is, it describes an incident in which a worker is explicitly addressed as a particular sort of person and acquiesces to the proffered definition. However, this process works through implicit as well as explicit statements and through meaningful practices as well as through language. Thus, although Taylor's interaction with Schmidt is remarkable for its verbal directness, he uses other rhetorical strategies as well. For instance, early in the conversation, Taylor wants to suggest that Schmidt is (should be) an individual, as opposed to a member of a class ("men in masses" is Taylor's phrase).[35] He accomplishes this not by saying so directly, but by contrasting Schmidt to the "cheap fellows" around him, implying that they differ on some inherent characteristic that would logically preclude their cooperation.

Despite the linguistic metaphor around which interpellation is defined, meaningful practices are as central to the process as language. This is abundantly obvious in Taylor's narrative, as the constitution of Schmidt as an individual is accomplished most powerfully in gesture.[36] At the outset, Schmidt is separated from his comrades and set to work alone, accompanied only by a supervisor. Taylor eventually trains every man in the gang, but like Schmidt, each is trained alone. Similarly, Schmidt works all day with a supervisor standing over him, literally directing his every move. This intensive supervision locates him as instrument rather than author and as tool rather than worker. Pace Braverman, Taylorism's "objective" capacity to keep workers from seeing the work process as a whole is only part of what is at stake here.[37] Through the absolute preemption of decision making, Taylor's strategy also evokes a particular workplace subject. The inability to see is not located in the process alone, it is also built into the newly constructed subject. Taylorism undermines the worker as creator, constituting a docile body in his place.[38]

Ransacking this story makes visible a phenomenon that is pervasive in global factories. Taylorist labor control is the managerial modality most famed for its disregard of worker subjectivities in favor of re-engineering the labor process itself, yet the production of subjectivity still glimmers just beneath the surface. Similarly, contemporary transnational managers and their critics both believe that third-world women workers enter the shop floor preconstituted. But here too, we can identify the primacy of managerial tactics which create, rather than rely upon, docile subjects.

The constitution of selves on the shop floor is of course more complex than the emblematic tale just presented. Following the explicit elements of Taylor's own account, I tell his story stripped down to reveal a single, unidirectional interaction. Manager and worker are the only two actors in the drama. The worker is addressed by the manager alone, and the manager himself is entirely unlocated. What's more, the man defined as Schmidt is produced only as a worker; his masculinity, nationality, and other social features apparently all sidelined in the process of interpellation. However, closer inspection of Taylor's narrative, not to mention of a living shop floor, reveals multiple complexities overlaid on the skeleton of these basic lineaments.[39]

First, managers are not the only people who can name others in the workplace. Although Taylor describes Schmidt's emergence as a worker in response to Taylor's actions alone, immersion in any arena of production reveals the possibility of multiple discourses and agents, with varied and fluctuating degrees of power. On most shop floors, managers, and the owners' perspective they express, create the primary frame. However, workers also address each other, with varying impacts. In an organized workplace, particularly one where the union operates on the shop floor, worker-generated rhetorics and practices can be powerful interpellatory forces. In addition, depending on shop-floor structure, workers can sometimes be powerfully addressed in less formalized social interactions, particularly those which occur across other power structures such as race or gender. Thus, the process of interpellation can operate between workers as well as from management to workers. Such multiple forms of address are in fact present in Taylor's story; his determination to deal with each worker alone is an often-explicit attempt to isolate the worker from otherwise present, countervailing addresses.

Second, although Taylor expends little energy excavating his own frameworks in this part of the narrative, managers, too, live in discursive structures which address, name, and describe them. These frameworks have fundamental consequences for how managers understand, and thereby control, their workers.[40] Unlike the more immediate structures which surround workers, the actors and discourses which address managers are often invisible from the shop floor.[41] Nonetheless, both the transnationally produced common sense about "normal" managerial behavior and the image of a salaried employee produced in a given company address managers, representing them to themselves. These processes shape managerial selfhood with discernible consequences for both technical architecture and personnel management in production. In taking seriously the notion of interpellation as a fundamental process of shop-floor control, the constitution of managerial subjectivity also rises to the surface, bringing the impact of meanings and the subjectivities they evoke into focus at all levels of the production process.

Finally, a fresh reading of Taylor's narrative reveals several non-production-related elements which go unmentioned (at least explicitly) by both Taylor and Braverman, yet which provide the conditions of possibility for the project as a whole. The first of these elements is the centrality of gender to the evocation of Taylor's working subject. Taylor does not ask Schmidt about himself as a worker or person, but as a "man." Whether "high-priced" or "cheap," the self modified is a masculine one. A woman referred to in such terms would be selling her body, not her labor. By the same token, Schmidt is chosen by Taylor in part because he is building a house. It is in this breadwinning role, and not outside it, that he is subject to financial manipulation. The second of these elements is the role of nationality. Schmidt, a "little Pennsylvania Dutchman,"[42] is addressed in accord with his "mentally sluggish type,"[43] made emblematic in the narrative through Taylor's phonetic rendition of Schmidt's speech, and by the pseudonym itself.[44] The meanings that imbue both an address and the subjectivity that emerges from it are thus gendered and raced, and it is the familiarity of these categories that in part accounts for Schmidt's matter-of-fact receptiveness. Thus, even in Taylor's schematic tale, we can make out the shadowy presence of non-production-related meanings behind the backs, as it were, of the actors themselves. Truly understanding the role of subjectivity in production requires that we investigate the role of gender and nationality in its formation.

Managerial control operates through the constitution of shop-floor subjects. This is a fully relational process. "Workers" are formed in dialogue with other shop-floor actors through comparison, contrast, and opposition to both multiple imaginaries and other shop-floor inhabitants. Managers are similarly socially located and formed, nested within their own set of constitutive relations. And depending on the terms of address, the content of workplace subjectivities can refer to many other categories of identity[45]—among them gender and nationality.

Like contemporary transnational managers, Taylor thought it was both possible and desirable to sideline worker subjectivities, although he structured production so as to bypass worker volition, whereas today's export-processing managers hire workers they believe to be pre-controlled. Nonetheless, both Taylor and these managers misunderstand the grounds of their own efficacy, for it is the description itself which constitutes the subject described. In addressing Schmidt as someone without will, Taylor creates conditions in which the subject he describes must emerge. Similarly, as I discovered repeatedly in the maquilas, in addressing workers through the trope of femininity, transnational managers create subjects they imagine to be preset. Envisioning subjectivity as fixed makes such processes invisible, thus making it impossible to see that femininity matters in global production not because it accurately describes a set of exploitable traits, but because it functions as a constitutive discourse which creates exploitable subjects.

Gender as Category

Just as they overestimate the durability of subjectivity in general, both academic analysts and popular critics of global production tend to give disproportionate credence to the mirage of eternal gendered meanings and permanently inculcated gendered subjectivities. In decrying capitalist exploitation of women's homemade docility, they locate it (although of course not its causes) firmly within the exploited worker herself. Within that framework, they assume a remarkable consistency of temperament, style, and enacted selfhood through time and space, as well as across different individuals within a single "population."

In so conceptualizing gender, they echo other early second-wave feminists, as well as much of the thinking prevalent in popular discussions today. Through the mid-eighties, mainstream feminist theory (like the movement from which it emerged) was primarily concerned with challenging the primacy of sex as a biological category,[46] and subsequently with analyzing the causes of male domination[47] and the social processes through which a controllable feminine psychology was constituted.[48] As a result, gender's fundamental inconsistency, malleability, and fragmentation disappeared from view. Wide differences in gendered meanings received little empirical attention or analysis. Commonalities between women of differing class, race, and other social locations were exaggerated,[49] as was the level of consistency in individual women's experience of gender over the course of a lifetime[50] or across social arenas.

The feminist poststructuralists who emerged following this period of theory building reopened the debate. Focusing on the tendencies toward "essentialism" in previous feminist theory, critics like Judith Butler warned that, in the process of delineating and analyzing the oppression of "women," notions of gender as a binary system were being re-inforced—replacing biological with sociological essentialism.[51] In rectifying this problem, they shifted focus from gendered subjects to gendered meanings—looking at the symbolic logics and internal patterns through which a particular discourse successfully "made sense" of sexed bodies.[52] This move made it possible to ask new kinds of questions. Queries such as "What is the hegemonic discourse within which managers understand 'women workers'?"[53] are fundamentally indebted to the theoretical ground clearing done by these thinkers.

The shift had certain costs, however. In the original Foucauldian formulation, discourses purportedly include the meanings embedded in the material world,[54] whereas in this literature, the move to the arena of meanings too often meant a move away from practices. As a result, much of the social world was left out of analytic focus, with symbolic systems disconnected from those who articulate them and from the practices through which they are enacted. In the process of questioning conventional gendered categories, these theorists fell into recounting the categories' history in isolation,[55] as if they existed in a universe filled only by language. This analytic focus misses the question of how such categories are built and practiced in daily interaction. Gender is thus essentialized anew.

The disproportionate attention given to language over practices had other consequences as well. Despite their commitment to developing a language capable of describing gender in all its palpable heterogeneity and fluctuating significance,[56] these theorists were more likely to cite than to explore gender's unpredictability and inconsistency. For the most part, the focus on linguistic structures kept theorists working in this tradition from exploring gender's lived specificity. Instead, much of their analysis remained at the level of the purportedly hegemonic discourses of a particular period[57] and took for granted the societal extension and resonance of a particular discursive understanding of gender.[58] The question of how these representations vary between localized arenas of domination, even those sharing elements of a common discursive framework, remained unexplored.[59]

In one sense, this literature's biggest failure is in not taking its own claims seriously enough. If gender is truly locally emergent and contextual, then there is *theoretical* work to be done in delineating where, when, and how this occurs. This requires bringing an ethnographic eye to bear on the ways that gender is practiced on a daily basis.[60] Without this empirical attention, at best, much of this theory remains at the level of inspiring and suggestive claims; at worst, the premium it places on linguistic processes obscures fundamental aspects of gendered experience. In the process, it misses gaps and breaks in gendered hegemonies that, as feminists, we would be well advised to illuminate.

Gendered categories are remarkably rigid and tenacious, thus playing a fundamental role in the experience of self. The content of these categories, however, is highly variable and their importance fluctuates widely across social situations. Too often, the characteristics of the categories are confused with their content and operation. Nonetheless, appearances to the contrary, gendered meanings are fluid, changing with social structure, intention, and struggle. Thus, when we conceptualize gender, we must begin with the intractable and unequal categories through which sense is made of human bodies and social actions. The particular sets of traits that come to fill those categories are analytically secondary. It is in fact just this combination of omnipresent but mobile categories and variable content which gives gender its tremendous capacity to interpellate subjects across a wide variety of social arenas and in the service of a multitude of interests and strategies.

This variation in content is both a response to local specificities and a structural element of how gender works as a social process overall. Femininity and masculinity are relational categories which operate fundamentally through contrast with each other—whether or not that process is made explicit in any particular case. As a result, as one moves through levels of social complexity, what counts as feminine or masculine often shifts, as at each level the attempt to see what goes where necessarily operates on the terrain of old oppositions, creating new contrasts in the process. Thus, "feminine" at one level can be "masculine" at the next. Take sewing leather gloves in a factory: one could imagine a cultural context in which it would be marked as masculine in contrast to work in the home; then within the category of paid work as feminine in contrast to construction work; and still again within the category of garment production as masculine in contrast to sewing lingerie. None of these activities are inherently either feminine or masculine, of course, but the process whereby they become gendered is an inherent aspect of how gender functions.[61]

While the potential for this sort of flexibility is built into gender as a process of meaning creation, the emergent content of gendered attributions emerges through the intentions, understandings, and limitations of the actors struggling in and over a particular social space. Although it has come to seem self-evident that gender varies through history and across the globe, I will demonstrate through the narratives below that what counts as feminine or masculine in fact shifts across much smaller expanses of space, time, and culture as well, as it is reconfigured, sometimes unintentionally, in the strategies, common sense, and power struggles of actors. Local rhetorics and practices of course make reference to larger frameworks, but they do not necessarily reproduce them. What's more, gendered meaning structures vary not only in extension, but in their longevity and durability as well, and thus in the speed at which they change over time. Some versions of femininity and masculinity span centuries or linguistic groups, others are hammered out in an individual workplace or family, dissolving and reconfiguring with a strike or divorce.

The dispersed origins and logics of the gendered meaning structures which meet in a given social space have crucial implications for how femininity and masculinity are lived by individuals on a daily basis. A given locale can be home to a variety of gendered meanings, some of which coincide and others of which clash, and which vary in both local importance and overall fixity. Thus, although we generally remain "female" or "male" as we move across social space, our experience and enactment of these categories can shift, sometimes radically, as we move across a landscape or through a day. Further, even within the confines of a given arena, individuals may find themselves interpellated within a veritable cacophony of gendered meanings.

This layering of dissonant gendered meanings is particularly evident in the Juárez maquilas. The explicitly, emphatically feminized nature of the industry as a whole means that factories within it are necessarily marked as feminine or masculine, as they are categorized either in terms of or in contrast to this gendered background. In this context, the meanings of work and the appropriateness of worker behavior are established on each shop floor in gendered terms. Thus, although workers belong to a single geographic, cultural, and industrial demographic, the subjects that emerge in different maquilas express and incarnate distinct shop-floor femininities and masculinities. What's more, in a given maquila, the relatively durable discourse of productive femininity that circulates among transnational managers coexists not only with a distinct discourse about women workers' promiscuity generated among local elites, but also with the more circumscribed, and therefore less stable, gendered production system of a particular shop floor. Grasping the productive and personal consequences of gender in the industry requires delineating the transnational trope of femininity as it emerges in the city, its idiosyncratic incarnations on individual shop floors, and its consequences for the daily work lives of these shop floors' inhabitants. Only in this way can we capture the fundamental complexity of gender at work.

Gendered categories are indeed persistent, rigid, intractable, and productive. However, these characteristics should not blind us to the categories' basic emptiness, and thus to their extreme contextual variation in content and function. Femininity and masculinity are defined through multiple and simultaneous struggles over power and desire, often occurring at varying speeds. In some social arenas, they are explicit areas of contest. In others, goals and intentions are focused elsewhere, but gendered meanings emerge as byproducts. In either case, subjectivities and structures of power are constituted through their invocation. It is precisely this duality—the rigidity of gendered categories versus the malleability and variability of gendered meanings—that accounts for the centrality and weight of gender in production.

In thinking of "women" as fixed production inputs, comparable in function to tempered steel or precut cloth, analysts of global production fundamentally misunderstood both the process of labor control and the nature of gendered selfhood. The content of "womanhood" or "manhood" does not inhere in the individual. It emerges in a changeable, multi-leveled set of enacted meaning structures. These local meaning structures cite a particular notion of gender and thus evoke individual femininities and masculinities in that time and space. A given individual, operating in a given social arena, will practice a particular version of femininity or masculinity. That version will have something in common with what that person practices elsewhere, but it will be fundamentally restructured and resignified within the meaningful practices of the current locale. Since gendered enactments are always simultaneously similar and different across time and space, the extent to which one chooses to focus on one of these characteristics is a theoretical and political rather than an empirically motivated decision.[62] In my judgment, the "essential similarities" between women working throughout transnational production has been overemphasized, increasing gender's visibility at the cost of undermining our capacity to recognize how gender functions in this context. Hence, I have chosen to foreground the crucial differences in gendered meanings and subjectivities that emerge even in closely situated arenas.[63] This strategy allows us to shift our questions. Rather than asking how women's patriarchally produced femininity is made profitable, we ask instead how gendered meanings emerge and are practiced, and how profitable, gendered subjects are evoked within them.

Making the Case

The current structure of transnational production may well be gendered in the aggregate, but a sociological understanding of how this gendering process works, and to what ends, requires immersion in the specific. On myriad global shop floors, managers assess what is possible and acceptable in gendered terms, measuring efficiency and productivity with reference to, and sometimes in terms of, the global icon of productive femininity. The consequences of these processes are significant, both for emergent gendered subjects and for corporate bottom lines, yet how this works cannot be inferred from the outside. It requires that we enter the social worlds of production and grasp the processes of subject creation that global processes are made of.

Like earlier analysts, I am struck by the predominance of "women in the global factory."[64] Unlike those analysts, I see this predominance not as a function of who women are (or have been trained to be), but of the way in which gender structures production overall. Thus, rather than seeing millions of women populating global production lines, I see a production process marked as feminine—"assembly"—replacing a previous process marked as masculine—"manufacturing"[65]—with clear consequences both for third-world workers' rights and experiences of self and for first-world profits and prices. This distinction is not merely semantic; it also makes visible important social processes.

Gender matters in contemporary transnational production. How it matters is the subject of this book. Through the case studies that follow, I will limn the consequences—empirical, intellectual, and political—of this shift in perspective. Different visions require different methods. Thus, the bulk of my data is ethnographic, culled from immersion in the daily life of global production.[66] This research process brings subjectivities to the forefront and makes it possible for me to investigate precisely how gender operates at work. The analysts and activists who first identified gender's role in transnational production took femininity and masculinity as givens, so they were untroubled by viewing these processes from outside the workplace—through either managerial accounts or labor market statistics. However, their sources of data obscured crucial aspects of the processes they described. In particular, by taking managerial statements as description rather than invocation, and by assuming that femininities and masculinities are used rather than constituted in production, these analysts misinterpreted the implications of their findings.

The contrasting perspectives on gender and subjectivity I have delineated here also generate contradictory empirical predictions. The primary difference lies in distinct accounts of the emergence of the "cheap, docile, and dextrous" women of international repute. The new international division of labor theorists expect these workers to be omnipresent in assembly plants, exhibiting a stable set of traits across time and place. If this were the case, then gendered subjectivities, particularly those aspects related to shop-floor discipline, should remain stable over time within the factory, and managerial work should focus on exploiting that docility, not evoking it. By contrast, I am arguing here that those shop-floor subjects who do embody the image are simulacra[67]— not "the real thing," but fantasies brought to life on and for the shop floor. If the latter is correct, then we should be able to describe the mechanisms through which global trope becomes local experience. Thus empirically, in any plant in which women embody this iconic image, we should be able to identify the particular local practices and rhetorics within which they came to do so.[68]

This initial difference has three corollaries. Each of these can be assessed through living the daily life of production. The first corollary involves the question of whether or not gendered subjectivities should vary between social arenas and within a "single" culture or population. Insofar as gendered subjectivity is fixed early and indelibly in the predictable patriarchy of home and family, the content of femininity and masculinity should be essentially consistent—whether individuals find themselves at home or in a particular workplace. On the other hand, as I argue here, if gendered subjectivities are evoked locally, then femininity and masculinity should vary widely, across social arenas and within the population which moves between those arenas. On the ground, then, we should expect to find variation in how femininity and masculinity are expressed and experienced on different shop floors, as well as between home and work.

The second corollary of this basic difference over the nature of the "third-world woman worker" is whether or not transnational production can function at all in its current configuration without female workers. If it is the presence of flesh-and-blood "women" that makes balance sheets and labor control practices workable in contemporary global production, then a typical low-pay, high-coercion global assembly plant will necessarily face problems in dealing with a largely male workforce. On the other hand, if labor control depends on managers' capacity to address workers in terms they recognize and accept, then not women, but resonant gendered discourses, are an essential element for successful production. The issue becomes whether managers are able to produce discourses in which male workers recognize themselves, not the gender of workers per se. If my analysis is correct, we should be able to find productive factories with male-dominated workforces, even in "feminized" global industries.

The third corollary disagreement is over whether the content of gendered subjectivities should ever become a direct subject of contention within production. If femininity and masculinity are constellations of individual characteristics that are set in childhood, then there is no reason for them to become an issue in shop-floor politics, and new international division of labor theorists do not predict that they will do so. On the other hand, if gendered subjectivities are malleable and emerge in response to contested local frames, their content can easily become a pivot of struggle, with significant consequences for the constellations of power in which they are embedded. Therefore, my analysis would predict that we should be able to find factories in which workers and managers struggle directly over the definition of legitimate femininity or masculinity, as part of a larger struggle over control of the shop floor itself.

The narrative that follows takes these questions into the field, looking to establish the role of gender in global production and to delineate its mechanisms of operation. The analysis has three interlocking strands. The first is descriptive and interpretive, narrating and making sense of the emotional, political, and productive dynamics of four maquila shop floors in their global and local context. The second and third are both theoretical, but speak with different intentions. The first theoretical voice is negative. Understood from this vantage point, each of the four shop floors becomes a contravening case, an object lesson illustrating a distinct problem with the essentialism that imbues much of the thinking about gender in global production. The second theoretical voice is constructive. Here again, the shop floors serve to illustrate a larger theoretical pattern, but this time they highlight the interaction of global discourses, managerial subjectivities, and gendered mutability that can account for the dynamics of the field. I give this voice the last word in the conclusion, where I discuss the role that meanings and the subjectivities they evoke play in economic processes more generally.

In Chapter 3, I delineate the process through which gendered meanings define a labor force and thus create a labor market. Although one could see the maquilas' early decades as confirming previous theories about the hyper-exploitation of young women and the more recent period as refuting them, the history presented here suggests a more complex reality. Here, the transnationally generated idea of productive femininity has structured the labor market through an ongoing citational process, evoking a highly specific, and at times resistant, labor force. The contradictory effects of this process provide the context from within which individual managers build hiring and labor control strategies.

I open this story with the gendered tropes of global capitalism, sketching the paradigmatic transnational worker—cheap, docile, dextrous, and female—against whose contours actual workers are judged. In Ciudad Juárez, a center for maquila production, this image has had material effects. A boom in maquila production in the early eighties, combined with the managerial assumption that only young women workers would do, combined to produce a marked shortage of precisely such cheap, docile, female workers. The resulting clash between global discourse and the local possibilities it generated and foreclosed has led to an industry-wide proliferation of gendered meanings and subjectivities, as well as of labor control strategies, as managers unable to put trope into practice have been forced to develop strategies to address previously unimagined subjects. This situation has been further complicated by local elites' publicly expressed anxieties at the increasing independence of young, female maquila workers and the perceived displacement of their male counterparts. This contradictory context highlights the gendered meanings in production and thereby makes it possible to trace their operations and grasp their mutable character.

Chapters 4 through 7 make up the ethnographic heart of the story. These narratives do not take the form of structured comparisons of a consistent set of "explanatory variables" across shop floors. Subjectivity cannot be "held constant." Rather, each case is analyzed as a unique configuration of structuring discourses within which the logic of local gendered meanings and subjectivities becomes comprehensible. In each case we discover why and how gendered meanings and subjectivities come to take the form they do—as I underline the highly idiosyncratic mix of local managerial decisions, worker responses, and resulting gendered subjectivities. Each chapter should thus be read as a unit, evidence for the way that particular gendered meanings are constituted in a specific context of domination and struggle.

Chapter 4 takes us into Panoptimex, a highly successful television assembly plant. Unlike the other factories I studied, Panoptimex stands out for the remarkable accuracy with which its workers incarnate the image of an inviolably docile femininity. An ethnography of Panoptimex's production process is thus of particular interest; it allows us to perform a genealogy, tracing the multiple forces which coincide to bring this paradigmatic woman to life. From the outside, it looks like Panoptimex managers got it right the first time, hiring embodiments of productive femininity and letting them roll. From the inside, though, things look different. On Panoptimex's shop floor, managerial control is established through addressing and thereby constituting these paragons. This chapter follows that process.

The transnationally based Panoptimex managers are visually focused—in hiring, labor control, and technical decisions alike. As a result of this attentional practice, the shop floor is designed to make workers visible, fostering self-consciousness as well as enabling literal super-vision. The logic behind this panopticon is also at work in populating and managing it. Managers accustomed to seeing factories full of young women take care to reproduce the image by hiring accordingly. Hence, when faced with a shortage of young, cheap, women workers, they import from a rural area outside the city, paying the costs of transportation in order to see their lines "look right." The enactment of managerial practices based on men watching young women creates a sexually charged atmosphere. On the shop floor, adorned and manicured young women work under the vigilant and interested eyes of male supervisors. Flirtation and sexual competition become the currency through which shop-floor power relations are struggled over and fixed. Women are addressed, and respond, as desirable objects, just as male managers are interpellated as desiring subjects. The few workers who are male become "not-men," with no standing in the game. We see, therefore, not preexisting clusters of feminine and masculine traits, wound up and released in production, but rather the creation of these traits on the shop floor. Panoptimex workers are simulacra, on-the-ground products of managerial "wishful thinking" set in motion by a highly particular conjuncture of transnational and technical discourses and subjectivities.

Shop-floor femininities, even productive ones within a single industry, can vary widely. Particimex—the auto parts assembler which is the subject of Chapter 5—also has an overwhelmingly female workforce, acquired in this case by moving out of Juárez to a small agricultural city where female—and "feminine"—labor is still plentiful. Despite this much-sought abundance, the content of productive femininity is redefined in the plant, so that shop-floor femininity diverges sharply, both from femininities enacted in local homes and families and from femininities described in transnational discourse. In fact, the productive femininity which emerges in this plant is formed in explicit contrast to first-world images of third-world feminine docility. As a result, this maquila makes particularly apparent the explanatory mileage gained by thinking about managerial use of gendered meanings, rather than about their use of "women" per se. Whatever it means to be a "woman," whether in the eyes of transnational managers or of the community in which Particimex is located, that category is reshaped on the shop floor.

Particimex's parent company initially opened this rural outpost precisely to take advantage of its purportedly tractable young women, who were becoming increasingly hard to find in Juárez itself. However, once there, young and ambitious Mexican managers decided to put themselves on the corporate map—making "quality" and "teamwork" hallmarks of their tenure. Thus, they instituted leadership training and teamwork in production, eroding the distinction between workers and managers. Not content with this emblem of "modernity," they elaborated an image of the ideal worker at whom this new production system would be directed. She is a young woman willing to make decisions and able to take charge—understood to operate in explicit contrast to the submissive women of "traditional Mexican culture" whom managers envision their workers to be outside the factory. This system, directed at young rural women accustomed to ongoing rituals of permission and deference, addresses and constitutes a distinctive shop-floor "femininity," one deeply implicated in production and ultimately highly productive, but not one marked by submission and docility. Thus, Particimex is a dramatic instance of the way in which the active constitution of local femininities, rather than the exploitation of previously established feminine traits, is responsible for feminine productivity in transnational production.

Particimex suggests that it is not a particular sort of woman, but femininity, which is at work. Andromex, the subject of Chapter 6, suggests that even femininity isn't necessarily the center of the story. In Andromex, femininity operates as the other against which "masculine" workers are identified. What appears to matter is not worker femininity, but management's capacity to successfully address workers in gendered terms which they can recognize. Andromex is a Juárez-based, mixed-gender hospital garments plant where the trope of the breadwinner/ producer frames manager-worker relations. The masculinity embedded in this category[69]—unlike the pointedly embodied image of productive femininity—need not be made explicit to function.[70] Thus, it is possible for both men and women to recognize themselves when addressed within its frame. In this context, managers at Andromex constitute women and men alike as "workers," successfully integrating them into production through negation of the transnationally produced association of femininity and assembly.

This situation results from the coincidence of a set of unusual historical and structural conditions. A violent strike in the early eighties, when the factory still employed primarily women, permanently disabused Mexican managers of the idea of women workers' innate docility. When women workers grew scarce, Andromex was among the first plants to cut out the feminized narratives and hire men. The pay structure into which these workers were hired is also unusual for the maquilas. Labor control is exercised and struggled over through piece rates, and the conflicts that result from this process are involving and constitutive, evoking masculine selves. In addition, due to the sterile nature of the work, workers wear smocks and caps that entirely cover hair and dress. Bodies are hidden, gender's physical markings obscured. Top management's "worker" rhetoric and explicit disinterest in references to femininity and masculinity, in combination with the invisibility of bodily referents, makes it possible to interpellate women and men alike into a single, implicitly masculine, framework. Thus, although this plant is remarkably productive, it depends neither on feminine traits nor on constituting femininity, but on evoking productive subjects through the more subtly masculinized category of "worker" itself.

Each of the previous cases reveals the utility of gender for producing controllable shop-floor subjects. However, gendered meanings and subjectivities can also become a source of tension and struggle of their own, eroding managerial control and shop-floor efficiency. This is the case at Anarchomex—the subject of Chapter 7—where managers' tenacious embrace of a fixed image of local femininity and masculinity has led to the formation of resistant rather than docile subjects, and thus to shop-floor chaos. Here gender's symbolic dimensions are particularly highlighted, as the content of masculinity and femininity is the ground upon which struggles over shop-floor control are fought, and ultimately upon which management loses control of the daily life of the factory.

Anarchomex belongs to the same corporation as does Particimex and makes virtually the same parts, albeit much less efficiently. Plant managers view workers as a factor of production; hence they focus on hiring the "right kind"—women—rather than on training and labor control. Unfortunately for them, plant size, industry history, and managers' own lack of organizational capacity combine to keep them from finding enough women workers to keep the plant running. As a result, their workforce is 60 percent male, but they continue to address all workers through the trope of femininity, deprecating male workers and eternally hoping they will eventually be able to hire the women they believe to be necessary. Their commitment to hiring rather than forming workers is reflected on the shop floor as well, where they rely on moving assembly lines, rather than on close supervision, to keep production going. These strategies make it possible for defensive and determined male workers, unwilling to recognize themselves in disrespectful managerial addresses, to take social control of the shop floor. Having done so, they compete over speed but not accuracy and initiate aggressive flirtations with their female co-workers. As a result, production is generally on-time but low quality, and struggles over the meaning of masculinity and femininity and the appropriate gender of the work become the center of shop-floor contestation more generally.

Each of these shop floors, like the labor market within which it is located, is a case study in the creative power of gender. In every narrative, we watch as gendered meanings constitute idiosyncratically configured subjects on the field of production, thus ultimately enabling or undermining productivity itself. Clearly gender matters here, but it matters because of its capacity to define and evoke appropriate shop-floor subjects, not because a particular version inheres in always-already docile women workers. To the contrary, the subjects who emerge are remarkably varied across shop floors, even emerging, as they do, from a single labor market defined by a dominant gendered discourse. This conclusion raises a final set of questions, and in Chapter 8 we turn from process to cause. Why is gender so intractable, yet so heterogeneous, across global factories? Here we move from a narrative of the ways in which each case contravenes an earlier set of theoretical assumptions to an account of why gender matters so much and takes such varied forms in transnational production.

The raison d'être of third-world assembly is "cheap labor." One might have thought, with access to low-wage, highly policed workers guaranteed through crossing borders, that seeking gender-based malleability in addition would come to seem gratuitous. Surprisingly, that does not appear to be the case. Instead, attending to managerial conversation reveals how the long-term, symbolic, and habitual links between women and cheap labor continue to bring gender front and center on today's global assembly lines.[71] As a result, the trope of productive femininity has become a cornerstone of transnational production, forming managers' expectations of workers before they even begin work in a particular global factory, and thus shaping production itself.

This persistence raises other questions in turn. Given the trope's stubborn centrality, why don't we find its clones at work in every global factory? We know that gendered meanings are flexible and locally constituted, but potential in no way ensures enactment. What impels the variety described above? Here the fundamental importance of subjectivity reemerges—but this time that of managers. Each transnational manager is located in a specific set of rhetorics and practices of gender, nation, and corporation, and his[72] sense of self and other emerges from that placement. This shapes understandings of and strategies for hiring and labor control, thereby generating the wide variety of gendered meanings delineated above. Thus, ultimately, subjectivities operate as causes as well as consequences in economic life. Gender matters in global production; how it matters is determined by the situated visions of managers around the globe.

The move from "woman" to "gender" can read as a move into abstraction, and thus as a move away from the shop-floor experience of transnational workers. However, global production is already structured around and through abstract explanations. Managerial accounts are distinguished from those offered here above all by the cloak of invisibility created by their absolute taken-for-grantedness. Certainly the managerial assumption of productive femininity is an explanatory abstraction with tremendous consequences for the lived experiences of women and men around the world. My goal here is thus to bring these frameworks into the realm of conscious critical analysis, where we can think about their causes and consequences and make decisions in that clearer light. Lenses which make visible gender's essential variability, both within and outside production, can help illuminate how selves are implicated in structures. Such a view can reveal the ongoing construction processes taking place behind the facade of gendered fixity, thereby suggesting potential sites and tactics of its productive disruption.

Trope Chasing

Making a Local Labor Market

---

*Today, from Penang to Ciudad Juárez, young Third World
women have become the new "factory girls," providing a vast pool
of cheap labor for globetrotting corporations.*

Annette Fuentes and Barbara Ehrenreich

Thus Fuentes and Ehrenreich introduced their pathbreaking 1983 analysis, *Women in the Global Factory.*[1] In bringing public attention to the presence of women, they made visible an important social phenomenon. However, in taking for granted the essential reasonableness (if not morality) of hiring women as a way of accessing "cheap labor," they obscured the discursive processes through which femininity came to be equated with cheapness and the consequences of such an equation in any given labor market. In Ciudad Juárez, managers indeed began by hiring young women, thus defining and shaping the local labor market through citing transnationally generated images of productive femininity. Over time, however, the tenacity of the equation of femininity with offshore productivity created a shortage of precisely such subjects, increasing the price and undermining the docility of local women workers and discomfiting local patriarchal elites. Thus, the story of the maquila labor market in Juárez is not only one of the hyper-exploitation of young women workers, but of the drying up of the "vast pool of cheap labor," of maquila managers' ongoing struggles to manage workers who aren't who they expect them to be, and of Juárez elites' (highly compensated) discomfort with the process. In this context, gender certainly shapes the export-processing labor market, but not through transnationals' capacity to leverage the ineluctable productivity of young, third-world women. Rather, gender intervenes because it is the terrain upon which the question of who looks like a maquila worker, and who doesn't, is decided, thus establishing the context within which hiring takes place and production is initiated.

Unemployed Men, Women's Work

When the program which established Mexico's maquilas was put into place in 1965,[2] it was already framed in public, gendered rhetorics. Yet, seen with the clarity of hindsight, the gendering looks doomed from the outset, for the framework was all about masculinity.[3] For decades, the U.S. government *bracero* program had imported Mexican men to work in the fields of the southwestern United States. Domestic pressures in the United States brought this to a halt in 1965, leaving both countries worried about the impact of 200,000 returning—and jobless—braceros on Mexico's border states.[4] The guarantee of tax-free entrée into the United States for the products of Mexican export-processing factories was intended to alleviate this problem by encouraging the establishment of businesses that could hire returning male farmworkers. On the face of it, the program was a phenomenal success. In 1975, a decade after it was established, maquilas employed more than 67,000 workers,[5] almost entirely at the border. By early 1992, when I arrived, they provided work for seven and a half times that number.[6] Unfortunately for this scheme, however, the jobs were not going to returning braceros; in fact they were not going to men at all. From the outset, young women made up over 80 percent of maquila workers.[7] Investors, while increasingly willing to participate in the program as the years progressed, had arrived with their own ideas about whom to hire.[8]

By the time the maquila program was established, free trade zones were already operating in East Asia, explicitly advertising the virtues of their feminine labor force.[9] Managers coming into Mexico took for granted that they would hire women. A 1966 report by the consulting firm Arthur D. Little,[10] oft-cited as a "smoking gun" in discussions of the exploitative dimensions of maquila hiring practices, explicitly suggested hiring women in order to increase the number of potential workers and thereby increase employer leverage. More telling, however, is an early treatise for prospective maquiladora investors, which simply assumed the workforce would be female and went on to enumerate Mexican women's many attractions: "From their earlier conditioning, they show respect and obedience to persons in authority, especially men. The women follow orders willingly."[11] This set of assumptions operated on the shop floor as well as in public relations. In a particularly fascinating example of this managerial common sense in the program's early years, we find managers looking to hire gay men when women were unavailable—for example, when women were still prohibited from doing night work. Van Waas describes a manager who requested gay men "as queer and effeminate as possible" and commented, "If I can't have women, I'll get as close to them as I can."[12] Similarly, in Anarchomex, a manager with a long history in the industry describes his experience supervising "the pink line." "They worked well, like women. It was very famous, that line."

Managers such as these claimed to be describing Mexican femininity, if not Mexican women, but they were in fact doing something else. Along with their colleagues in Asia, they were developing a new set of meanings for "femininity" that freed it from its location within the family, even potentially from its connection to female bodies at all, and reconstituted it as a set of transferable characteristics, including cheapness, natural docility, dexterity, and tolerance of boredom.[13] In the process, their description became prescription, and the transnational trope of productive femininity became the new standard for maquila workers, women and men alike.

Such rhetorics were particularly believable in a labor market like that faced by the maquilas in the early years. In response to ads seeking "little ladies" (*damitas*), unemployed young women flocked enthusiastically to maquila jobs. A woman who managed to get work in one of the first plants recalled stringent entrance requirements, the thrill of getting in given the "gigantic line of people trying to enter," and the amazing experience of being paid in dollars without having to cross the border.[14] In 1979, a union spokesman still described the many "little ladies" who "aspired" to work in the maquilas, adding that the quantity of female labor in the area was "inexhaustible."[15] In the same period, the manager of a General Electric plant in Juárez explained at a conference that, given the 25 percent unemployment rate, they were able to hire two or three of every twenty-five applicants.[16]

In marked contrast to the sanguinity of transnational managers about these desirable new workers, the preferential employment of young women in the maquilas elicited troubled discussions in local media and conversation about the erosion of "traditional" patriarchal structures.[17] These anxieties were—and are—particularly evident in Ciudad Juárez, where concerns about the industry's preference for women were sharpened by the city's economic dependence on the maquilas and its national reputation for deviant sexuality and gender roles. A city of roughly a million people,[18] Ciudad Juárez is geographically isolated within its home country, linked instead with its U.S. "twin city" El Paso, in the midst of a windy desert. As a result of this placement, the city was barely subsisting on the traditional border "industries" of cheap liquor and prostitution in 1965. It was hungry for jobs, and starving for "respectable" ones, when the maquila program was established.[19]

Early discussions of the program by local elites were imbued with anxieties about working-class women's sexuality. As the program began, these statements focused on the consequences of women's problems finding work.[20] In 1965, a union official commented "crudely" that "many women have stopped being honorable upon not finding sources of decent work."[21] As the industry grew, the emerging solution to these concerns only instigated new anxieties. A 1971 article, "The Maquiladora Plants and the Border Woman," encapsulated the city's conflicted attitude toward the industry's hiring practices. In quick succession, it worried about the high number of single mothers in the plants and the local scarcity of maids and lauded Mexican women's special aptitude for maquila work (comparable even to that of their Asian counterparts) and the plants' role in slowing the growth of prostitution in the city.[22] In these few lines, the article captured the mixture of pride and shame, as well as the close links between discussions of women's work and women's sexuality, which characterized, and continues to characterize, local discussions of women's work in the industry.

This elite ambivalence was only heightened by women workers' increasingly assertive self-presentation as their preferential employment continued. In interviews from the period, workers recounted newly found "independence" from formerly controlling fathers and husbands.[23] Writing in the early eighties, Fernández-Kelly described the emergent assertiveness of these young workers, including scaring away men who showed up at "their" bars by jeering at them.[24] That these developments provoked anxiety in the city[25] is evident in articles like two written in 1979 in Juárez and printed in both the *Los Angeles Times* and a major Mexico City paper. In huge letters, the first headline declaimed, "MAQUILADORAS: Evil Exploitation of Women's Work: Fracture Tradi-

tional Mexican Family Structure." The next day its sequel added, "FAIL-
URE OF THE BIP [the maquila program] TO EMPLOY BRACEROS: A Labor Force That Displaces the Man as Breadwinner."[26]

The linked anxieties reverberating through this article about familial
disintegration, male displacement, and female misplacement continued
to echo through local media coverage throughout the seventies and
early eighties. In 1972, a bureaucrat was quoted in a local paper complaining that the maquilas "hadn't served the function for which they'd
been created" because they'd hired women rather than men.[27] Calls by
union leaders and local intellectuals to hire men were constant; they
claimed that only by employing men as well as women could the maquiladora industry halt the "assault on family unity."[28] Throughout the
seventies, Juárez papers enthusiastically reported each new promise of
the imminent advent of "heavy" industry, expressly geared to the employment of male workers.[29] The Belgian consul made headlines in 1977
by saying that he intended to encourage Belgian investment that would
provide work for men.[30] When a maquiladora "for men" finally opened
in 1979, its eighty-eight new jobs received tremendous attention, and
local unions continued to laud its existence despite a quickly earned and
well-deserved notoriety for toxic work conditions.[31]

By 1980, promises of a surge in "men's jobs" had become more dif-
fident. A local bureaucrat, discussing his "confidence" that "this year"
the maquilas would hire men, added: "To be honest, we must recognize that as of now, nothing is guaranteed, and all we have is the faith
that this will happen."[32] In 1981, in the context of an expanding industry that showed no sign of changing its employment practices, an article
used one of many reports of the imminent arrival of men's jobs to express elite anxieties about the erosion of local working-class manhood.
"The husband, without work, lives off his wife, either losing his value as
man of the house, if he still has it to lose, or otherwise, openly establishing a gigolo's existence."[33]

Media coverage was almost as perturbed by the women working as
by the men who weren't, worrying over women's new and unnatural
"emancipation."[34] Local pundits discussed young women's "premature
growth" and disproportionate authority in the home.[35] Newspaper
headlines blared about the dangers of "liberated women" in the plants
carrying venereal diseases to an unsuspecting public through unregu-
lated prostitution.[36] A Justice of the Peace announced that divorces
were increasing because male unemployment generated "a false independence among the women."[37] And public functionaries repeatedly

appeared in the media to obsess about maquila workers as mothers, whether the issue was the impact of their "dissolute lifestyle" on the health of newborns or ambivalent reports of their "liberated" decisions to register illegitimate children.[38] In 1980, a union began offering self-improvement courses for women workers, "so women workers save their moral and human values."[39]

There is of course a certain irony here. Young women were brought into the maquilas as ineluctably "feminine" and addressed as such internally. In the process of referencing this purportedly homegrown personality, transnational managers frequently succeeded in constituting it in the factory. Nonetheless, young women in Juárez, often migrating from cities further south to work in the plants, were less and less likely to live in traditional patriarchal homes[40] and were increasingly expressive of this newfound freedom outside the factory.[41] Thus, as transnational managers celebrated women workers' familially induced suitability for the rigors of assembly, local elites worried over their increasing assertiveness in the home, and about their male counterparts' consequent displacement in both spheres.[42] The few Mexican plant managers, members of transnational and local communities alike, ultimately articulated a perspective which reflected both celebration and unease. Thus, their viewpoints occasionally diverged from that of their more numerous foreign counterparts. In the following period, as women workers' shop-floor docility came under suspicion as well, these differences would come to be significant.

When Women Stop Acting like "Women"

In the early eighties, the industry romance with its workers began to fade. The U.S. economy went into a downward spiral, and maquila workers immediately began to feel the effects, not only in decreased hiring, but in mass layoffs and enforced "time off." After years of double-digit growth, the number of workers employed by the plants in Juárez fell by 6 percent between 1981 and 1982. By 1982, formerly "docile" workers were losing patience. The years 1981 to 1983 saw a burst of worker "demands" against their employers before the labor board (the Junta de Conciliación y Arbitraje).[43] Local papers reported in June 1982 that there had already been more formal strike threats in six months than there had ever been before in a full year—.8 per maquila.[44]

In 1980 and 1981, two strikes became the focus of dramatic media coverage. In mid-1980, a conflict between two unions[45] erupted at Andromex (see Chapter 6), and for seven months, the public was treated to the sight of women workers yelling at their bosses, barricading themselves in the plant, and forcefully asserting their right to be heard. The following year, at Fashionmex, workers legitimately concerned that the company would close down without paying the legally required worker indemnifications took their complaints to local authorities, to the streets, and to the media. They marched through downtown handing out leaflets proclaiming "For the union of all maquila workers!!" and forcibly stopped a truck full of company products from leaving the city before workers were paid.[46] At the same time, a newly radicalized COMO (Center for the Orientation of Women Workers)[47] weighed in on the side of "working women" in general, supporting both the Fashionmex and Andromex struggles and loudly proclaiming working women's right to self-determination.

The maquilas responded to these challenges either by leaving town[48]—or, more commonly, by threatening to leave—or with highly publicized blacklists intended to keep out "conflictive people."[49] Although they complained loudly of worker intransigence, they showed no sign of reevaluating the gendering of their hiring strategies. Local media, on the other hand, narrated the developments through their usual troubled gendered lens. Thus, stories of maquila workers' resistance were imbued with sexual innuendoes and mockery. At the end of the Andromex conflict, one paper reported that weird unfeminine hairstyles and a hysterical woman worker running nude through the plant were "the last straw" for workers after a bad year.[50] Six months later, a cartoon of the women at Fashionmex showed them busty and miniskirted, ooing and ahing over their union boss,[51] and the day a recount went in their favor, a local paper buried the victory—reporting it inside an edition whose red, inch-and-a-half front-page headlines screamed "PROSTITUTION IN THE MAQUILADORAS."[52]

Amid this charged context, 1982 brought a drastic peso devaluation—the first of a series that would follow over the upcoming decade. Between 1981 and 1982, the dollar value of the peso was cut in half, and average maquila wages fell from US$234.30 weekly to US$105.60.[53] The following year, maquila employment in Juárez jumped 26 percent. Even more dramatic devaluations followed in 1986 and 1987. By the end of the decade, in dollar terms, the peso was worth a mere fraction of its value at the outset of the maquila program,[54] and maquila employment in Juárez had tripled.[55]

The soaring demand for workers had immediate consequences. In December 1982, the first sarcastic headline appeared: "TWO COMPANIES SEEK 120 WORKERS; but . . . the CROC[56] 'doesn't have anyone free.'"[57] Four months and a half-dozen articles later, the tone was anything but sarcastic. "MARKED ABSENCE OF FEMALE LABOR FOR THE MAQUILA-DORAS: In the unions controlled by the CROC they need five hundred young people; yesterday only one hundred showed up."[58] By May the tone was frankly hysterical: "'DEFICIT' OF LABOR FOR THE MAQUILA-DORAS: With Sound Systems They Look for Workers in the Shanty-towns."[59] The union leader who only four years earlier had claimed that the female labor force was "inexhaustible" now announced that it was "obvious that all the women of Ciudad Juárez are already employed"[60] and began suggesting importing labor from rural areas farther south.[61] Current personnel managers who worked during the early eighties communicate the mood of their departments at the time through the black humor of the period: "In personnel in those days, all we needed was a mirror. If they were breathing, they were hired"; or, "We'd hire anyone with ten fingers."[62]

Despite the sudden scarcity of young women workers willing to work at maquila salaries, after industry wages' initial collapse, pay stagnated,[63] with real wages falling throughout a decade legendary among managers for the severity of its "labor shortages."[64] In 1983, the plants began offering benefits such as free lunches, transportation to and from work, and credits at nearby chain stores, but base pay remained low.[65] Industry representatives made much of the external factors which prevented them from raising wages, including pressures from the Mexican state, which was concerned with protecting international competitiveness,[66] and pressures from local domestic industries, which were unable to afford wage inflation computed in dollars.[67] However, local management was also limited by the image of maquila labor elaborated in home offices[68] and accepted as common sense in their border outposts, which took extreme cheapness as a defining feature of appropriate export-processing labor. Thus, discussion of substantial raises in pesos, even if their costs were constant in dollars, remained taboo. Instead, managers frequently referenced the "irrationality" of workers, who, it was said, could be assuaged by benefits and shows of appreciation, but not by wage increases. As a result, the maquilas in 1984 paid less than half what they had just a few years earlier and far less than comparable national industries in Mexico City.[69] By 1988, even *Twin Plant News,* the industry's English-language newsletter, was remarking that "earning $3.50 or less for a full day's work simply doesn't seem attractive to many people."[70]

As the value of maquila wages fell, women workers who had become reliant on higher salaries looked elsewhere. Local newspapers reported them moving into better paying "men's jobs"[71] and crossing the border to "earn dollars."[72] It was this set of decisions which, in tandem with management's inflexibility on wages, produced the "shortage" so dramatically presented in personnel department accounts. This was occasionally recognized at the time. In May 1988, *Twin Plant News* tartly lectured its readers. "Many companies believe that [because of] the large number of maquila plants that have been started in the last few years . . . there aren't enough people to go around . . . we would like to point out . . . that the number of 'employable' operators is still larger than the number of vacancies."[73]

Transnational managers expected "feminine" workers. That meant workers who were as inherently cheap and docile as they were sexed. However, cheapness and pliancy are at least in part market products, and tight labor markets rarely produce them. Thus, despite maquila managers' experience of the grueling labor shortage of the eighties as something like a natural disaster, it was substantially of their own making. In defining the paradigmatic maquila worker as simultaneously cheap, female, and docile, they created a market which eventually undercut the conditions of existence for such a creature. Many young women were still willing to work in the plants, of course, but there were no longer enough to keep all industry lines running at once. Ultimately the demand for cheapness made some shift in the demographics of maquila workforces inevitable.

The rigidity of transnational management's image of an appropriate maquila worker not only diminished women worker's availability, it also eroded the "docility" of those available. The alarmism of the early eighties notwithstanding, maquila lines never came to a halt for lack of workers. However, in the context of high labor demand, idiosyncratic benefit packages virtually invited workers to shop around. Thus, although maquila wage policies did not stop production, they did produce turnover.[74] In February 1984, the head of AMAC (the maquiladora industry association) said as much when he dismissed the notion that there was a labor shortage on the border: "What is going on at this time . . . is that there are 7,000 unstable workers . . . [who] go from one industry to another to where it's most convenient for them to offer their services, and this is reflected in the plants that don't bring their benefits up to the level of their competitors."[75]

Women's growing leverage in the labor market produced a similar phenomenon on the line, and after years of calling the shots, managers found themselves at a disadvantage. A supervisor who'd been a worker in the seventies lamented the new order: "In the beginning it was marvelous, when the maquilas started, because you took care of your work, you knew there were 200,000 more willing to do it."[76] This comment, and others like it, were encapsulated in tropes that, like the labor shortage jokes, were repeated in interview after interview with personnel managers who had been in the industry during this period:[77] "They always knew they could get work on the other side of the street"; or, "All a supervisor needed to do was look at her crosswise and she was out the door." Newspaper reports of the period took the same exasperated tone. Early in 1983, one complained: "Due to the current scarcity of women workers in the maquiladoras . . . the women change employment when they feel like it."[78] Three months later, the same paper reported: "Yesterday, maquila operators were found enjoying the labor shortage facing the plants; they don't worry about arriving early or being fired. At the Juárez Monument, Guadalupe Cárdenas and Laura Lozano . . . commented that they were already late; both said that, because of the labor shortage, they couldn't fire them, and that's the way it is, because the one thing there's plenty of is work in all the factories."[79] Women workers' "bad behavior" was directed at new male workers as well as at their bosses. A frustrated union leader complained that the few men who entered the plants were forced out by catcalling women co-workers, who were gleefully taking advantage of their unusual numerical superiority.[80]

On the heels of women workers' increasing assertiveness, the first cracks in the maquila managers' implacable image of the "docile woman worker" emerged in the spring of 1983. Fresh from a year of shop-floor militance, and in the midst of soaring male unemployment rates,[81] Andromex's new Mexican plant manager was among the first to recognize that "docile" was as scarce as female in its current workforce, and to announce that he was hiring men.[82] By March of 1983, others were quietly following suit, although they were reluctant to admit publicly that they were breaking with tradition. The head of the CROC announced that several companies the union worked with "had seen themselves obliged to hire men." He refused to name them, commenting that if he did so, "they wouldn't hire them anymore."[83] Obviously, these companies were not the only ones. In June, men made up three of every five workers hired,[84] although they would not make up this high a percentage of the total workforce until the end of the decade.

Despite the burst of men hired in 1983, management remained skeptical about the utility of men for assembly work. In a typical statement from the first uptick in hiring men, the union boss responsible for hiring for a group of maquilas commented: "The hiring of men is done with more rigorous selective criteria given that they are more disobedient, irresponsible, and prone to absences; distressingly, in Juárez, men already got used to not working."[85]

Newspaper ads from the first half of the decade reflected this attitude, continuing to request women.[86] By the end of the eighties, though, industry representatives were frantic. Turnover was well over 100 percent annually,[87] and industry complaints about shortages and increasing training costs had reached a fever pitch.[88] Still focused on getting their hands on femininity, however embodied, a few plants hired transvestites. One manager recalled, "The need for people was so great that we had men who walked around the plant dressed as women," adding parenthetically, "We don't permit that anymore." Maquilas paid workers to bring in friends,[89] established "gentleman's agreements" not to hire workers who'd left previous jobs "without clear reasons,"[90] and even considered setting a single salary and benefit structure for the industry as a whole.[91] In this context, they began to publicly discuss broadening their worker profile for the first time, acknowledging the possibility of hiring men, albeit in the most disrespectful terms. Their first public statements on the subject coincided with assessments of the feasibility of contracting senior citizens and the handicapped,[92] and although discussions of these latter two groups were pitched in the most self-congratulatory terms,[93] the possibility of hiring men was consistently framed as a compromise. Although women are "more careful and responsible," commented the head of AMAC in 1988, men had also been found "acceptable."[94]

Not surprisingly, men responding to these mixed messages were slow to enter maquila doors. In the spring of 1983, amid reports of the first labor crisis in the maquilas, their pace drew the ire of the editors of a local paper. A picture of men sitting under the trees was glossed by the caption: "Despite the many maquiladora factory announcements soliciting male workers, it seems that the *juarenses* have declared war against work and prefer to face the heat in the shade of a tree."[95] In 1988, the head of AMAC reiterated these complaints, commenting that "despite the invitations to take positions, there are very few [men] who are interested in working."[96] Managerial ambivalence and male workers' responses meant that the proportion of women in the maquila workforce did not go into free fall. Rather, between 1982 and the end of the decade, the percentage of men increased between 2 and 6 percent yearly. It was not until 1988, in the third year of over 10 percent growth in the

city's maquiladora workforce, that there was finally a surge of advertisements directed at men as well as women.[97] Not until the end of the
decade did men constitute a stable 45 percent of the industry's direct
local workforce.[98]

The causes and consequences of the inflow of men into maquila work
have been much debated.[99] As cheap, docile, and female became an increasingly difficult combination to find among flesh-and-blood job applicants, one might have expected that the tenacious feminization of
maquila work would erode, especially as thousands of men filled shop
floors with no noticeable impact on industry productivity. Yet the trope
of productive femininity, nourished by ongoing links to a larger transnational imaginary, remained in place.[100] In the fantasy world of "offshore production," docile women continued to hold the microscope
and thread the needle. Maquila managers, ongoing participants in a
larger, transnational system of meanings and taken-for-granteds, continued to cite the "maquila-grade female" as a standard against which
to measure maquila labor.[101] As a result, for the most part (see Chapter 6 for a telling exception to this pattern), men were hired, but
marked upon entry as lacking, with complex consequences both for
their own sense of self and for shop-floor control.

Increases in the number of men in the maquilas did little to assuage
local unease over changing gender roles, as the industry's ongoing preference for women kept the spotlight on changing familial structures. In
an emblematic moment in 1985, the Mexican president met with (female) maquila workers during a visit to the city. His response to their
complaints about transportation, housing, and other public services
was a revealing non sequitur: "The fact that a large portion [of maquila
jobs] are filled by women is inducing changes in our social and productive life, phenomena with which we Mexicans were previously unfamil-
iar and which present us with challenges which we cannot always resolve
quickly."[102]

Between the president's perturbed comments in 1985 and a 1991
hiatus in the industry's breakneck expansion,[103] local media kept track
of working-class women and men's role failures and sexual trespasses
with grim zeal. In the financial sphere, local newspapers worried over
women moving into "men's jobs"[104] and turning down employment as
maids.[105] In the social sphere, reports were even more persistent and
damning. Women were joining gangs in which they were "as dangerous
and aggressive as men."[106] They were drinking and carousing,[107] prac-
ticing "free love" and using condoms,[108] divorcing, and having children

out of wedlock.[109] In a particularly acidic report, a large local daily reported that the city was increasingly seeing an "unusual discrimination" against northern—that is, local—women in favor of their counterparts from the south in the area of paid domestic work. "It's as if women from these latitudes have forgotten the ritual of 'bed making' and of 'homemade *mole*.'"[110] Young working-class men were less constant a target, but the few comments were saturated with disdain. Men weren't working because "they really didn't want to find work,"[111] yet their "machismo" led to divorces when their wives worked.[112] More damning still, they were engaging in "the oldest job in the world" in the service of their employed female counterparts, and their consequent "lack of restraint" was evident in their participation in beauty contests and "ladies' only nights."[113]

Despite dramatic shifts in the demographics of the maquila workforce during the eighties, the frameworks surrounding it proved remarkably stable. Both transnational managers' tenacious image of innate feminine docility and local anxieties over shifting gender roles and behaviors remained constant, framing workers' understanding of maquila work, the ways in which they were brought onto maquila shop floors, and the labor control strategies which greeted them upon arrival. This period proved to be somewhat easier for the few Mexican plant managers, as their participation in a local discourse about the erosion of femininity provided them with at least some framework through which to grasp and respond to a changing situation. Nonetheless, they were in a clear minority, and in the booming industry of the eighties, the transnational trope of productive femininity continued to create conditions which undermined its very existence locally. As hundreds of managers sought ever more desperately after the iconic feminine maquila worker, she moved farther and farther out of reach, making hiring and labor control an ongoing challenge and leading to tremendous variety in managerial strategies throughout the industry in the decade which followed.

Proliferating Genders

The demographics of the maquila industry in its first decades and the public rhetoric of its plant managers over time suggest that early analysts got it right: the edifice of transnational production was built on the preconstituted cheapness and docility of third-world women workers.

The demographic situation at the end of the eighties and later suggests that early analysts got it wrong: femininity was not an essential element in the structure of third-world assembly. In my opinion, neither of these interpretations captures the complexity of the situation. Certainly, global production does not depend on the existence of a fixed and pre-set "femininity." Just as surely, however, the trope of "femininity" does matter in transnational production's development. Both discourse and demographics provide important information about the way in which gender operates at work. The idea of femininity structured, and continues to structure, production in the maquilas. It provides the norm against which workers are assessed in hiring and labor control, both in terms of their fitness for the work and in terms of what is possible and acceptable to expect of them in production. As such, although "women" are not necessarily a cornerstone of global production, the idea of who they are continues to structure its daily operations and on-going evolution.

In the Juárez maquila industry of the early nineties, when I arrived in the city, this structuring process was particularly evident. The difficulty of finding flesh-and-blood workers who approximated managerial images meant that each manager was left to himself to find a way to make sense and profits of an unexpected workforce. Thus, each shop floor became a tiny experiment, an arena where a fluid set of gendered meanings was fixed and harnessed in the service of shop-floor control—and occasionally in the service of its undoing (see Chapter 7).

In late 1991, the industry was contracting in response to a recession across the border, and the number of men had stabilized at close to half the workforce. In an interview, the head of AMAC explained male workers' ongoing presence at the end of the boom as a consequence of their metamorphosis from highly "problematic" into something very much like "maquila-grade females." "It was a process of acculturation for men to incorporate themselves into production . . . with the years they have changed; now they have a mentality oriented toward the industry." [114] Outside his office, opinions of male workers were far more varied and less sanguine, however. [115] Despite the thousands of men working in the maquilas, there was still no trope, no structure of meaning, within which "male maquila worker" made sense. At 45 percent, they remained the ubiquitous exception.

A decade after the introduction of men into maquila work, the meaning structures around productive femininity remained fully evident and remarkably firm—still providing the narrative framework within which most maquila managers imagined, hired, and supervised workers. Even in this period, roughly half the ads in local newspapers specified women only, and many still requested "*Señoritas*" and "*Damitas.*" Although there were exceptions (see Chapter 6), most managers continued to treat women's dextrous fingers, malleability, and capacity to withstand routine as "facts of life," even in the face of massive evidence, even personal experience, to the contrary.

For individual managers, the persistence of the trope of the "maquila-grade female," alongside the ongoing scarcity of workers who fit that description, created the quandary of how to hire and discipline a shop-floor labor force in such a context and have the project make sense. Immersion in the dailiness of four maquilas in the area made it possible for me to track the highly varied ways in which they addressed this problem, and to see the multiple gendered processes behind the mystery of the industry's demographics. The managers of the plants I will describe below each created their own path through this set of challenges, some more successfully than others, but all making meaning, if not profits, along the way.

In Panoptimex, transnational managers committed to a factory that "looked right" went to great lengths to import a workforce that matched the industry image, thus giving birth to a shop floor full of simulacra they perceived as originals. In Particimex, a plant established outside the city precisely in order to access a home-disciplined female workforce, Mexican managers addressed women workers in a rhetoric that explicitly challenged their transnational colleagues' celebration of Mexican women's "traditional" docility. In Andromex, Mexican managers found their few remaining images of feminine pliancy shattered by women workers' shop-floor militance. In response, they restructured their hiring and labor control strategies around the image of an (implicitly male) "worker," regaining shop-floor control in the process. And finally, in Anarchomex, transnational managers, stuck both in Juárez and in the common sense of the maquila industry, inadvertently created a shop-floor struggle over the content of worker masculinity, much to the detriment of production quality.

Each of these arenas of production constitutes a case study in the operations of gender at work. No individual case is either "typical" or "representative." Instead, it is the uniqueness of each plant which is of interest and importance. In taking the measure of these idiosyncrasies, we come to see how a globally constituted rhetoric operates through local conditions and subjectivities, creating facts on the ground whose wide variability in no way diminishes their indebtedness to global forces. This chapter told the story of the making of a labor market. The next four chapters travel to the shop floor, delineating the variable ways that members of the industry-defined labor force actually become "workers" within the arena of production. In so doing, we move from newspapers and interviews to participant observation, bringing shop-floor practices and ethnographic experience to the fore. In each of these factories, we will watch as the market discourses described above are shaped and restructured by local strategies and intentions, thereby evoking idiosyncratic local subjects on the shop floor.

4

Bringing Fantasies to Life

Panoptimex

On first encounter, the Panoptimex shop floor is eerily familiar: the docile women workers of managerial dreams and feminist ethnography, theory, and nightmare seem come to life in its confines. Rows of them, smiling lips drawn red, darkened lashes lowered to computer boards, male supervisors looking over their shoulders—monitoring finger speed and manicure in a single glance. Apparent embodiments of availability—cheap, malleable labor, willing flirtation—these young women make flesh the image of productive femininity upon whose existence an entire global political economy claims to have staked its success. Nonetheless, a quick recollection of the actual panicked labor market stirring just outside the factory's gates, replete with tales of shortage and insubordination, transforms my resigned "of course" into puzzlement. Where have all these icons of paradigmatic femininity come from? If no one else has been able to find them in the Juárez streets, how have the Panoptimex managers done so? The answer, as is so often the case, lies in reformulating the question. These paragons have not been found, they have been made. As Panoptimex workers respond to managerial descriptions of how they always were, they come to incarnate these images in the here and now.

Immersion in Panoptimex's daily life reveals not only that gender matters in assembly; it also shows how it matters. Of all the factories I will discuss, Panoptimex best fulfills the expectations embedded in the stereotype of the preconstituted, passive, nimble-fingered assembly worker. Thus, an analysis of this plant operates as something of a limiting case. Insofar as we can expose the process through which feminine productivity is created *here,* we are well on our way to being able to take apart the mechanisms through which production produces, rather than relies on, the (in)famously docile and dextrous third-world woman.

Panoptimex is part of an enormous electronics transnational I call Electroworld. It produces televisions, and since moving into its new building several years ago, that production has been remarkably successful. Its speed and quality levels rival those achieved by the same corporation at far higher cost in the United States. Recently, another TV assembler in Juárez was so taken by its competitor's results (and look) that it bought Panoptimex's building blueprints for its second plant. This success is directly, if unintentionally, related to the extreme feminization of the plant's basic production tasks and the concomitant sexual objectification of its workforce.

In Panoptimex, visually oriented managers have created a structure of labor control in which everything is designed to produce the right look. In the process, they have designed a machine that evokes and focuses the male gaze[1] in the service of production.[2] The panoptic shop floor[3] is full of high-heeled young women, gleaned with great effort from Juárez and beyond. Around them stand critical, attentive male super-visors whose eyes invite both performance and self-vigilance. Through obsessive watching, managers create a shop floor of voyeurs and their objects, and labor control operates through the sexualized, gendered subjectivities which emerge in this lopsided interaction. The rare male worker is a third wheel here, consigned to irrelevance by his inability to look. Neither labor control processes which make no reference to gender nor the imported docility of feminine workers can account for the quiescence of workers in this plant. To the contrary, it is through addressing workers' gendered subjectivities that managers fulfill their own desires, building TVs among them.[4]

Over-seers

In Panoptimex, management's common sense is remarkable for its consistent bias toward visual signs and symbols of success or failure.[5] This visually skewed attention is the product of a cluster of forces, both institutional and discursive. Standard maquila accounting practices, the erosion of profit margins in the production of low-end TVs, and the high internal mobility of top Electroworld managers combine to undermine a focus on costs and profits for their own sake and to encourage a focus on impressing headquarters instead. At the same time, these institutional predilections are solidified and underlined by the more general visual rhetoric of TV production, in which "the picture" is the frame within which everything is understood and evaluated.

This attitude has distinct consequences when it is turned from managers' bosses to their subordinates. Once focused "down"—both literally and metaphorically—this visual attention is imbued with nationalist and gendered understandings. Top (hence foreign) managers' nationalist chauvinism toward the Mexicans they supervise further incites their tendency to see workers as children to be conditioned, rather than as intelligible adults. At the same time, the focus on the "look" of the factory, combined with a long tradition of women workers in electronics, leads to a rigid form of job gendering in which filling the lines with young women becomes a goal in itself. Together, these institutional routines and attentional habits lead to a highly gendered and sexualized pattern of hiring and labor control. As we will see below, this pattern ultimately proves both pleasurable and titillating (if also disturbing) for the young women on the shop floor. Partly because of this, it proves remarkably effective in shop-floor control.

This attitude also has consequences for my position in the plant. When I first meet Dave Jones, Electroworld's regional personnel manager, he immediately launches into a critique of my undoubtedly "radical" ideas and, without waiting for a response, accedes to my request to observe production on the grounds that it will let me see me how good work conditions "really are" in the maquilas. Unlike his counterparts in other plants, however, he refuses to allow me to work on the line, even for a day. In explaining this decision, he emphasizes that he is concerned neither for the quality of the TVs I might produce nor for my personal safety. He is concerned instead that, in a context where watching is power, a worker might "look back," see me, and report me to the Mexican department of labor. Nothing I say can sway him from this conviction. Thus, in Panoptimex of all places, I find myself wandering the lines with "nothing to do"—but watch! In the ultimate gendered panopticon, I am placed as both ogled woman and observer of the observers—my status ambiguous enough to garner me invitations to managerial meetings as well as worker parties, and uncomfortable enough to unnerve supervisors and embarrass myself on a daily basis.

PROJECTING UP

Production at Panoptimex occurs in a highly symbolic system in which appearances are as much the currency as dollars. To an extent, this is an issue throughout the industry. Most maquilas are far from any point of sale and their accounting systems are organized to "make their budget" rather than to make a profit.[6] As a result, local managers find themselves more subject to the managers at corporate headquarters who set that budget than to external competition. Their energy tends to be directed accordingly. However, in Panoptimex, the tendency to make headquarters' approval the primary goal of work on a daily as well as a long-term basis is particularly accentuated.[7]

Late in my sojourn in the factory, Carlos Figueires, the plant manager, invites me to a series of meetings he has called to assess the year's results.[8] The plant has not made its budget, he announces to assembled managers. The deficit, in his view, is minimal. But how is he to communicate his "success" to corporate headquarters? Several meetings are devoted to this question. When he presents the meeting's results to the chief of Juárez operations, his superior matter-of-factly agrees—cost overruns are not a problem since their causes are out of Carlos's control. The issue is one of allocating blame, not of concern for the "bottom line." A damage control operation during this period shows the same dynamic. Electroworld is slated to prove its compliance with demands by international creditors that it cut its workforce 10 percent across the board. The response in Panoptimex is a major effort—but only one of bookkeeping. No one is fired. No money is saved. But 10 percent of salaries are moved to the "miscellaneous" category of the budget. Looking credible is enough; there is no countervailing price or profit pressure direct enough to undermine this entirely symbolic solution.

Two sets of institutional forces—intense price competition in the international TV industry and Electroworld career trajectories—frame Panoptimex's operations and evoke these responses. The first of these, the low profit margin in TV production, is a rarely discussed backdrop against which daily decisions are made on the shop floor. "TVs are not a business," the manager of Electrofeed, a local Electroworld parts maker, tells me early on. "If you had to face stockholders with only a TV business . . ." He shakes his head soberly. The profit margin on the low-end TVs produced by Panoptimex is so slim, according to Carlos, that not "making budget" frequently means literally selling below cost. So why produce TVs at all? Because, they say, it's worth it to Electroworld to keep its name in the marketplace. Once that is accomplished, profit can be made elsewhere, for instance, in VCRs. Here, it is not only Panoptimex managers who treat costs symbolically. The overall corporate decision to continue TV production is predicated on the calculation that it is worth it even under conditions in which such production may not turn a profit on its own.

This sense among Panoptimex managers that appearances are paramount, and that the relevant audience is headquarters, is further encouraged by Electroworld's corporation-wide managerial placement policies. Electroworld is an American subsidiary of an even larger European corporation. Panoptimex managers report to bosses in the United States, but their personal career trajectories move throughout the corporation as a whole. Top managers around the world are brought in for several-year periods, then moved on to keep them from being overly attached to—and hence losing their "objectivity" about—the factory they are running. As one of the managers calmly explains, "The truth is, I'd get less emotional about fighting for this place than for my little radio plant in England." This external staffing policy has obvious implications for the perspective of those—the current Panoptimex manager among them—brought in from the outside. Carlos is a Brazilian on a three-year contract. He began with Electroworld in Manaus, but most recently ran a plant in Singapore. He makes quite clear that his sights are set far above Panoptimex. He spends the better part of a first interview drawing detailed diagrams of the corporation's overall structure and explaining where he'd like to be and when. These are no idle daydreams. His attention is firmly fixed on those who have the power to move him where he would like to be.

These institutional patterns—a market in which profit cannot be the primary criterion for success, a structure of career opportunities in which top managers are not deeply tied to "their" factories, and a set of accounting practices which formalize local managers' absolute reliance upon headquarters—together encourage a highly symbolic attitude toward production. TVs must be produced, of course, preferably of reasonable quality and without huge cost overruns. However, top management attempts all this with an eye on neither "the consumer" nor "the competition," but instead on the boss.

SEEING IS BELIEVING

The institutional patterns described above encourage a focus on appearances, but they do not ensure it. These institutional structures are far more common among the Juárez maquilas than is the plant's overwhelming focus on the look of things. What makes such structures so significant here is that they create an appearance-directed context within which the visual rhetoric available in TV production can, and does, frame managerial perspectives on the shop floor. In listening to Panoptimex managers, the sight-related criteria through which success and failure are assessed is striking and pervasive. Ultimately, this visual rhetoric is both symptomatic and constitutive of the habit of watching as a practice of control.

The general visual focus held throughout the factory emerges almost obsessively in Carlos's conversation—most clearly as the centerpiece of his triumphal autobiography. It erupts in a set of photos—pulled with a practiced gesture from his desk's top drawer—of the factory he ran in Singapore. "It was all shit, just shit, girls working with garbage all around. Dark, ugly, I change all that. We paint, we make it nice." He slams down the before-and-after pictures for emphasis, expostulating on the importance of color scheme and pointing out details of the change. The color scheme is of particular importance, he points out, and his first act on arrival in Juárez was to paint Panoptimex in identical tones. His commentary on more daily management reveals the same emphasis. He discusses his capacity to see production from his office window at great length, describing calls down to supervisors on the floor to check on problems and remind them he's watching. This focus is even expressed when he discusses the importance of politic ignorance. Covering an eye with his hand he comments, "I have to keep my eyes closed here all the time."

This emphasis on watching as a modality of control is also evident among other top Electroworld managers in Juárez. For instance, the chief Juárez quality manager begins discussing the programs he has instituted in Panoptimex by pointing out that workers are first shown a quality video and then sign a "quality badge" they wear afterward as a visual reminder of the experience. He goes on to describe the brightly colored quality charts facing each worker. "Workers are involved in quality because we keep track of all that they do, mistakes, everything, and they see it all the time." The manager of Electrofeed follows Panoptimex's lead on production-area structure, installing a set of windows on the shop floor. Simultaneously invoking both their metaphorical and literal purposes, he explains that the windows increase "transparency"— "So that I can see them [workers] and they can see me."

This visual idiom of control is most clearly embodied in the physical structure of the Panoptimex shop floor. Clean, light, spacious, and orderly—the production area is the very image of a "well-run" factory.

Top managers are highly aware of, and invested in, this fact and they often boast about the plant's attractiveness. The factory floor is not merely easy on the eye, however. It is organized for visibility—a fish bowl in which everything is marked. Yellow tape marks the walkways, red arrows point at test sites, green, yellow, and red lights glow above the machines. On the walls hang large, shiny white graphs documenting quality levels in red, yellow, green, and black. Just above each worker's head is a chart full of dots—each color an assessment of the worker below. Workers' bodies too are marked: yellow tunics for new workers; light blue tunics for women workers; dark blue smocks for male workers and mechanics; red tunics for (female) group chiefs; orange tunics for their (female) assistants; ties for supervisors. Everything is visually signaled.

Ringing the top of the production floor is a wall of windows, with a manager behind every one. They sit in the semiprivacy of the reflected glare, watching at will. From on high, they "keep track of the flow of production," calling down to a supervisor to ask about a slowdown, easily visible from above in the accumulation of TVs in one part of the line, gaps further along, or in a mound of sets in the center of a line, technicians clustered nearby. From here, managers show the factory to visitors, standing on the glassed-in balcony boasting about the plant's large capital investment and unique labor process. At one point, men with cameras watched for stealing from behind the glass walls, and it is common knowledge on the shop floor that cameras are still embedded in the ceilings for this purpose. They have set it up so that even the walls have eyes.

This highly objectifying modality of control encounters an added incitement in the intense national chauvinism and cultural disrespect with which top—hence imported (symbolically "American")—managers view Mexicans in general. These attitudes make it possible for Electroworld's regional personnel manager, Dave Jones, to speak virtually no Spanish after almost fifteen years in the job, and for the Brazilian plant manager to be far more fluent in English than Spanish. It makes it possible for a top Juárez manager to say to me of one of Electroworld's rare Mexican plant managers, "There are some things we can say here and now across this table that you couldn't say with him." And it makes it possible for Jones to say openly that he could offer a U.S. plant manager 20 percent more than his top offer for a Mexican, and that for that sort of money, he'd prefer "to hire a U.S., they're more mature, more innovative, more versatile." And, conveniently, it makes it possible for Jones to refer disparagingly to the "Mexican mind" whenever supervisors or workers raise labor complaints. The actual inability of most top managers to communicate with their employees, combined with a venerable U.S. tradition of assuming Mexican cultural and racial inferiority, adds a final element to the labor control logic in which listening to workers makes no "sense" and watching them thereby becomes imperative.

HIRING FOR LOOKS

Panoptimex managers' focus on the look of things is expressed particularly clearly in the plant's gendered and sexualized hiring practices. The five years since Electroworld began producing entire TVs—including the two years since that production process was moved into this "showcase" factory—have all been characterized by a dramatic "shortage" of young female labor in Juárez. Nonetheless, the plant has almost invariably had at least 70 percent women on the line, and has rarely had under 75 percent. The average age on the shop floor continues to be under twenty, and a man has yet to be placed in the chassis-building section. Although electronics plants generally have an easier time hiring women than do other maquilas in Juárez,[9] Panoptimex's figures remain unusual.

When asked about their absolute commitment to hiring women for most line jobs, Panoptimex managers tend to point out that electronics—certainly Electroworld—*always* hires women, whatever country they're in. Panoptimex's last manager comments matter-of-factly that "electronics traditionally uses female types" when I ask about the decision to hire women even when they're much harder to find than are men. Other managers offer similar narratives.[10] Supervisors request not only the number of workers they need for their line, but the genders of each position as well. The personnel department puts a great deal of daily planning and energy into hiring the "right" genders for the jobs available. Irene Pérez, the head of personnel in the plant, details criteria for most line jobs, beginning with being female and young and continuing with being slim and having thin hands and short nails. The criteria also include not being pregnant, using birth control, and being childless, or, if absolutely necessary, having credible childcare arrangements. The most basic of these requirements is being female, and as a result, on hiring days guards admit all the women applicants who come to the maquila gates, but only a previously specified number of men. The few men hired for what are known as the line "heavy" jobs are not subject to the bodily strictures required of their female counterparts, but in their place are a substantially more demanding set of social requirements. Unlike their female co-workers, they must have someone in the plant vouch for them, and they must present a certificate of high school graduation.

These criteria and practices are not unheard of among other Juárez maquilas. What sets Panoptimex apart is the lengths to which management went to ensure a female workforce during the shortage of young women workers in the late eighties, even as colleagues in other maquilas reluctantly began hiring men. Panoptimex managers, stubbornly refusing to acquiesce to the new labor market demographics, decided to recruit workers from a village with what they called an "agrarian economy" an hour beyond city limits. In an extended "PR" campaign involving all levels of the personnel department as well as top managers from other departments, they first courted the mayor, then treated the whole village to a picnic with mariachis, then knocked on all 150 doors in the village with pictures of the plant, and finally offered to pay transportation for all young women willing to come work in the factory. Four years later, these young women still work the lines, and Panoptimex is still paying for their transport.

Managers' framework in Panoptimex is relentlessly visual; this perspective is expressed not only in their dealings with their superiors but in their hiring and labor control practices as well. As a result, they hire assembly-line workers who are overwhelmingly female and young—the age to be beautiful and to be invested in that beauty—then monitor them through obsessive observation. The essence of their hiring criteria is most succinctly expressed by a woman supervisor in another Electroworld plant: "In Panoptimex they don't look for workers, they look for models—short skirts, heels, beauties." Not that Panoptimex workers are more beautiful than young women in other maquilas—at least not to my eye. However, Panoptimex workers *are* hired as "models"—hired to look the way managers expect workers to look.

In the Fishbowl

Panoptimex managers' focus on control through vigilance is expressed throughout the factory in a hierarchy of seeing. Top managers sit behind windows above the shop floor, looking down. Supervisors walk the lines below, observing the workers sitting before them. In front of workers, however, there are only routinized tasks and individualized quality charts—co-workers glimpsed from the corners of their eyes. Shop-floor control is orchestrated through a set of embedded panopticons: managers watch supervisors and workers, supervisors watch (most) workers, workers watch themselves, and when they can, each other.

This hierarchy of seeing, however, is defined as much by gender as it is by the relations of production. Rather than depicting the scene as one in which managers watch supervisors and workers, one might aptly describe men watching men watching women (and ignoring a few emasculated men). Or, more accurately, one might describe the scene by including *both* production and gender: a panopticon in which male managers watch male supervisors watch women workers and ignore a few male workers.

Managers' attentional practices and the physical space they spawn have constituted a highly visual system of labor control that differentially affects women and men. The women are central objects of supervisory attention, whereas the men are peripheral objects of supervisory disregard. This system is enacted by top managers, supervisors, personnel staff, and union delegates both within and outside the arena of production. Although it can be described with no reference to gender, its tremendous interpellatory power comes from its gendered organization of desire. Even the most cursory tour of the shop floor reveals intensely accentuated gendered styles, and conversations with workers add to this impression. These subjectivities in turn have repercussions for the level of managerial control on the shop floor, accounting both for the shop floor's intense atmosphere of titillation and control and for its highly successful production record.

SUPER-VISING

Unlike Electroworld's other maquilas in Juárez, Panoptimex produces a final product. From the beginning to the end of its long, looping lines, hundreds of tiny components are combined with monitors and cabinets to emerge as TVs, ready for sale. Production takes place in five lines—each one a perfect replica of the next. One hundred and twenty workers make up each line. Backs to their supervisors, eyes to their work, they repeat the same gestures a thousand times during the nine-and-a-half hour day.

The first part of the line assembles the TV's innards. This is chassis, the plant's most "critical" operation. Here, several hundred miniature electronic parts are inserted into prepunctured boards. The work is done by forty seated young women, each of whom inserts six to eight tiny color-coded parts during every thirty-second "cycle." The chassis is then tested before moving on to "final" at the end of the line, where ten young men, standing, attach it to monitors and cabinets. Turning the corner, the now-recognizable "TV" reenters the women's domain. Here the electrical system is assembled, wires soldered and twisted— the facsimile made real. On to the "tunnel," where young women peer at the screen, seeking straight lines, ninety-degree angles, and clear pinks and greens. Finally, the TV is ready for use. Once again, it moves into male territory at line's end. Here it is packed, boxed, and marked with one of a half-dozen brand names, finally rising to the ceiling in a glass tube and vanishing from sight. Soon it will reemerge in warehouses on the other side of the border, its last stop before the large chains that bring it to consumers throughout the United States.

As in almost all maquilas, the workers who produce these TVs are paid poorly, even for Juárez.[11] Most workers take home roughly US$40 weekly.[12] This is not a negligible amount of money, but it is well below what is required to live independently in Juárez, and as in many such plants, portions of even this amount are contingent on perfect attendance. Missing a single day of work costs a third of the weekly paycheck. Seniority provides no respite here. Workers can, and do, work for years without promotion of any kind. Most do not stay that long, however. Three-quarters of the workforce must be replaced over the course of the year. Not surprisingly in this context, most workers are teenagers and live with family—whether it be parents, siblings, more distant relatives, or (occasionally) working spouses. Given this pay structure, labor control cannot depend too heavily on financial incentives or the hope of promotion. This is where the tremendous scrutiny under which workers operate in the plant, and the self-consciousness that emerges from that scrutiny, becomes fundamental.[13]

Lines are "operator controlled." The chassis comes to a halt in front of the worker, who inserts her components and pushes a button to send it on. There is no piece rate, no moving assembly line to hurry her along. But she hurries anyway. In this fishbowl, with managers peering from their offices above and supervisors observing from the floor, no one is willing to be seen with a clogged line behind her or an empty space ahead of her. If she does slow momentarily, the supervisor materializes. "Ah, here's the problem. What's wrong, my dear?" He circles behind seated workers, monitoring "his girls" just as he is monitored from above.

There are layers upon layers of supervision. Above the shop floor hover those known below as "the Americans"—top managers who, regardless of their international origins, are associated with the U.S. headquarters to which they report. Their presence is often noted by workers and supervisors seeking to explain the difference between Panoptimex and other Electroworld plants. A Mexican assistant manager in personnel comments that at Panoptimex, "there are visitors all the time, and the windows all around . . . all the time you know they're watching you." And they do not only watch from a distance. In the late afternoon, Carlos and his production manager descend to see more closely. Hands clasped behind backs, they stroll the plant floor, stopping to berate a supervisor about a candy wrapper lying on the floor or to chat with workers on the line.

Below the production manager are the supervisors. Two to each line, they are all Mexicans, all men, most in their early thirties, all but one with some technical or managerial training.[14] Both watching and watched, they are particularly sensitive to, and reflective of, the prevailing visual idiom in the plant. They spend virtually all day standing just behind workers' shoulders—watching. As the hours pass, they alternately compliment efficiency and deride mistakes, decide who can still work if they arrive late and who can't, initiate and bar conversations, commandeer and offer forbidden candies, lecture and cajole whenever quality or speed falter. Their attentions are not evenly distributed, however. Although they are responsible for their entire half of the line, supervisors in chassis can generally be found in the section where components are inserted by hand, and supervisors in final can usually be found in the testing tunnel. The rest of their lines are left to the care of "group leaders."

Group leaders are on the lowest level of this supervisory hierarchy. They are all women, promoted workers who earn almost twice entry-level wages, but far less than the supervisors they assist. They have little autonomy and no disciplinary authority, serving primarily as extensions of their supervisors. Their job is to keep an eye (and an ear) on workers and pass any information up the line, even as they communicate supervisors' wishes down the line. They also collect the line quality and productivity statistics demanded by top management.[15] The ratio of group leaders to workers in chassis is almost double that in final assembly. This has predictable effects on the level of surveillance on the line, and final is generally considered "calmer" and "freer" than chassis.

The sense of being watched comes not only from direct visual surveillance, but from the managerial production of signs and symbols that are then available for perusal. Above each worker's head is a chart, fully visible to her at all times, as well as to anyone walking by. Group leaders fill them out each day. Gold stars mark perfection. Green dots mark errors. Red dots mark trouble. This public exposure has consequences for workers' sense of self and self-worth. A woman whose chart is full of green and red dots comments, "I feel ashamed. It's all just competition. You look at the girl next to you and you want to do better than she does even though it shouldn't matter." At the end of every day, announcements echo over the shop floor as each line finishes its daily thousand TVs. In lines far from their quota, the group leader begins circulating anxiously at 3:00, an hour before shift's end, saying they should "get a move on" or they'll be the only line that doesn't make it. The line always picks up speed at this point. When I ask a woman generally notable for her jaundiced attitude what's going on, she shrugs: "When they start congratulating the other lines for having finished and we haven't, you feel bad. Competition makes you work harder."

Off to the side of this shop-floor structure stands a parallel disciplinary edifice, the personnel department. Situated outside the physical space of the panopticon, personnel office staff rely less literally on sight than do supervisors on the shop floor. However, practices in this arena too speak to workers' images of themselves. Personnel staff members, all women, are known as "social workers." Their main focus is on questions of appropriate appearance and behavior, rather than on the work itself. Throughout the day, supervisors send in workers who arrive late, who quarrel on the line, who answer back. No one is simply reprimanded for working too slowly or sloppily. Whether the problem is production quality or dissatisfaction with one's job, it is dealt with as a problem of out-of-control emotions and inappropriate attitudes. Thus, petitions to be moved to another position are always treated as signs of immaturity rather than legitimate requests. And when a technician on a temporary contract takes a job elsewhere as a supervisor, one of the "social workers" lectures him not for leaving the plant in the lurch, but for not being "serious."

Personnel staff's focus on changing who workers are is legitimated in part by their title of "social workers" and by the attentive, "listening" stance this represents. This is enacted informally in the repeated pseudo-maternal insistence that workers tell them their problems. It is also enacted more formally. For instance, personnel staff poll workers about food quality during lunchtime. Responses are then posted in large "quality" graphs that attest to managerial "responsiveness" in living color. This official role is further legitimated by the presence of the "union delegate" in the office as a member of the personnel staff. Her daily responsibilities are practically indistinguishable from those of her co-workers in the office, and her direct supervisor, the one who excuses latenesses and approves days off, is the Panoptimex personnel manager. As a result, rather than supporting an oppositional subjectivity in the plant, her presence increases management's personal leverage with workers by providing credibility to the personnel staff's highly psychological style.[16]

Labor control in Panoptimex is achieved through practices— primarily but not exclusively visual—that speak directly to workers' sense of self. Whatever their center of attention in any single situation, managers' ultimate goal in the factory is to see that TVs get built to their bosses' satisfaction. They achieve this indirectly, however, by focusing on who workers are rather than on the work they do. In this process, worker subjectivities are directly addressed, and their success or failure as workers is easily conflated with their success or failure as human beings in general. This merging of work and personal identities gives management tremendous leverage on the shop floor, a leverage whose results are immediately obvious in workers' ongoing and anxious attempts to secure signs of managerial approval.

This is not the whole story, however. This leverage is achieved by addressing neither a concrete "worker" identity nor a more abstract "human" identity. The subjectivities addressed on the Panoptimex shop floor are gendered and sexualized, and the narrative of shop-floor quiescence only begins to make sense as we investigate the substance of the subjectivities that are constituted and spoken to in the panopticon. Thus, we will revisit the scene with the "empty places"[17] filled— investigating the impact, not of bosses watching workers, but of male bosses watching young female workers. It is here that the depth of shop-floor control becomes evident.

OGLING AND DIS-REGARDING

The visually defined practices that typify labor control in Panoptimex are imbued with sexual energies and gendered meanings when they are practiced in this girl-filled, guy-dotted space. Here, managers and supervisors are situated as voyeurs. Inside the panopticon, women workers are at the center of attention. Monitoring becomes the gaze of sexual objectification as soon as it locks on them. Male workers, on the other hand, are at the periphery, outside notice. Neither watching nor watched, they are emasculated even as their female co-workers are objectified. Thus, the visually defined practices described above frame a highly sexualized set of meanings in and for production. Women and men on the shop floor are allocated distinct and interdependent roles in the scenario. It is on that stage and within those characters that labor control is struggled over and ultimately established by management.

Supervisory subjectivity reflects and embodies this symbolic framework. As the plant's official watchers in this gendered space, supervisors, as much as their charges, are located in a sexual relationship. This is expressed in their initial self-presentation, as well as in their routinized daily behaviors. They are generally married with children, yet they openly flout their marriages on the shop floor, mentioning their children only in joking references to their manhood. They are required to wear ties, and from the booted, blue-jeaned "cowboy" to the "serious professional," each stamps his line with an idiosyncratic version of this symbol of masculine predominance.

Beneath the gaze of these monitors, female and male workers are incorporated into production in distinct ways. They are given different sets of identification numbers, different types of uniforms, and different jobs, and they are subject to different modes of supervision. Women do "detail" work such as inserting components and checking quality; men do the "heavy" work of assembling the cabinet and packing the finished product. Although there was a period before the labor shortages of the eighties when all positions were filled by women, managerial consensus now is that only men are capable of doing the "heavy" jobs, and there has been an almost total collective amnesia about the fact that it was ever different. All other jobs are assumed to be "women's jobs," and the notion of their being done by men seems positively ridiculous. On top of this base, other differences rise. Women sit, men stand. The center of the line is a female domain, its ends are male. Chassis, with its fifteen-to-one ratio of group leaders to workers, is all women. Final assembly, where there is a twenty-seven to one ratio, is almost half men. Within final, the group leader does all communicating with the men. This leaves the supervisor free to spend all his time with the women in his line. The cumulative symbolic and practical effects of these differences are overwhelming. Women are central—watched, constrained, pinned down. Men are decentered—ignored and relatively free to move around.

The differences between women and men—and between the meanings of femininity and masculinity in the plant—are marked as much by ongoing managerial behavior as by their initial setup in the structure of production. Every afternoon, Carlos walks the lines, all masculine and proprietary expansiveness, and "jokes" with women workers; male workers are ignored. Among the women too, only some are recognized. As he walks, he stops and talks to the "young and pretty ones" (as they say on the line)—to those known as "*las famosas*" in personnel department gossip sessions. These conversations are flirtatious and titillating, full of teasing on both sides, with mild, blushing self-revelations on the part of workers and pseudo-paternal supportiveness on his part. He does not stop at speaking, either. It is well known in the plant that he has a mistress on the line, as does the production manager. Thus, every conversation is tinged by ambiguity and the flavor of forbidden sexuality.

The plant manager is not alone in this. His example is echoed down through the ranks, and in any case follows a plant tradition that predates his tenure. Non-hourly male workers, from low-level engineers on up, prowl the lines in search of entertainment of all sorts. In this context, supervisors take full advantage of their position. One of the workers favored by Carlos's attentions discusses her co-workers pitilessly. She reports that the supervisor on her line propositions everyone, and that some make the mistake of going out with him, hoping that it will lead to promotions. But she doesn't. It's obvious he won't really pay up. Another supervisor has a worker pregnant and is currently dating another, both on his line. As the due date draws near, personnel staff tease him flirtatiously, threatening to tell his wife or to throw him a baby shower. He struts complacently. The norm is best encapsulated by workers' approving comments about one of the expectant father's (also married) colleagues, who they all agree is different from the others. "Why, as far as I know," says one woman, "he's only gone out steadily with one girl on his line, none of this using all the workers [*operadoras*]."

Supervisors not only use their position in production for sexual access, they also employ a highly sexualized discourse around workers as a means of labor control. It is striking to watch them wandering their lines, monitoring efficiency and legs simultaneously—their gaze focused sometimes on "nimble fingers" at work, sometimes on the quality of a hairstyle. Often supervisors will stop by a favorite operator—chatting, checking quality, flirting. Their approval marks "good worker" and "desirable woman" in a single gesture. Each supervisor has a few workers he hangs around with, laughing and gossiping throughout the day, and it is not lost on their co-workers that these favorites eventually emerge elsewhere, in slightly higher paid positions on the line or in the plant beauty contest. A young woman recounts a conversation with her supervisor and several co-workers in which he told them that a woman should never marry a man who makes less money than she does— legitimizing their low pay in the process of accentuating their femininity. Throughout each day, managers and supervisors frame women workers as sexual beings and sexual objects. In the process, women workers are subjected to an ongoing evaluation in which desirability and productivity are indistinguishable.

Women workers are of course not the only ones whose shop-floor experience is structured through a heterosexual matrix.[18] This is also the arena in which managers and supervisors struggle for predominance— both in individual cases and in the larger symbolic context. The shop floor is rife with complaints by both supervisors and managers about ways in which the other group's sexuality undermines shop-floor discipline. There's the supervisor who complains that Carlos's tendency to talk to some and not others undermines "motivation" on the line. There's the supervisor who tells of being forced by the production manager to allow a worker in on a day she arrives late. "OK," he reports, having resentfully agreed, "But then I'm not the supervisor any more." In personnel, there are constant stories about how Carlos countermands personnel and supervisor decisions about his favorites. There are stories of a line where the production manager's mistress throws her weight around, making the other girls cry and remaining exempt from sanction. And then there is the corporation's British "Organization and Efficiency" (O&E) manager for the region, who comments, "In the Mexican environment . . . you can imagine what are the other things a young girl can offer to a supervisor . . . we've tried to crack down, but within the limits of the culture . . . macho is strong here." In these incidents, supervisors and managers jostle for control of the shop floor in order to legitimate and affirm their masculinity—which in this panopticon is about sexual mastery (or in the case of the O&E manager, about mastering their sexuality); and they jostle for control of women workers in order to legitimate and affirm their shop-floor power. In the process, a configuration of production and labor control processes is established that is as much about gender and sexuality as it is about efficiency and TVs.

These struggles over and through the mantle of masculinity also mark relations between management and male workers, although it is an unequal battle from the outset. Top managers casually belittle men who work on the line. Jones, the regional personnel manager, off-handedly exempts male line workers from the category of "men" in explaining why they are not included in his general policy to pay men more than women: "From a macho standpoint, a guy wouldn't take an operator's job." The O&E manager summarizes this emasculating view straightforwardly: the men who work on the line are "drifters" by definition; real men "wouldn't do production line jobs." Supervisors are less offhand but equally scathing in their assertions. A supervisor finding a young man behind one afternoon is withering in his commentary, "Just like I said, you have to keep an eye on these guys. He thinks he's some kind of Latin Lover." His target, a shy young man new to Juárez, looks at his shoes and hurries back to work.

Managerial claims always have more clout than those of male workers, in large part because they are built into the structure of daily life in the factory. And just as women workers are disciplined within an essentially visual framework, so are their male co-workers. However, rather than being placed at the center of an immobilizing optic, male workers are relegated to its periphery—actively ignored. This process begins during hiring; the personnel assistant addresses the mixed-gender group as "*todas*"—employing the feminine form of the pronoun and thus effectively negating the presence of the men in the room. A young male applicant turns to me. "I already feel bad," he says, "After all, *I'm* here!" [19] This pattern is repeated on the shop floor. Men are physically segregated, standing at the line's ends. The plant manager does not even slow down as he passes them during his daily perambulations, and the supervisor is conspicuous for his absence. Only the group manager's assistant hangs around during the day, and when the supervisor wants something changed, he sends the group leader to relay his order.

Marginalization does undercut male workers' capacity to enact legitimate masculine defiance on the shop floor, but as a mode of control, disregard also has its dangers for management. Men on the line are subject to little direct supervision. They move around relatively freely, trading positions among themselves and covering for each other during extra bathroom runs, joking and laughing, catcalling women as they pass by. After a couple of months in the plant, I notice that the guy who attaches the label clamps it down only on every few TVs, rather than on every one, as he'd done when I first arrived. He laughs at my noticing, admitting that at the outset he'd been afraid I was a supervisor, so he'd done the job to specifications. On realizing I was not part of management, he went back to his normal way of doing the job in my presence.

This sort of cutting corners is far more possible—and likely—in the men's section of the line than in the more highly monitored women's section.

Nonetheless, male workers' relatively autonomous physical location, while permitting some freedom of movement and a few masculine rituals, also provides a powerful tool for managerial control. Even though male line workers are peripheral, they are still men to the extent that they "do the heavy work." If a male worker gets out of control, supervisors can always move him out of male territory, and occasionally they do just that. When men on the line get too cocky, the supervisor materializes and immediately stops the fun. Abruptly, he moves the loudest to soldering, where he sits in conspicuous discomfort among the "girls," while the other guys make uneasy jokes about how boring it is "over there." Ultimately, the supervisor has the last word in masculinity. Male workers can challenge his behavior, but he can reclassify them as women. In such moments, he retains control precisely through this capacity to throw into question young male workers' shop-floor-bounded gender and sexual identities.[20]

If we return to the personnel department with this optic, we can see that the sense of self "social workers" are addressing in workers is also highly gendered.[21] One day, a supervisor brings in a young woman for fighting. It turns out that her ex-boyfriend is on the line and showed her old letters to their co-workers, leading to relentless teasing. The response of the "social worker" is neither to castigate those involved for disrupting production nor to suggest they would all feel better if they found satisfaction in doing good work. Instead, she suggests to the young woman that she find ways to be better liked, writing an aphorism on a post-it for her to memorize: "It's nice to be important, but more important to be nice." After the young woman leaves, the entire office gets involved. Her boss Irene is particularly indignant. "Dragging that poor girl's name through the mud!" she exclaims. The ex is then called in. "That's not manly, a man with *trousers* wouldn't behave like that!" the "social worker" lectures. Being a better worker is not the central issue, it's being a better woman or man that matters. In a similar incident, Irene's cousin—a line worker—is brought in for fooling around on the line. Irene is extremely upset about the way it reflects on her, not because of the insubordination, but because she's also been hanging around the plant holding her boyfriend's hand. "A girl from a decent home," she fumes. Behavior, attitude, and demeanor are indeed what is adjudicated here—yet as related to gender and sexuality, not to work.

Productivity at Panoptimex is elicited through a discourse constitutive of, and directed at, workers' localized sense of self. The subjectivity addressed is not that of the "producer" or "creator," however; it is that of the "woman" or "man." Labor control is established as supervisors conflate sexual desirability and productive capacity—judging workers' status as desirable women or "real" men on a moment-by-moment basis. In this context, young women are recognized as women in being marked as sexual objects, with all the attendant constraints and pleasures implicit in such a process. Young men are actively not addressed—neither super-visors nor objects of desire, they are excluded from the factory drama. Yet there are fewer differences here than meet the eye; both women and men become "Panoptimex workers" through their admission to a gender category dependent on managerial affirmation. These processes produce not only compliance, but shop-floor selves, selves which in turn retain traces of that process of incorporation.

MAKING "MODELS," MAKING "DRIFTERS"

A glance at the Panoptimex shop floor reveals a sea of shimmering legs and high heels, rows of meticulously curled bangs and brightly manicured hands, and women painting their lips on every line. It is difficult to be a woman on this shop floor without being self-conscious. The light, the windows, the eyes, the comments—each and all are persistently, glaringly evident. This gaze affects women at all levels in the plant. Women in personnel, from Irene down to the union delegate, walk the shop floor in thigh-high skirts and plunging necklines, flirting as they go. One young woman shows how much it matters, mentioning that she missed work the day before because she slept too late—too late, that is, to do her hair and makeup and still make the bus. To enter the plant as a woman is to be immersed in objectification—to be seen, to watch, and so to watch and see yourself.[22]

A young woman on the line recounts her story of transformation. When she started work she used no makeup and always wore dresses below the knee. Soon her co-workers began telling her she looked bad, that she should "fix herself up." So encouraged, she decided to be less shy. Today, mini-skirted and made up, she reports she finally feels self-confident in the plant. As she speaks, her best friend surveys her physique with an affectionately proprietary air. "They say one's appearance reveals a lot," she remarks. Later, they both appear in the Electroworld beauty contest, a poorly organized and attended affair except for the fifty contestants, many of them from Panoptimex, who infuse the occasion with a deep symbolic seriousness. The stories traded over cookies and shared lipsticks revolve around the lack of courage shown by those who "chickened out" at the last minute and the value of participating, whether or not you win, as an act of bravery and an assertion of self-worth. There are also extensive discussions about those left behind, about the importance of representing those on one's line who lack the necessary courage to be present themselves. To claim one's own desirability becomes an act of pride, independence, and solidarity all at once.

The ultimate arbiters of desirability, of course, are supervisors and managers. Workers gossip constantly about who is or is not chosen. On every line, they can point out those Carlos speaks to and those the supervisor favors—women only too happy to acknowledge their special status. For those so anointed, the experience is one of personal power. "If you've got it, flaunt it!" Estela comments gleefully, her purple-lined eyes moving from her black, lace bodysuit to the supervisor hovering nearby. This power is often used more instrumentally as well. On my first day in the plant, a young woman—well known as one of those favored by managerial notice—is stopped by guards for lateness. She slips upstairs and convinces Carlos to intercede for her. She is allowed to work after all. The personnel office is incensed and the lines sizzle with gossip.

Gossip is the plant pastime and weapon of choice, as well as its most-cited cruelty. "Did you see him talking to her?" The lines bristle with eyes. Quick side glances register a new style, make note of wrinkles that betray ironing undone. "Oof, look how she's dressed!" With barely a second thought, women workers can produce five terms for "give her the once over"—words that shade in meaning from "gossip about" to "cut down" to "censure." The issue of favoritism is a constant source of conflict, and everyone is always watching. Estela is a frequent target of sexual rumors, and she is torn about whether to be hurt by or proud of her notoriety. The first time I meet her she boasts, "The other girls don't like me, I get on their nerves." She turns to a co-worker. "Isn't that true?" The other girl nods matter-of-factly. Another favorite on the line says there's lots of jealousy, and she describes a period in which another girl on her line was taking her components. It stopped only when the supervisor, production manager, and plant manager collectively lectured the line. When I ask if the incident hurt her feelings, she comments disdainfully that the problem is that the other girls don't try to "improve themselves," but then they are jealous of her success. In this bounded space, femininity is defined and anointed by male supervisors and managers. Women workers have little to offer each other compared to the pleasures of that achievement and the perils of its loss.

If the young women in this plant can provide each other little recompense, the young men on the line have even less to offer. One unfortunate young man says he came here precisely for all the women. "I thought I'd find a girlfriend. I thought it would be fun." "And was it?" I ask. There is a pause, "No one paid any attention to me," he responds finally, a bit embarrassed, laughing and downcast. His experience brings scenes to mind: women on the line discussing the gendering of production, mocking men's "thick fingers" and lack of attention to detail, giggling helplessly at the notion of a male group leader. I hear again a comment made by one of the women workers who returned to the factory after having quit. "It's a good atmosphere here. In the street they [men] mess with us, but here, we mess with them a little. We make fun of them and they get embarrassed."

In the face of such commentary, men on the line struggle to affirm a legitimate masculinity in production. They are quick to expound, for instance, on the objective meanings of the plant's spatial gendering. When I ask why they chose to work here, in jobs known outside as "women's work," Pedro objects. "Down there [gesturing toward the center of the line] is women's work; this is men's work." When I ask how he knows, he shrugs at such an obvious question, "Women there, men here." Within their small domain at the end of the line, they attempt to create an autonomous community. Final assembly is known to be more "unified" than the rest of the line, and in fact when one worker has a crisis, all the rest contribute to make him a sizable short-term loan. At the same time, they tease each other unmercifully, and the banter occasionally erupts into physical fights. Making a virtue of necessity, they use their isolation to constitute livable identities among themselves.

Like their female counterparts, they also look to supervisors to affirm their gendered location. Unlike their female counterparts, however, both what they want and how they attempt to get it require confrontation rather than intimacies. Eschewing indirect appeals for legitimation, they make constant, carefully ritualized demands that the supervisor acknowledge their masculinity, both on the shop floor and off. In sotto voce rebellions in the plant, they impugn their supervisor's manhood and imply his fear of theirs. "If he has a problem, he should come tell us himself, not send Mari [the group leader] down. He's just afraid it could come to blows," complains Juan in a characteristic (and characteristically quiet) critique. A group in final excitedly tells me what happened after I left their line's Christmas party. The supervisor showed up late and they asked him, "So what's the story here, do we talk to you like the supervisor or like a man?" Needless to say, he said like a man. "So we gave it to him, almost insulting his mother!" they reported with relish.

Despite such performances, the plant's very structure undermines male workers' capacity to enact a viable local masculinity, and supervisors have no reason to undercut this. To the contrary, male workers' desperate desire for respect becomes a potent tool of control. When supervisors tire of the constant challenges and move male workers into female territory, the effect is dramatic. Once snatched from the male domain and relegated to the "womanly task" of soldering, even eye-stinging black smoke amid broken ventilators evokes no complaints. In Panoptimex, to be male is to have the right to look, to be a super-visor. Gender and production relations are discursively linked. Standing facing the line, eyes trained on his work, the male line worker does not count as a man. In the plant's central game, he is neither subject nor object. As a result, he has no location from which to act—either in his relation to the women in the plant or in his relation to factory managers. Just as his female co-worker becomes a productive subject through her response to managerial discourse, so does he. However, in her case the process has its pleasures. In his case, it is the lure of fixing things, the recurrent desire to remake an untenable, local gender identity, that ties him into factory life. Nine hours of objectification prove less stultifying than nine hours of invisibility.

Putting Trope into Practice

Panoptimex women workers are classic simulacra,[23] copies of an elusive "reality" that preceded them only in the imagination. Thus, gender matters, but not because young women enter ready-made for managerial purposes. Gender matters because women workers are addressed and constituted within the confines of a particular set of gendered meanings—made anew on the shop floor in the transnationally produced image of nubile pliancy. These global images of femininity are filtered through on-site managerial intentions, desires, and strategies, joining the many more idiosyncratic symbolic structures which configure the daily life of production on the shop floor. Contrary to appearances, therefore, Panoptimex provides us with an opportunity to see, not "women," but gender at work, constituting the shop-floor selves who make global production tick.

Although the images are transnational, the form in which they enter the shop floor and the consequences of their presence are specific to this plant in this moment. Panoptimex managers work in a corporate context whose very reason for being is "the picture," and the visually focused habits of that universe imbue their labor control strategies. For these managers, things are under control when they can *see* they are under control. The shop floor reflects these attitudes. The factory is set up to be seen, and to look a particular way. The young women seated in long lines complete the appropriately feminized picture—in their own sexualized daily experience as well as in that of managers. Managers at all levels strategize to ensure the continued presence of these young women. Their decision to bus young rural women to work on a daily basis is only another indication of their obsession with seeing a primarily female labor force. These young women are hired into a panopticon for the same reasons that they are hired at all—because the managerial framework for labor control is to ensure that production looks right.

In an arena peopled primarily by male supervisors and female workers, this objectifying modality of control constitutes a highly sexualized, and productive, set of gendered subjectivities. For both supervisors and women workers, laboring and sexual identities merge on the shop floor. Supervisors revel in their location. Young women workers take pleasure in the experience of being desirable and in their use of this delicious if limited power. For the few men on the line, however, it is a different story. Their inability to watch makes it impossible for them to assert a legitimate local masculinity, and their attempts to assert an alternate masculinity only make them vulnerable to the managerial capacity to undercut these assertions. As a result of these processes, the gendered and sexual subjectivities of everyone on the shop floor are at stake in production. Thus, Panoptimex owes its success to a set of meaning-imbued labor control practices in which workers are constituted and incorporated into production primarily as women and men and only within that framework as workers. Workers are literally engendered—they come into being as workers in the same moment in which they come into being as "women" or "men" within the shop floor's terms.

Re-forming the "Traditional Mexican Woman"

Particimex

Panoptimex showed us how the ostensibly preconstituted femininity of third-world women workers is actually made on the spot. Particimex will make clear how productive femininities which contradict transnational images can also be manufactured in global assembly. Particimex is, if anything, a bigger success story than Panoptimex, particularly compared to plants owned by the same corporation in Juárez (see Chapter 7). Costs per hour are low, and the plant won four company-wide awards for quality the year before my arrival. Yet while workers in both Panoptimex and Particimex could be poster girls for the managerial strategy of hiring young women in third-world assembly, a closer look at their modes of femininity suggests entirely different processes of control, and in consequence, distinctive femininities at work. Managerial applause and feminist critique notwithstanding, productive femininities are neither home generated nor, consequently, all-of-a-kind. On the contrary, they are idiosyncratic, evoked in the distinctive intentions and constraints of each shop floor where they are employed.

Particimex is part of Autoworld, an enormous, U.S.-based auto producer. Like many other maquilas owned by Autoworld in northern Mexico, Particimex produces parts that are assembled back in Detroit. Unlike most maquilas, however, Particimex is a long, empty, six-hour drive from the border. In response to the shortage of willing young women in Juárez in the eighties, Autoworld managers established an outpost in Santa María,[1] a small, agricultural city where paid work opportunities for young women remained scarce.

Given this history and given the conclusions of a decade of feminist analysis of transnational production, one might expect the plant's un-usual success to rely on a bevy of classically docile young women. This is not the case, however. Despite a workforce of mostly young women, traditional images of feminine docility are neither elaborated nor re-inforced on the shop floor. Instead, the maquila's symbolic practices around femininity highlight independence, assertiveness, and the ca-pacity to make decisions. These qualities contrast sharply not only with the more sexualized tropes evident in Panoptimex, but with those de-scribed in transnational managerial discourses and displayed in the com-munity outside the factory. In fact, managers' disciplinary strategies ap-pear set on undermining the very characteristics that purportedly led them to hire young women in the first place. What's more, these new femininities appear to be just as productive as the old. In the pages that follow, we will trace the institutional structures and situated manager-ial subjectivities which produced these new, unexpected subjects and which account for their remarkable productivity. In the process, we can better grasp the extreme malleability of gendered meanings and subjec-tivities and thus refine our understanding of the ways that gender shapes and is shaped by global production.

Border Managers

It's a summer afternoon in El Paso, and the mall is packed with window shoppers escaping the dust and the blue-blinding heat. I see Jesús across the perfume section, shopping bag in hand—a tall, fair, boyish-faced man, at ease in a sea of English. I'd known him in Spanish, six hours back across the border, running the only maquila in a small city set amid chile fields. Now a visitor, he nonetheless seems as at home here as he did there.

Jesús is the Particimex plant manager. He is thirty-two, born into a well-to-do family in a small, rural town in northern Mexico. He gradu-ated from a technical college in 1982 and turned to the maquilas. In the state of Chihuahua, these were the logical choice for a young man with technical training and a yen to succeed. He was immediately snapped up by Autoworld. Like many of his colleagues, he began work in Ciudad Juárez. Since then he has moved up steadily. Today he is Autoworld's youngest factory manager, and one of only a handful of Mexicans at this level. Most of his staff is like him—tall, self-confident young men with technical degrees and ambition to spare, whose primary work experi-ence has been within the Juárez maquila industry.

Mexicans running plants in the maquila industry face a particular set of challenges, since their reason for being hired—being Mexican—is also their biggest impediment to advancement in the larger corporation. Disparaging comments about Mexican managers are routine among their North American superiors and counterparts. In interviews with transnational managers throughout the industry, Mexican managers and managerial prospects are described to me—without apology, mitigation, or even circumspection—as variously "unsophisticated," "underdeveloped," "authoritarian," "inflexible," "macho," and sexually predatory.[2] Nonetheless, there is substantial pressure to begin building a Mexican managerial workforce, both from the Mexican state and indigenous elites and from maquila headquarters in the United States looking to lower labor costs, increase local expertise, and placate indigenous power-holders. Thus, when purportedly inferior Mexican managers are hired, it is not just in spite of their nationality, but also because of it. As a result, the few Mexican plant managers in the industry are constantly juggling—trying to emphasize their Mexican insider and outsider status simultaneously.

In the case of the Particimex managers, this issue is further complicated by the fact that, although when seen from Detroit they and their workers are "all Mexicans," when seen from Santa María they are also urban *fronterizos* versus rural northerners, opposed social categories which neither abrogate, nor are abrogated by, their shared nationality.[3] Thus, Jesús and his colleagues experience themselves, and want to be experienced by others, as both like and unlike their workers—as Mexicans, but not Mexican peasants. Their work is thereby tripled as they struggle to stress the absolute otherness of their workers, even as they retain a claim to authentic Mexican-ness and demonstrate their cosmopolitan capacity to move in global circles.

The Santa María managers are thus true border occupants—no longer geographically, but ever-more-so psychologically. They are Mexicans, working in Mexico for a U.S.-owned transnational, and at work they describe themselves and their countrymen through the reflections they see in the eyes of their North American bosses. "We have a different culture [than the gringos]. There's still a lot of 'that's the way it goes' here," Jesús comments as he describes a quality innovation. "We're working on it, but there's a long way to go." They are fiercely and conventionally patriotic, yet they have a profoundly objectifying relationship to the "Mexico" in which they work. Returning from company meetings in Ciudad Juárez, Jesús comments matter-of-factly, "Production in Mexico is no longer cost-effective. We're going to open factories in Central America next year."

The combination of primary identification with Autoworld and bona fide "Mexican-ness" allows these managers to put forth arguments about and for Mexican workers that their U.S. counterparts do not feel free to make. Thus, when I ask the assistant plant manager about below-subsistence wages, a problem generally acknowledged by U.S. managers, he responds, "We're not like Americans. They're more materialist. We Mexicans want other things—recognition." He goes on to tell a story about a car wash owner who tested one of her workers on her own car. The worker did such a good job that she tipped him. Instead of being grateful, however, he was offended, saying, "This is my work and that's why I do it well." He smiles at me and specifies the moral: "That's the way we are." It is precisely this double vision, the claim to be privy to Mexico's honorable "essential nature" while still being willing and able to recognize its "faults," that gives these managers legitimacy in the company at large.

These young men, and others like them, occupy a special place in the complex U.S.-Mexican relationship. Unlike their poorer compatriots who work in the United States illegally or their more privileged countrymen who go to the United States for graduate degrees, they show no inclination either to work outside of Mexico or to deemphasize their nationality. On the contrary, their conversation is laced with "we Mexicans" and "but in *our* culture." Despite the tensions caused by working for the transnational sector as "locals," it is their "Mexican-ness" that makes them useful and gives them leverage within the corporate structure. As a result, managerial conversation is framed against, and in terms of, stereotyped and static notions of both "Mexican culture" and "the way the gringos do things." These two sets of images are permanently at work, built into the very structure of production, hiring, and labor control in the Santa María factory.

It is within this context that gender comes into play. Gender is a terrain on which modern and traditional are clearly demarcated,[4] and this is particularly accentuated within the U.S.-Mexico relationship, where the very notion of overbearing masculinity has been marked as Mexican.[5] For Mexican managers positioning themselves vis-à-vis North American bosses, separating themselves from the stigma of "macho" is an important first step. Publicly addressing women workers outside tropes of docility is a way of making that move. In their capacity to remake Mexican women, they demonstrate both their distance from and their connection to "their culture." Gender thus functions as a landscape within which managers can locate themselves—in their own experience as well as in the eyes of their transnational colleagues—as Mexican exceptions.

Particimex managers are institutionally as well as culturally bound by their peripheral location. This is most clearly evident in the budget, which defines what counts as managerial success or failure, and what elements of production are within the maquila manager's purview. The plant budget is written in Juárez, and it includes only the costs of running the factory's physical plant and salaries. The costs of materials and transportation are omitted. Thus, if the plant manager confronts cost overruns, virtually the only way he can balance his budget is by squeezing workers. When I ask Jesús about the relationship between the value added in his factory and the value of the plant's assembled product, he doesn't know the answer. He is judged only on whether he "makes his budget."[6] The rest is not his concern.

The effect of the overall structure is to give plant managers very little room for maneuver. This is true from the daily handling of petty cash through larger issues like decisions over inputs. "We don't handle cash here," the finance manager reports simply. The money is kept in a bank in El Paso. Every expenditure must be called into headquarters in Ciudad Juárez. At headquarters, they contact the bank in El Paso, and the money appears in Santa María the next morning. This is simply a "formality," the finance manager comments. Indeed it is, but it is a formality that defines and redefines on a daily basis the relationship of center to periphery, of who asks and who grants.

Not surprisingly given the success of Mexican managers' claim to a privileged relationship with their compatriots, the one spending area that does not require authorization from Juárez is severance pay. Under Mexico's progressive labor law, even workers who are fired with cause are due some severance pay. Although the specifics of these laws tend to be honored in the breach, workers expect and generally receive something. The plant finance manager comments, "That way, if they tell me, 'I don't want to see him here again!' I can pay him off right there." This unusual, if minor, financial leeway is partially due to the minimal amounts of money at stake. However, other, remarkably petty, expenditures do require Juárez's authorization. Rather than a simple question of amounts, this small arena of financial autonomy is an indication of where the "niche" for Mexican managers is located. Dealings with personnel issues is the one area where Mexican managers are ceded expertise by their U.S. bosses.[7]

This particular configuration of strengths and weaknesses has led

Particimex managers to adopt a set of explicitly ungendered, participatory management practices for labor control. Gianini, the iconoclastic North American head of Organizational Development at Autoworld's Juárez headquarters, had been trying to get one of the Autoworld maquilas to try a system of "work teams and total quality control"[8] (however gendered) since he arrived in Mexico in 1977. This was a project he understood in frankly national terms: "We're moving from an authoritarian Mexican system to a more participatory model. . . . [Participatory management] is a maturation on the part of our Mexican staff. They have to learn to be a leader not a dictator." His efforts met with little success at first. However, in the late eighties, he finally convinced Santa María's first (Mexican) plant manager to come see the system in one of Autoworld's U.S. plants. The plant manager came away a convert. In 1988 the plant embarked on a new system of production and labor control they nicknamed "Cambio" (short for "Change in Motion"). It is Cambio, and Gianini's investment in it, which accounts for my presence in Santa María. Gianini offered me access to the plant, as well as to another in Juárez (see Chapter 7), because he was interested in my "impressions" of the differences between the two.[9]

Today, the Santa María managers are enamored of what they have wrought. Their simultaneous identification with and "othering" of their workers make it appealing to employ participatory management practices that simultaneously "involve" and "improve" workers— particularly insofar as these processes occur in the arena of gender. At the same time, Cambio solves several institutional problems for managers. It addresses the problem of rigid budget constraints by allowing them to cut supervisory and excess production workers while legitimating these decisions through a language of modernity and Americanization. Cambio also improves Mexican managers' marginal status in the larger organization. In agreeing to use participatory management, they exhibit their personal capacities to move away from the "authoritarian Mexican system" so casually named by Giannini. The new management practices' trendiness gives them global cachet. The focus on personnel management builds on their earlier credibility as those who understand "their people." And their reversal of gendered discourses marks them as unconstrained by "local customs." Over lunch, supervisors and managers gossip about how, when they go to meetings in Juárez with all the other (American) plant managers, "Everyone tries to act like they have work teams." Particimex may be a provincial outpost, but Cambio has put it on the map.

As was evident in Panoptimex, Particimex managers' situated selves have direct ramifications for the production and labor control processes that are employed on the shop floor. These managers see themselves as simultaneously like and unlike their transnational colleagues and their Mexican workers. In locating themselves so as to express this experience, they are drawn to labor control mechanisms which address their workers as a new sort of Mexican, able to transcend both transnational stereotypes and local gender mores. As a result, the Particimex shop floor evokes new working subjects and a new productive femininity, one in which workers experience themselves not as compliant vassals but as those directly responsible for productivity.

Lateral Controls and the
Evocation of the Working Subject

The system Particimex managers have created operates directly on and through workers' sense of self, thus enabling the radical shift in gendered subjectivities that we will explore later in the chapter. Understanding this system's logic requires entering the shop floor and watching how it shifts and obscures power relations in production. Cambio blurs distinctions between workers and management, thereby implying that they have a comparable interest in good production results. It minimizes the difference between deciding how to carry out externally determined goals and determining the overall parameters of production—thus giving workers a tremendous, if not always warranted, sense of personal responsibility. And it makes a team of peers the most basic unit of production. This breaks down the separation between workers' responsibilities to their friends and their responsibilities to the company, and thus between social and work identities. All of these border erasures invoke a dependent shop-floor subject. But while Panoptimex workers look for personal, often sexual, affirmation from managers, Particimex workers depend directly on efficiency and productivity indices for such reassurance.[10]

Seen from the road, Particimex resembles nothing so much as a "Spanish-style" hotel. It is a large, flat, rectangular building—off-white walls ringed with enormous, arched, brick-trimmed windows. A brick plaza in front is studded with trees and bushes. Off to the side, white umbrellas dot the terrace, and at intervals during the day workers can be seen eating at white cast-iron tables beneath their shade. Inside, the production area is light and pristine. Shiny floors are highlighted by yellow tape, and workers stand on green carpets. Beside each assembly line is a rectangular wooden table with benches bolted to the floor—often filled with workers in fervent conversation. Above each workstation is a picture of an attractive young woman with long hair, smilingly holding an example of a common mistake. Nearby, joking reminder notes and encouraging messages are posted. "Your work area speaks of you," says one. Music plays loudly: varieties of *norteño,* dance music, and sad ballads, all supplied by workers.

The plant produces harnesses—car electrical systems. A few workers splice multicolored wires into cables at stationary posts. The majority assemble these into electronically specified sequences. During first shift, eleven assembly lines are in motion, staffed by roughly four hundred workers. Upright boards rotate methodically around moving assembly lines. Each board is about five feet square, studded with knobs and hooks, and covered with colorful dangling cables. Each worker stands at a station. As the board goes by, she routes, inserts, or wraps a particular series of cables. Each insertion is accompanied by a rewarding electronic beep. It takes about a minute for a board to pass a given station, so individual workers repeat the same set of gestures close to five hundred times a day.

Participation is remarkable for the self-conscious absence of status demarcations within its walls. My first day, I arrive and ask the receptionist for the plant manager. She turns to a tall young man in a light blue smock. "Jesús," she says, using the familiar form of address, "someone to see you." Everyone in the factory wears the same light blue, short-sleeved smocks and ID tags adorned with underexposed black-and-white photos. Managers even gave up their ties, they remind me repeatedly, donning them only for visitors. For safety reasons, high heels and jewelry are not allowed, and everyone on the production floor must wear plastic, aviator-style glasses. In this final regulation, the entire plant, including managers, is in league against the guards, who report people for not wearing glasses even when they're not on the line. During an interview with the quality manager in an office just off the production floor, we both take off our glasses. Every few minutes he hisses "glasses" and we hastily replace them, removing them as soon as the guard has retired once again. These symbols and representations of equality are at the heart of the maquila's disciplinary system: obscuring sharp distinctions of power and privilege between managers and workers is crucial to increasing workers' sense of personal involvement and investment in their work.

This blurring of boundaries is also reflected in my position in the plant. Unlike in Panoptimex, managers evince no discomfort with my request to work in the plant. Instead, they quickly assign me to a work team and put me through training, expressing concerns only about my safety in production. Unlike at Andromex and Anarchomex, on the other hand, my presence in production does little to impede my access to management. Given the leveling symbolic practices in the plant, neither my dress nor my physical location makes me entirely other. In other plants where I worked on the line, I met with managers only by making appointments with their secretaries; in Particimex, I can buttonhole them on the shop floor or knock on their doors.

Cambio is structured around "teams" which are collectively responsible for production. Each line is divided into four groups of six to ten workers. The team is the primary site of labor control, as well as of production. Each team has one member who is not in a fixed position—a "coordinator"—and half have an additional assistant known as a "support." The coordinator is the team's central figure, the crucial link in making Cambio work. Coordinators' formal job is keeping track of quality indices in writing and reporting them monthly to management. However, their fundamental responsibility is to make sure these numbers (quantity, quality, labor efficiency) come out right. Supports help workers when they fall behind and fill in for those who need a break, usually to go to the bathroom. They also replace colleagues when they are sick. Both jobs are officially filled through voting. More often than not, however, supervisors pick people, and voting merely ratifies their decision. The jobs are supposed to rotate every six months. Nonetheless, although the coordinator does receive a small bonus, it is not generally enough to tempt those who feel the job is too much responsibility. This feeling that not just anyone can do the coordinator job is encouraged—often consciously—by supervisors, who worry about their own production results whenever an inexperienced coordinator enters the position. As a result of these pressures, many coordinators are in the job for several years at a time.

Supervisors deal almost exclusively with coordinators. They rarely interact with individual workers or monitor the line directly. This system not only decreases the possibility of worker/management conflicts, but cuts labor costs as well. The team structure has allowed management to eliminate half the factory's supervisory and all its assistant supervisory positions. In their place are four coordinators per line, actually helping in production, and earning roughly a fifth of supervisor wages. Thus, one of Cambio's primary effects has been to push responsibility down to its cheapest possible level.

The team is the plant's central social structure, and record-keeping practices institutionalize the team's position. Mistakes are registered by both workstation and team, but the team register is far more important. Every error is marked, and those not caught before they reach the end of the line are tagged with "red tickets" and recorded. When a mistake slips through, everyone checks to see not which individual, but which team, is responsible. In one team meeting, we commit to making no more than five defective harnesses in the next two weeks. When we exceed that limit within the first week, my contribution a disproportionate *two* red tickets, my fieldnotes seethe with guilt and embarrassment. The woman next to me is practically in tears, as a second red ticket from her station rolls around the corner. Auditors who do random checks throughout the lines don't even record their findings by individual station, only by work team. When I comment flippantly that mistakes don't matter that much since no one gets in trouble personally, an apparently nonchalant young woman on my team responds intensely, "But if you were the best team, then you're not anymore!" The plant's assistant manager sums it up: "Now they don't feel pressure from above, they feel it laterally, from their own co-workers. They don't want to look bad in front of their workmates."

This sense of responsibility toward co-workers is enabled and fomented by what management calls "auto-control," in which workers are given tools to understand and perform the work, as well as salient (if limited) elements of control over the labor process. During the initial training sessions, auto-control is defined: "You plan it, you do it, you check it, you fix it if necessary." However, there are more limits than the script implies. For instance, the pace of the line is set collectively, but within a range established by supervisors. Similarly, if a team decides to sit down and talk, no one will question them, but if as a result the required number of harnesses isn't produced, the supervisor will complain. Or a work team can cover for an absent teammate and decide to have her paid. But if her absence impedes production, the supervisor will object. This ultimately allows supervisors to appear more casual than workers about production. One day my coordinator, Cara, reports to our supervisor that we failed to make our daily quota of four hundred harnesses, missing it by twenty. When I ask if the shortfall is serious, the supervisor says no, "It's only twenty minutes of production." "That's what I mean," Cara immediately corrects her acerbically. Those minutes of production still must be made up, and it is the coordinator who is responsible for making sure that happens. One of the young trainers comments, "In a traditional plant, workers give little of themselves because they're not trusted. Here they're trusted." "Auto-control" is contingent upon getting the job done as management thinks it should be done—within quite narrow limits. In the process, workers are given just enough leeway to feel accountable for the results.

At one point, the support on my team is so stressed that he threatens to resign if people exercise their official right to three bathroom breaks a day. Since no one else is willing to take his place, everyone agrees to forgo a bathroom break. They would not agree to such a decision mandated from above, yet they accept it with little discussion when it appears that the only alternative is having to rotate as supports themselves. In such a transaction, a managerial decision—to provide too few workers for all to take their allotted breaks—appears as a worker decision to bow to necessity. Cambio functions by implying that workers have control and thus engendering a sense of tremendous responsibility for production.

All these processes work on and through the constitution of a new self. This personal remaking begins during the initial week of training, which includes exercises such as describing yourself to the group and being led around blindfolded and then discussing how that felt. In weekly sessions held over the following six months, teams discuss problems ranging from interpersonal conflicts to how to manage a supervisor who doesn't support teamwork enough. During the initial course, workers are told to see themselves as "collaborators," responsible for telling their boss what they think. They are encouraged to speak up, to participate, to assert their presence and point of view. The young trainer, who himself began on the line, comments, "The training changes people. It gives you the opportunity to learn and it gets rid of the fear of speaking up." In discussing the trainings, the department manager comments that workers "leave the course transformed," and in his introductory comments he exhorts the group that these lessons are "applicable in your personal life, too." The effect of such exhortations is visible in workers' suggestions that women workers in the plant are beginning to postpone marriage. Workers' willingness to take on the maquila as an identity is apparent, too, in their tendency to wear their smocks home, rather than removing them as soon as a bell sounds, as do their counterparts elsewhere. The shop-floor impact of this training is of course the most obvious, and these new selves can be seen on a daily basis in workers' responsible, assertive, and anxious attitude in production.

This invocation of worker responsibility is a delicate balancing act for managers, and it took them a while to get it right. When Cambio was first implemented, the discrepancy between managers' and workers' understanding of the idea of worker "independence" precipitated a violent strike that lasted nearly a month and entirely shut down the plant for several days. One of the few women who walked out who remains in the plant has a more critical analysis than her newer co-workers. With Cambio," she explains, "You're more tied down—to the work, the team, the responsibility—than you were before." Managers describe the shift differently. They claim that Cambio gave workers more "autonomy," but that initially trainers didn't know how to explain it correctly. Workers misunderstood Cambio as meaning they would be "free" in the plant to do what they wished. Now, in the initial training, managers are careful to define the freedom they really mean: "The coordinator says what, you decide how." The years of quiescence since the plant's initial walkout testify to the efficacy of these revisions. Constituting productive selves is a tricky business, but for the most part, Particimex managers seem to have succeeded.

In Cambio's current structure, the role of the coordinator is particularly crucial in linking the team vertically, ensuring that it operates in the interests of production and not of worker resistance. Coordinators are peers and friends of those on the line, yet their personal credibility is also at stake in production. Through them, a sense of responsibility and anxiety over speed and quality is transmitted to other members of the team. When we make too many mistakes, our coordinator Cara lectures, "I help you so that you don't fall behind, but you have to help me too." Team members look abashed. Later Mari comments, "We knew we'd been careless, so we felt bad." In a particularly telling decision, Cara tells me just before I leave that she's decided to begin giving people on the team little presents when they make no mistakes for the week. "They've been demanding it of me," she comments. A coordinator on another line tells me, "It's like being a supervisor, but when they get mad, people can't say anything. After all, they chose you." Thus, the figure of the coordinator is the nexus of the system of labor control, as it allows for a high degree of control without weighing the system down, and presses workers' social relations and sense of interpersonal responsibility into the service of production goals.

These dynamics are most clearly visible during weekly "quality treks," in which a cross-section of production lines report results to the plant's top management. A group of managers walks from line to line. At each stop, work continues while the coordinator of the team in question stands with microphone and pointer in hand and graphs nearby, explaining the monthly numbers. During these rituals, line workers do their best to support their vulnerable representative. On one such occasion, during a trek stop at my line, the work suddenly gets easy. I soon realize that the support has slipped to the other side of the line and begun doing most of the first position's job so that we look more efficient. As I listen to the presentation behind my back, the coordinator's tone shifts back and forth from calm and technical as she reports on good results to childish and apologetic when she comes to a cluster of bad ones. Addressed simultaneously as worker and supervisor by management and as friend and supervisor by co-workers, the coordinator is the crux of Cambio's operations.

Standing at this crucial intersection, coordinators most clearly display the system's effects and contradictions, both in their deep commitment to Cambio goals and their frustrations with its limitations. Despite the language of teamwork and collaboration, pay remains low, averaging a little under a dollar an hour, and there are no automatic raises or promotions on the basis of seniority. What's more, workers in Autoworld's U.S. plants can be compensated for production innovations, but not here, and workers and managers alike complain about the unfairness of the distinction.[11] Many coordinators have passed a test to become "expert operators" and earn 50 percent more than their co-workers. Nonetheless, because Santa María has long sent seasonal labor to the U.S. heartland, workers in general have a clear sense of how little that is compared to the wages of those doing similar work in the United States. More important, while preparing to become "expert operators" and again as coordinators they hear far more than other workers about the ways that the factory's success depends on them. The obvious discrepancy between this rhetoric and their own prospects in the plant generates a constant if quiet grumbling among this group which the higher wages can't quite appease. While most workers take the lack of pay and promotional opportunities as givens of the job, coordinators "buy into" the system and therefore resent its inconsistencies. Their complaints reveal the difficulties of instituting participatory management in a plant whose raison d'être is cheap labor.[12] Yet the sense of disappointed expectations also reveals Particimex managers' success in convincing workers of their commitment to participatory management's basic tenets, even in this context.

Although coordinators' unhappiness requires management of its own, the fact that they critique Cambio in its own terms ultimately does more to legitimize than to undermine the system's functioning. The depth of coordinators' acceptance of Cambio's fundamental claims is apparent in the following story, recounted by a proud and bemused supervisor. One of the teams on his line had had a fourteen-week run as winner in the plant's internal quality competitions. During the coordinator's presentation at a quality trek, she made a mistake that cost the team its position. As soon as she realized this, she fled to the bathroom, crying inconsolably at the thought that her team would lose its place. The supervisor had to coax her out, telling her that he was pleased to see her crying, as it signified how important it was to her, but that everything would be alright. The plant's disciplinary structure makes labor control internal, allowing supervisors to experience and position themselves as those who mitigate the discipline's most oppressive effects, instead of those who enforce it on a daily basis. The imprint of this structure can be seen throughout coordinators' practices and rhetorics as they enact their emotional investment in successful production.

Cambio is successful because it addresses workers in terms that are both pleasurable and productive, constituting useful shop-floor subjects in the process. "Training" imparts substantive information about neither product nor production process. Instead, it focuses directly and explicitly on remaking workers' selves—on evoking a "Particimex worker" who comfortably wears her work smock home through the streets, whose sense of self is tied both to the maquila and to her teammates, who takes active responsibility in and for production, and who experiences both pride and shame as a routine part of her job. The Particimex shop floor operates with the same technology as do a multitude of less efficient Autoworld maquilas nearby. The difference lies in the selves who use that technology, and they emerge through Cambio's interpellatory processes.

The Terrain of Gender

The analysis above sounds exhaustive, the story finished. But in its current form, the narrative merely reproduces the silence which structures the shop floor itself. Particimex was initially established to take advan-

tage of a gendered form of labor. The Autoworld managers who decided to open the plant sought not unspecified "good workers," but
gender-coded, "docile, dextrous, and cheap" workers. That is, they
sought not generic obedience, but the transnationally elaborated image
of productive femininity. What's more, current Particimex managers
continue to employ an overwhelmingly female workforce, and they cast
their ostensibly ungendered notion of appropriate shop-floor behavior in terms of its contrast with that enacted by young women outside
the plant. Thus, "productive femininity" functions as an other to be
negated—it is not absent. Cambio's silence around gender is expressive,
successfully addressing particular gendered subjects. Delineating the
mechanisms through which this silence operates allows us to grasp the
way in which new shop-floor femininities emerge and become productive in this unexpected context.

Managers' complex practices and rhetorics around gender function
in relation both to the plant's internal logic and to workers' external
social universe. Particimex workers—the many women and rare men
alike—inhabit a social world outside the factory in which gender is
deeply, consistently, and pleasurably accentuated. For the young
women who make up the bulk of the workforce, daily life is filled with
rituals of deference and request that emphasize their gendering in more
frustrating terms. Against this background, Cambio's gender-neutral
rhetoric of worker assertiveness and leadership is appealing and salient.
The fact that neither the rituals of submission nor those of respect
correspond directly to actual levels of independence changes, but does
not diminish, the importance of these rituals. New, productive feminine
subjects are still produced in these interactions.

Gendered meanings do not merely address shop-floor subjects. They
also mitigate a set of contradictions in Cambio itself. The rhetoric of
Cambio promises a level of shared leadership that it cannot possibly deliver. Within the shop floor's persistent trope of homemade feminine
diffidence, Particimex's women workers have come to understand their
own implacable feminine distaste for power to be the explanation for
the system's evident limitations. The plant's few male workers, on the
other hand, tend to rise through the Cambio structure, as there is substantial affinity between the natural masculine self assumed by factory
discourse and the ostensibly ungendered object of managerial address
in Cambio. Thus, the system's inherent tensions are resolved by gendered frameworks. Managers effectively instantiate gender in the process of negating it, invoke it each time they insist on its absence. In the

process, they produce a highly successful form of shop-floor control, one which owes its success to the very gendered discourses it denies.

SANTA MARÍA—RITUALS OF REQUEST AND WAITING

Santa María is in many ways typical of the complexities of contemporary northern Mexico. Not long ago it was a rural town. Today it has roughly 70,000 inhabitants, its population having soared with a flood of recent arrivals from the south. Many area residents still live largely off the produce from their small farms, and the primary local wage-earning industry is commercial chile farming, followed by a single, large, Mexican-owned bottling company. The paucity of local jobs leads to seasonal migration, and much of the area's income comes from agricultural work done on the other side of the border. Young men who have never been to Mexico City speak knowledgeably of remote farming towns scattered throughout the U.S. heartland. All these sources of income are primarily available to men, although women sometimes work in the chile harvest. The maquila is the only place that hires large numbers of women. At any given time, it employs close to 20 percent of the young women in the area. Many of the rest are not working for wages at all.

Despite the city's sudden growth, it has retained much of its small-town flavor. This is primarily because it is the economic hub of a set of small rural towns, many populated by relatives of Santa María residents. Close to half the Particimex workforce comes from these towns, rather than from Santa María itself. And wherever they live, for local young people, the towns are the main theater of interaction. Despite the presence of more "modern" discos in the city, the weddings, *quinceañeras*,[13] and dances that take place in the plazas of local towns attract a steady stream of the area's younger residents to dance, drink, flirt, show off, and keep track of their neighbors.

These dances are the pivot around which the maquila week revolves. Tuesdays and Thursdays, plans are made; Wednesdays and Fridays, blouses glitter beneath light blue smocks; Thursdays and Mondays, complaints of exhaustion are savored. The dances themselves are theatrical affairs, with young men in cowboy hats and boots, and young women made up and shining. A live band plays *norteño,* and the town plaza or basketball court is flooded with light, momentarily transformed into a stage for high-speed *corridas* and sexy *cumbias,* filled with dancing couples.

For all the wildness, however, the revelry has its rules. Only men can enter the dancing crowd at will. Women stand at the light's edge, still and restless, looking meaningfully at the dancing pairs. They watch the men drinking in groups and wait to be asked. Unlike in Juárez clubs, they are entirely dependent on the circulating men. Dancing with a girlfriend is not an option. And they can refuse a bad dancer, but only at the risk of an angry accusation—"Stuck up!"

One night I am impatient after a string of bad dancers, and now no one is asking. I recognize men from the maquila. "Can't I just ask them?" I beg Rosa, the woman in whose house I'm staying. "That's not done," she responds implacably. She is as impatient as I, but more practiced at waiting. I am reminded of the evenings she spends in constant enquiring trips to the window, looking for her boyfriend. Sometimes she waits for days. Suddenly from behind us there are hands on our elbows, and we are steered onto the dance floor. Rosa is smiling. I look up at my partner, all young bony limbs and a cowboy hat, and wait for that first subtle inclination that will allow me to move. We dance.

Unlike in Juárez, where many workers live away from their birth families and almost all reside outside their community of origin, young women in this area live in families and communities where everyone knows them, and everyone is watching. Rosa, a young divorced mother, never allows her boyfriend into the house, even for a minute. When he comes by, he stands in the street talking to her through the window. They spend hours hiding out in the countryside during evenings I am available for baby-sitting. People know, but they haven't actually seen anything. Appearances matter. Even when the vigilance isn't judgmental, it is tenacious. When I dance with a plant technician throughout a country evening, the entire maquila comments the next morning. "Here comes your dance partner," murmur my co-workers every time he passes.

The constant surveillance is particularly treacherous for young women because of the danger of jealousy. Men "suffer" from jealousy. It is referred to as an uncontrollable disease that sweeps over a man at the most minor indication of his wife or girlfriend's wavering attention. When a man is in the throes of jealousy, almost any behavior is forgivable. Wild drinking binges are the norm. During a period of floods in which workers from outlying villages stay in local, company-paid hotels, husbands and boyfriends forge the swollen rivers to make sure wives and girlfriends are really at work. Late in my stay in the area, a young technician shoots himself in front of his new (maquila worker) wife. He was jealous, workers recount matter-of-factly, and she tried to leave. Discussion over whether she is to be blamed or pitied goes on for days. "She's very pretty," says one of my co-workers in apparently self-evident explanation. The young widow is never able to show her face in the plant again.

The threat of jealous rages is part of what keeps young women careful, but they are also subject to more direct rules and pressures. Whether they live with their fathers or husbands, "asking permission" for young women is an ongoing ritual—one with varied practical applications depending on who is being addressed. When women living with their birth families want to go out, fathers must be asked, but they generally consent. New husbands are another matter. A young wife on my line explains that she spent a half-hour wandering in the town market with a friend on the way home the day before. When she finally arrived at 4:30, her husband was steaming. "He gives the orders at home," she explains simply. Another young women tells me, "I don't want to get married now. My sister just got married, and now she can't go to the dances. Horrible. I have a boyfriend, but he can't tell me no. I don't belong to him."

This sense of marriage as ownership is pervasive among the single and newly married women who make up the bulk of maquila workers. It is less so among the older women, who make up a minority of the workforce. Particularly after the arrival of children, many women carve out a space of autonomy at home. A married woman, already a mother, explains that she initially got married because her parents wouldn't let her go dancing anyway. At first her husband wouldn't allow her to go anywhere either. Now she just leaves him a note saying where she is. "You've got to stand up for yourself," she says. Her younger co-workers don't respond. This is not yet an option for them with the men in their lives.

Young women are of course not passive in these situations, and as Rosa's country hide-outs suggest, they often greet restraints with schemes for circumventing them. Certainly the fact that 20 percent of the women in the maquila are single mothers is one indication of the high level of noncompliance with at least some of the community's formal strictures. Nonetheless, young women's daily lives are structured by rituals of request and waiting. In families, with their boyfriends, at dances, young women are expected to respond, not initiate. This set of external structures thus provides a context for all that occurs in the factory, a background against which managerial practices are interpreted, experienced, and appreciated. Set against the rituals of home, shop-floor practices play as "liberatory" and invite women workers to inhabit profoundly appealing selves.

"I TELL THEM THEY CAN DO IT, BUT THEY WON'T TAKE THE LEAP"

The managers of Particimex are not from Santa María, and they sharply distinguish their view of the world, and of gendered realities, from that of their workers. At the same time, they do not share the pragmatic utilitarianism of their non-Mexican colleagues when confronted by these differences. Instead, in seeking to distinguish themselves from their Mexican peasant workers, they focus on re-forming the intractable "traditional femininity" of women workers in the plant. In so doing, they position themselves as insiders who can see out—as a modernizing force in their own land. Thus, their shop-floor rhetoric is ungendered, but pointedly so, addressing the young woman worker as Cambio's ideal, decision-making subject.

Within this context, and against the backdrop of their experiences at home, young women in Particimex experience and enact a new sort of self-respect and self-direction. In an arena where their opinions are solicited and formally noted, many hear the potential authority of their own voices for the first time. Simultaneously, the voices from home that define it as unfeminine for young women to occupy positions of authority are reinforced by managers' "concern"—reiterated in interactions outside of Cambio's formal structures—that they cannot overcome these pressures. This two-tiered discursive structure effectively naturalizes feminine submissiveness, while underlining heroic managerial efforts to counteract these deeply rooted traits. Thus, shop-floor disciplinary practices constitute a split feminine subjectivity within the factory. The few young men in production have a simpler time of it. Getting hired is difficult. But once hired, men are encouraged to follow their natural "daring" and become leaders within production. As a result, a single set of meanings allows both young men and young women to constitute livable—and productive—subjectivities on the shop floor.

The decision to establish a Santa María factory in 1987 was aimed at accessing the docile young women workers who had become increasingly scarce in Juárez's tight labor market. The move has been an unparalleled success. Young women with few other employment options have proved ready and eager to work. When I arrive, five years after the plant's inauguration, managers still have the latitude in hiring decisions that brought them there to begin with. Turnover is extremely low for a maquila:[14] it has not surpassed 3 percent for a couple of years. Roughly seventy-five people—fifty women and twenty-five men—apply for work every month. As a result, during the intermittent hiring periods, managers can pick and choose, contracting about half the women and a quarter of the men who are available at any given moment.

Demographic hiring criteria remain both explicit and effective. In the interview schedule for production workers, the interviewer is reminded that the factory goal is to hire 80 percent women. The head of personnel sounds no different from his Juárez counterparts, waxing eloquent about women's quiescence, patience, and concentration. Age is also emphasized. He comments, "Young people, they're not spoiled. They don't bring bad habits from other work. You form them here." Women constitute 70 to 75 percent of workers at any given time, 85 percent on the line. They average seventeen years of age; the men are a couple of years older. Nondirect jobs are even more skewed by gender. All of top management, twenty-seven of thirty supervisors, all maintenance technicians, and almost all material handlers are men.

When the factory opened and began hiring young women, it encountered a fair amount of local suspicion. Early rumors described it as a "deflowering" factory. Today, the plant makes explicit attempts not to come into direct conflict with the authorities in women workers' external lives. The interview schedule instructs the questioner to look for "emotional stability," and interviewers comply by asking about relations with boyfriends or husbands. Similarly, the schedule asks about permission to work from parents and husbands. When describing the hiring process, the personnel manager who does the interviewing raises the issue of husbands as well: "If her husband isn't in agreement with her working, I won't hire her. She won't last." A quarter of women workers are married and about two-thirds of these have children.

Despite the maquila's unwillingness to hire women against their husbands' wishes, once it does hire them, management tries to keep these women even in the face of trouble at home. Yet personnel staff members are explicit about trying to avoid stepping on husbands' toes. Retention of women workers is engineered by accommodating husbands, not by challenging husbands' authority. As a result, it is not uncommon for the personnel department to give a woman a week off to "work out her problems at home."

Outside of personnel, in production, the official language around gender is far more muted. Gender differences are scarcely mentioned by supervisors and managers on the shop floor. When asked directly about the differences between male and female workers, they tend to frame their responses in terms of Cambio. Thus, they focus on temperamental rather than physical differences, and on women's ability to create peer relationships, rather than on their manageability. Women work better in groups, they support each other more, they "spoil" each other. Men are more assertive, more individualist. However, even these comments are rare. The official line in production is that gender is unimportant.

This studied shop-floor disregard of gender has markedly gendered implications given shop-floor demographics and Cambio's internal logic. Young women make up the overwhelming majority of the direct production workforce itself—the arena in which the Cambio is most developed. Thus, they are the primary group addressed within Cambio's language of independence, participation, and responsibility. Consequently, the simple fact of omission—that Cambio fails to mention gender, that its rhetoric about assertiveness, taking chances, and ongoing learning neither acknowledges nor accommodates the gender makeup of its primarily young, female audience—is in itself of tremendous significance. And this rhetoric does result in concrete developments on the shop floor. On the line, women make up 71 percent of expert operators, 58 percent of coordinators, and 64 percent of supports. In production, women are frequently in positions of authority.

The intensity of the discourse that addresses young women as workers leaves little room for alternate, managerially promulgated subjectivities within the factory. Sexuality, for instance, is neither underlined nor mobilized by supervisors on the shop floor. A supervisor tells me that until recently he had an assistant on his line, but he found him other work to do. In stark contrast to Panoptimex, where sexualization is part and parcel of effective management, the supervisor felt his assistant's constant flirting had disrupted overall control on the line. Because discipline is exercised through the constitution of young women's subjectivities around work, the introduction of an alternate managerial discourse around sexuality only interferes with that process.[15]

Young women in the factory respond assertively to these frameworks. One day, soon after my arrival at the plant, I notice a woman packing finished goods—a job generally described in the industry as too "heavy" for women workers. She explains that she's part of an all-woman team, and team members want to keep it that way. They rotate jobs. "We had a man on the team. He thought he was something. . . . He just wanted to sit around and order everyone about. We called him *el influyente*. He left to be a support person and we told the supervisor we want only women. We can do all the jobs." The supervisor comes by to ask a question about the week's quality numbers, then hurriedly retires. A co-worker smiles. "Last week he was on top of us all the time. He kept coming over and correcting us, instead of talking to the coordinator like he's supposed to. We had to have a meeting and point it out to him." Men in the plant recognize the same shift, although they do not necessarily respond as positively. The supervisor of maintenance tells me that (male) technicians had a hard time after Cambio was first instituted. "The gals started to order them around and speak rudely to them," he comments. "They weren't accustomed to being spoken to that way."

The experience of the woman who puts me up in Santa María is emblematic of these processes, and of the ongoing contrasts between these shop-floor experiences and life at home. Rosa is the oldest daughter of a local family which, like many of its neighbors, owns a small farm and supplements its meager yield through seasonal work in the chile harvest. Just before she began working at Particimex, she married, and the couple had a child shortly thereafter. She and her new husband entered work together. Fortunate enough to enter immediately after the strike, she was quickly promoted through Cambio, moving up and off the shop floor into the training department. He, on the other hand, began drinking and was eventually fired. Over time, these differences placed unbearable strain on the relationship, and they were divorced a year before my arrival. Her plant status is such that, when her younger (single) sister was discovered to be pregnant in a routine exam prior to starting work at the plant,[16] it was Rosa, not her father, who was informed of the familial problem. Nonetheless, despite her evolving responsibility and clear, assertive, somewhat demanding persona within the maquila, she continues to practice local feminine reticence in interactions with her current boyfriend. In his presence, she is pointedly, expressively passive. She never contacts him, never asks where he's been, never even seeks him out at local dances. Her first relationship was a casualty of the different demands of home and work. She does not seem inclined to repeat the journey. This time, the contrasts have become routine elements of a dissonant daily life which is increasingly the norm—not only for her, but for other women in the plant.

Not surprisingly in this situation, women workers often favorably contrast their treatment in the plant to their experiences in the community outside. A young woman speaking of being bossed around by her husband says, "Here, really, they don't order you around. You're responsible for your own work, for what you do." A co-worker describes her older sister's confining marriage, commenting, "Maybe I won't get married. They don't let you do anything. . . . Now that we work here, we're different than before." [17] The young married woman who works next to me spends the last hour of work planning out the chores she has to do when she gets home. Her husband "feels like it's plenty" to help take care of their daughter, she comments acidly. Maquila work is easy in comparison. In managerial discourse around production, young women are required to enact assertiveness. At home, these same young women, particularly those working out new relationships with men, are expected to perform compliance. Whatever the actual constraints and possibilities that underlie these rituals, the enacted contrast between them is glaring.

This set of contrasts shapes life on the shop floor. But this is not only because workers note these differences. It is also because managers do. As ongoing participants in transnational discussions of "third-world women's" intrinsic docility, Particimex managers are quick to remark upon its signs in their workers. In daily discussions, the rigidity and persistence of workers' notions of femininity and "macho" is a frequent and routine point of reference. These references serve several functions. They enable managers to distinguish themselves from workers, emphasizing their relative advancement. They also reify and naturalize "femininity" itself, establishing it as a shop-floor presence. Supervisors rarely suggest women workers for coordinator jobs, but complain at length that no matter how much they encourage their women workers to be coordinators, "They won't make the leap." Jesús says that he thinks half the supervisors should be women, but unfortunately, "*la cultura mexicana* . . ." He looks pained. Miguel says there are "beliefs" about women locally . . . Leo shakes his head in mingled despair and admiration over a fight. "Mexican jealousy, it's something else," he says. These regretful comments serve a function in the daily life of the factory, confirming the continuing inequality of men and women in production, while implicitly attributing it to the backward culture from which workers (but not managers) come.

Not surprisingly in this context, many women in the factory are reluctant to take on positions of authority, and despite the relatively high percentage of these positions filled by women, they are still underrepresented compared to their proportions in the workforce. In direct production, most expert operators are women. Yet only 13 percent of women workers are expert operators, whereas 27 percent of men are. Similarly and more importantly, whereas 7 percent of women on the line are coordinators, 28 percent of the men are. Another way of assessing this last discrepancy is that if there is a position of authority open and a man available to fill it, he will do so 85 percent of the time, rather than one of the five to nine women also on the team.[18] Women do take leadership positions in production, but generally only when no men are available to do so.

Managers' ongoing complaints about gendered meanings and practices outside the factory's walls give these discourses form and solidity within the plant itself, effectively producing them as ongoing points of reference internally. The participatory structure is thus kept within controllable bounds. Men are told they can move into positions of authority, and they do. Women are told they can move into positions of authority, but that they probably don't want to sacrifice their femininity to do so. Not surprisingly, for the most part they don't. Thus, the overrepresentation of men as coordinators and supports makes it possible to have a credible rhetoric of shared leadership, without most workers ever really imagining themselves in scarce leadership positions. The fact that workers themselves are in part responsible for these decisions through "elections" only makes the system more stable.

Thus, we can see the coexistence in the factory of a powerful language directed at young women that contests external norms, even as a subtext simultaneously laments the "natural" rural Mexican character that makes this contestation only partially possible. This subtext, and the managerial practice of pushing women to do everything except become coordinators, makes it possible for managers to involve both men and women within Cambio—women as those who "should" risk taking on authority and men who actually do so. Women are addressed in a deeply pleasurable, liberatory language; yet this is coupled with a narrative that accepts and sustains the naturalness of male power. It is this double elaboration of paradigmatic femininity—responsible and independent within the factory, "naturally" retiring externally—that makes managerial discourse around gender such a powerful address and therefore such an effective form of labor control. We can understand Cambio's effectiveness as a disciplinary system by analyzing the gendered meanings that infuse practices of labor control in the factory.

New Women on the Line

In Particimex, managers have instituted a disciplinary system that directly addresses and incorporates the laboring self. The quiescent, in-

volved, even enthusiastic workforce attests to the success of this recon-
stitution of selves on the job. This process of remaking the self occurs
on a charged, gendered field. The plant's hiring and labor control practices invoke external gendered tropes, both to invert and to reinforce
them. In so doing, they evoke a set of feminine subjectivities that operate in contradiction to those outside, while constituting masculinities
in keeping with external norms. Within this process of challenging transnational tropes and constituting not–"traditional Mexican women,"
Particimex managers cement their privileged status as Mexican emis-
saries who can modernize "their people" within the transnational structure. And by addressing gendered shop-floor subjects—new femininities and old masculinities—managers establish and guarantee the quality
of their harnesses.

If Panoptimex demonstrates the idiosyncratic social process behind
the emergence of gendered subjects who might otherwise appear eternal, Particimex illustrates how more unexpected femininities can also
be constituted in the service of global production. Located in a social
world where cheap, docile, and dextrous women would appear to be
available for the taking, Particimex managers choose a less obvious
strategy of shop-floor control. In acting to free themselves from the
stigma of the local, these managers address their workers in contradiction to both global expectations and local experiences. In establishing
the icon of the third-world woman worker as the other in contrast to
whom Particimex workers are to be evaluated and to evaluate themselves, they produce new, although still productive, shop-floor femininities. As a result of the success of these strategies, women workers at
Particimex resemble neither transnational nor local injunctions, and
they enact distinct femininities on and off the shop floor. This process
highlights the variable content of the category we know as "femininity"
and reveals its capacity to shift over both space and time. It also demonstrates the utility of this flexibility for managerial control, thus suggesting still another reason for gender's central role in global production.

6

Manufacturing "Workers"

Andromex

In Panoptimex and Particimex, we indeed found women on the line in the global factory, but it was the category of femininity which was at work. What's more, the category itself proved remarkably malleable. In Panoptimex, local conditions conspired to reproduce the basic lineaments of global images of productive femininity, whereas in Particimex, the transnational icon became an other against whom local femininities were evoked. Thus, femininity remained central, but its meaning proved variable. In Andromex, we see a shop floor even further removed from global expectations, as here the feminization of assembly work itself becomes an object of contest. In consequence, gender continues to shape shop-floor selves, but the workforce is half men, and the subjects who emerge—male and female alike—are masculinized rather than feminized.[1]

How and why this unusual gendering emerged is in itself a story worth telling. It is doubly significant for present purposes, for it further illuminates gender's crucial but varying role in transnational production. In a labor market where jobs are explicitly named as women's work, managers and workers alike already operate on gendered terrain. Thus, the decision to address a maquila workforce through tropes taken from manufacturing rather than assembly immediately implies a distinctively gendered subject, even if that new gendering is never made explicit in language. As a result, like their counterparts throughout the industry, Andromex workers become productive subjects through their interpellation in a gendered meaning structure, even though that structure is not femininity.

Andromex is one of the oldest and largest maquilas in Juárez. It is a subsidiary of the transnational Pharmaworld, and has been producing sterile, disposable hospital garments in the city since 1970. From its opening with forty workers, it has grown into a Juárez institution, employing more than 2,000 men and women in three daily shifts. The plant manager was long ago disenchanted by his experience of women's purported docility, and he insists that gender is not a concern in hiring. This discourse is reinforced on the shop floor by the caps and coveralls required of workers producing a sterile product, making gender difficult to distinguish at first glance. Nonetheless, a closer look at the daily life of production suggests that the subjects who are enacted are not ungendered; they are implicitly masculine—responding to a managerial framework which accepts legitimate struggle for a family wage as the shop-floor norm.[2]

The plant manager is a Juárez native who revels in working-class masculinity, and in the context of the feminized maquila industry, masculinizing work is easy. Since gendered meanings are always established through contrasts, sewing and folding at Andromex can be framed as "men's work" through only minimal increases in wages and shop-floor autonomy. Thus, once men are hired, they are addressed in terms they are able to acknowledge. Male workers respond by enacting a combative masculinity, performing their capacity to work and their right to do so unmolested throughout the day. At the same time, since the masculinity referenced here is both disembodied and implicit—assumed within gendered categories, rather than named[3]—women, too, are able to recognize themselves within shop-floor frameworks. Thus, gender continues to matter in the shop-floor politics of this plant, but workers are addressed in contrast to, rather than in consonance with, the larger feminized expectations of global assembly.

Masculinizing "Women's Work"

In the context of global and local labor markets organized around the cheap, docile, and dextrous woman, a mixed-gender export-processing shop floor structured around contentious masculinity begs for explanation. In the case of Andromex, where production was indeed initially set up around productive femininity, this anomaly emerged through a parallel and mutually reinforcing set of changes in gendered meanings and labor control structures. Today, the shop floor more closely resembles a first-world manufacturer staffed by a conventionally unionized male workforce than a third-world assembler staffed by docile women workers. This shift required both the shattering of the image of productive femininity and the emergence of a set of labor control methods organized around, and constitutive of, masculine subjects. In the following pages, we will see how a conflictive history, a demanding set of production imperatives, and a powerful "native" plant manager converged, first to open the shop floor to men, and ultimately to evoke masculine subjects in this previously feminized context. Faced by a history of resistance, a skill-dependent labor process, and a desire to make transnational production work in his own backyard, Roberto Gómez, Andromex's Juárez-born plant manager, has established a "hegemonic regime" on the shop floor.[4] In this framework, productive subjects are evoked in ritualized shop-floor struggles which sometimes increase wage packets but which unfailingly affirm both managerial control and worker masculinity. In the process of creating this unusual structure, Gómez has successfully incorporated men into the work of the global assembly line.

UNWOMANLY WOMEN

When I arrived in the early nineties, Andromex immediately stood out for its mixed-gender workforce and for the respectful tone used by the plant manager in addressing and referring to his workers. This had not always been the case. To the contrary, during the plant's first decade of operation in the 1970s, Andromex management employed the same predominantly female workforce and dismissive rhetoric as did the rest of the industry, and work conditions, wages, and disciplinary practices were if anything worse than those nearby.[5] The shift from an earlier mode of labor control to that which I found upon arrival pivoted on a crucial strike in 1980, during which furious women workers forever disabused management of the easy assumption of feminine docility.

Midway through that year, a relatively small national union (the CRT) jockeying for a place in the Juárez maquila industry began organizing the plant's predominantly female workforce against both management and their purported union "representatives" (the CTM). By all accounts, neither union was much concerned with workers' welfare,[6] but the challenger's efforts found fertile ground in the plant's abysmal conditions.[7] For months, the plant swung between management lockouts, worker occupations, and slowdowns punctuated by furious meetings and strike threats.[8] Management took out full-page ads in local papers announcing their imminent departure from the city. The CTM sent male members from other industries to retake the plant, armed with clubs, pistols, and tear gas. Women workers supporting the CRT demonstrated in front of the locked plant, and pictures of them, complete with warlike headbands and clubs and surrounded by their (unarmed) husbands, ran in local papers.

The conflict finally ended with the "help" of a government mediator, rumored to have threatened CRT leaders with the loss of other contracts if they persisted. The final deal guaranteed CTM's right to represent workers and resulted in the firing of hundreds who had organized for new representation. Despite the utter failure of democratic process, the strike inaugurated a new era in the factory. The new union leadership, while still under the CTM umbrella, needed to win over a radicalized workforce if it was to operate effectively in the plant. Thus, while supporting the ongoing weeding out and blacklisting of "troublemakers" from the conflict, it also began to present itself as workers' advocate.

The six-month struggle was followed by new management as well as by new union leadership. Gómez, the new plant manager, is still running Andromex today. Unlike his predecessor, he brought a rhetoric of respect and an interest in negotiation to his dealings with workers. The combination of a union semi-obligated to workers and a manager invested in working with the union made the emergence of a hegemonic shop-floor regime possible.[9] And that system bore fruit. Production efficiency rates soared, going from 78 percent in 1981 to 109 percent today.

From beginning to end, the managerial decisions which led to this remarkable turnaround were made on an (often explicitly) gendered terrain. Initial managerial hiring criteria were a foregone conclusion given the transnational trope of productive femininity and the ensuing hiring practices in the industry locally. The consensus around this understanding ran so deep that when the plant hired ten men in September of 1980 it was straightforwardly described by local media as preparation for a violent strike.[10] Why else would Andromex hire men, after all? They clearly were not appropriate Andromex *workers*.[11] In a context in which women meant docility, hiring men was understood as fighting words, by management and onlookers alike. This foundational belief in the gendering of docility and violence was one of the major casualties of the strike. The current plant manager recalls taking astonished note from his vantage point in electronics as women workers talked back, walked out, shouted, and even fought, all in the blazing light of the media's cameras.

An article that appeared at the end of the strike suggests that women workers inside the factory interpreted their shop-floor resistance through gendered lenses as well, and that the experience was a conflicted one. The article reported that the last straw for several young women working in the plant was when some of their (female) co-workers adopted the "outlandish" fashion of head shaving. Worse yet, one worker took all her clothes off and ran through the plant, as a co-worker lamented the loss of "Our femininity! Our femininity!"[12] Some women, the newspaper reported, were urging the press "to deliver a message of decorum to their co-workers so they'll stop 'burning' us so much."[13] Whether they responded to the strike's stresses by challenging or reaffirming their "femininity," it was gender which became the ground upon which this distress was articulated. For workers as well as their bosses, the conflict shook received notions of gendered meanings and subjects, making possible the dramatic shifts in hiring policies and shop-floor culture that followed shortly thereafter.

Hiring policies did not shift immediately after the strike, but as soon as the labor shortage of 1983 set in, the plant began to hire men. Neither union leaders nor managers were willing to forgo production in order to hire women whose docility had already proved unreliable. By 1984, 40 percent of the labor force was male. Even more striking, managerial perceptions of the labor force were shifting. In 1985, rather than echoing fashionable complaints that men didn't want to work, management began attempting to reform them within the plant. The front page of the plant newsletter in November 1985 was dedicated to a paean to manhood beginning and ending with the injunction "LET'S BE MEN" and filled with thirteen exhortations to responsibility in the guise of definitions of manhood:

> TO BE A MAN is not just to be male, a mere individual of the masculine sex; . . .
>
> TO BE A MAN is to be the creator of something, a home, a business, a position, a system, a life;
>
> TO BE A MAN is to do things, not to look for reasons to show that they cannot be done.[14]

Real men were workers; real workers were men. The symbolic transition from feminine assembly to masculine manufacturing was well under way.

The 1980 conflict was a turning point for Andromex, establishing patterns that persist more than a decade later. Today, the daily creation of consent has replaced shop-floor coercion and a mixed-gender workforce enacts masculine bravado in an arena once organized around "femininity." Despite the qualitative break in production relations between the period before and after the strike, however, the new set of relations cannot be attributed solely to the conflict itself. The new system took root only because it was well suited to the production process already in place on the shop floor.

VALUABLE WORKERS, BREADWINNING WORK

Sewing is valuable; sewing is difficult. It is at the intersection of these facts that the results of the period of struggle can be explained. The ongoing presence of experienced workers is essential for a factory to function in the international market in disposable hospital garments. This situation gives Andromex workers something to bargain with, unlike their counterparts in many other maquilas, and the impact of their position is visible in daily life on the shop floor.

According to Gómez, the overall orientation of the Pharmaworld corporation is toward sales rather than production.[15] This means that the entire transnational structure is geared, not to producing widgets and then selling them as quickly as possible, but to getting orders for widgets and then filling them as quickly as possible. This corporate self-understanding has consequences at the level of production, the most important being that having experienced workers available when necessary is *the* top managerial priority in the company's manufacturing division. Labor costs always matter, of course, but ultimately they are secondary. This attitude is visible all the way down through the supervisory structure. Group chiefs are expected to get out production—at any cost. If they must pay overtime to get out an order, so be it. Gómez says simply, "We must be able to react. . . . If you want to make money, you have to pay. You make more money if you pay more."

The impact of this attitude is heightened by the grueling and practice-dependent character of industrial sewing. Workers in the plant report that the work is far harder than at other maquilas, and even those who have been in the plant for years describe certain positions as "killers." The woman responsible for vetting new workers—significantly a job in and of itself in Andromex—says she's "always hiring," and new employees leave in droves in their first few months. An experienced worker in the factory comments, "The new ones get desperate, but you know you handle the material, the material doesn't handle you." This level of mastery doesn't come easily. Even formal training time is far more substantial here than in other maquilas. The most skilled operation, attaching sleeves to the smock, requires twelve weeks in order to bring workers up to speed. In this context, when an experienced worker quits, it's a serious loss.

This has some predictable effects. Management aims to pay at the top of the maquila scale in Juárez, making it possible, although difficult, for a worker to support a small family alone. Base pay is comparable to that in other large maquilas, and most earn exactly that. However, with incentive pay, skilled workers can sometimes even double their wages; as a result, average earnings are about 25 percent higher than in Panoptimex and other major Juárez plants. For those whose positions require the most training, a portion of this bonus is guaranteed. For the same reason, workers wanting to return to the plant after having quit are welcomed back. Whereas in most maquilas the default decision is not to rehire such workers, in Andromex the default is to embrace them. Workers' value is similarly evident in the lamentations of personnel staff, who describe battles with other medical supply plants over experienced workers and complain of their best workers being "lured away."

The most important effect of the company's dependence on its experienced workers, however, is not so much financial as social. Unlike in other plants, where pay is frankly "supplementary," here workers and management alike can, and sometimes do, refer to something like a family wage. In addition, insofar as the plant needs experienced workers, it is less likely to fire them impulsively, even in response to shop-floor resistance. Similarly, insofar as their capacity to bring up their wages increases, workers are less likely to quit impetuously, even in response to difficult work conditions. The result of this mutual dependence is the emergence of a space for, and a tolerance of, struggle on the shop floor.

The period of resistance politicized the shop floor too deeply for management to simply return to the old unilateral practices of labor control. However, the emergent pattern of conflict might have proved impossibly disruptive to production if workers had had no resources apart from incipient shop-floor radicalization. If every conflict were met by firings or resignations, ongoing shop-floor tussles would not be a workable practice of shop-floor control. What makes this set of practices viable on the Andromex shop floor is the high value of the worker, a value that has consequences for both management and workers. Management is motivated to keep workers by paying more and negotiating worker demands, and workers are motivated to keep their jobs. Only in this context can there be sufficient tolerance all around for hegemonic control to operate successfully.

The vibrant jockeying for control which characterizes daily life in the plant is further enabled by both the nature of supervisory workers and the structure of pay. Sewing is not a highly technical process, but it is a highly skilled one, and this has consequences for the allocation of shop-floor management. The factory has always given primary supervisory responsibility to promoted workers rather than to formally trained supervisors. The head supervisor of the smock section entered Andromex nineteen years ago as a worker and has been supervising for eighteen years. Below her are ten groups of forty workers, each in turn supervised by a "group chief." These too are women who were promoted in the maquila's first years of operation or immediately following the walkouts. Their position is not an easy one. Separated from those they supervise by little more than luck and ambition, group chiefs struggle to maintain their authority, and workers comment constantly on how little distinguishes them.

Similarly, the wage structure is an invitation to struggle. Industrial sewing has historically been paid on a piecework system,[16] and this tradition continues in the maquilas. It is a system full of opportunities for conflicts over production, and in a context in which workers are addressed as breadwinners, such conflicts are legitimate. From minimum production levels to incentive pay to compensation for time lost when materials are unavailable, each step of the process requires judgment calls that open abundant areas of possible disagreement. In the context of a hegemonic system of labor control, these struggles become the terrain upon which contradictions are adjudicated and consent is established.

The constant minor conflicts that make up daily life in production at Andromex are not always pleasant, but they are invariably compelling, and participation evokes contentious, masculinized subjects. As workers, women and men alike enact rituals of "standing their ground." In the process, they are interpellated as a particular version of the industrial worker—the manly producer, locked in ongoing but necessarily respectful conflict with management.[17]

A MANAGER AT HOME

The legacy of the 1980 labor struggles, the mid-eighties shortage of female workers, and the production factors inherent in industrial sewing go a long way toward accounting for Andromex's conflict-ridden and efficient labor process, and for the implicitly masculine subjects it ultimately evokes. But factories don't run themselves, history and industrial structure notwithstanding. This is particularly clear in the case of Roberto Gómez, the longtime Andromex plant manager.

Gómez stands out among maquila managers. He carries himself more like the owner of a Mexican factory than like a manager within a large, foreign transnational. His attention is on "his" city, "his" factory, "his" workers, not on his ascendance within the corporation. Unlike the plant managers I observed in other maquilas—Mexican and non-Mexican alike—he is not angling to move up and out of the "hinterlands." Juárez is his ultimate destination. Once I have known him a while, I realize that even my initial contact with him was characteristic in this respect. I was initially referred to him not by another maquila manager, although he is well known among them, but by the Mexican personnel manager at Anarchomex—a personal as well as a professional acquaintance. For all his transnational connections and credibility, Gómez is a true *juarense*. Understood in this light, Gómez's decision to remain in the city makes sense. Nonetheless, it is sufficiently unusual for someone in his position (even his brother-in-law is already working in Chicago) that he feels compelled to justify it to me at length during an interview. He notes his wife's desire to remain near her family, his own fear that away from the border, his ability to bridge two cultures would simply become inadequacy in one of them, and his belief that northern Mexico is on the cusp of being an important global industrial center. Above and beyond his own decision-making process, however, this commitment to the local is made possible by a set of underlying features, both in the Andromex structure of production and in Gómez himself.

The work done in Andromex makes up a significant portion of the overall cost of its products, given the low level of capital-intensivity in the labor process and the general cheapness of materials. In the maquilas discussed earlier, labor accounts for only a small percentage of the value of the final product—for instance, labor constitutes only 1.8 percent of the wholesale cost of the average television in Panoptimex. In Andromex, on the other hand, labor accounts for anywhere from 12 to 17 percent of the value of the maquila's finished products.[18] The obvious importance of dealing effectively with workers in this context gives the factory, and by extension its manager, clout within the corporate structure.[19] This position is only getting stronger. During my tenure in

the plant, all cutting for Andromex products is done in El Paso to sat-
isfy U.S. quota regulations. However, plans are in the works to shift
these facilities to Gómez's turf in Juárez,[20] and he is often to be found
in El Paso, evaluating the current binational production process. As
plant manager of Andromex, Gómez already operates with sizable autonomy and control.

In the context of this independence, Gómez's personal history takes
on particular importance. Son of an elite Juárez family, he trained to
be an engineer, with an eye toward working in Juárez from the outset.
As a teenager looking for a summer job, he took work in TVA, one
of Juárez's first—and today largest and most prestigious—electronics
maquilas. The investment was rewarded after he finished his technical
training in the early seventies, when he landed one of the still-scarce
engineering jobs in the Juárez maquilas in TVA itself. It was from the
comparative calm of TVA that he was recruited to pick up the pieces in
Andromex in 1981, as local elite anxiety over working women displacing
men was reaching new public heights. He has been there ever since, or-
chestrating the rebuilding of the workforce to include men, a new set
of relations with workers, and a soaring efficiency index.

Like his countrymen at Particimex, Gómez is faced with the challenge of locating himself in a cross-border structure in which his nationality is both a primary reason for his employment and his greatest liability within the corporation. One of the rare Mexican plant managers
in Juárez, he has had to work to establish credibility with his American
bosses. During an interview, he tells an emblematic story, evidently
painfully engraved in his memory, of his own learning process. During
his first meeting in the States, he showed up in the white shirt and tie
he wore on the shop floor, "with my head full of production figures."
Everyone else came in designer suits, whose jackets they took off
during the meeting to reveal elegant vests. When they went to dinner,
he was the only one without a jacket. Worse yet, instead of asking
him about production, they asked him about Mexico, and he didn't
have answers. As soon as he got home, he swore he'd never be "*el pobre
mexicanito*" again. He bought *Dress for Success* and started reading the
newspapers. Today he is "one of the best dressed of them all" and is
something of an authority on "his country."

In his need to manage his relationships with his North American superiors, Gómez is not unlike his Particimex counterparts. But he differs
sharply from them in his relationship with his workers, whom he recognizes as compatriots, despite their evident differences. At one point

he quotes himself talking to the union representative: "What's the difference? You're from Juárez, I'm from Juárez. You and I are the ones who make this plant. We can't fool each other. The guys from Chicago wouldn't know [if they'd been fooled], but we would." This allegiance goes beyond alliance to the performance of a shared (urban, *fronterizo*) masculine self. Within the plant, Gómez's body language and speech style announce his links to a cultural world generated by Juárez's working class. He greets visitors to his office with the complex series of handshakes that are de rigueur on the shop floor and elsewhere among non-elite men in Juárez. In interviews with me, he speaks rhythmically, throwing his body back in the chair, then swinging back up, slapping his leg for emphasis. His conversation is peppered with local, typically masculine slang (*guey, jale, lana*[21]) and his inflections echo the street. His stories, too, perform these connections. At one point he describes what I learn only later and elsewhere was a summer job as "working his way up from the bottom" starting "almost [as] a janitor."[22] His accounts of his tenure at TVA are full of lighthearted tales of his interactions with (women) workers on the line. "They'd call out to me, 'Roberto, honey!' and I'd act nuts, like I didn't hear them and then, 'Come here, *güero*!'[23] . . . I hang with the workers."

Gómez's identification with, rather than othering of, his workers is reflected in his overall managerial style. Critically contrasting the workplace he was trained in to the one he has built, he comments, "In many respects, the people in TVA don't matter. The person is practically another machine. It's different here." He is convinced that "you have to give a lot of authority to people." Thus, unlike other managers I observed or interviewed, he is willing to direct a shop floor organized around conflict and negotiation. This is his world and these are "his people." He deals with them in this framework.

Gómez's autonomy and control mean that his frameworks set the shop floor's tone. In this context, his attitude toward workers makes it possible for the tendencies inherent in the history of resistance and the structure of production to crystallize into a coherent system of labor control through conflict. At the same time, his personal style of masculinity and membership in a social world consumed by anxieties over working-class male displacement have converged to establish an idiosyncratic set of gendered meaning structures on the shop floor. Rather than struggling to find women when they got scarce, he hired men, integrating them into the center of shop-floor life and legitimating the contentious breadwinner as the normative shop-floor subject. Thus,

Gómez's understanding of himself and his workers ultimately led to the labor control practices we will see below—practices that address combative masculine subjects within an otherwise resolutely feminized industry.

Mastering Work, Making Masters

> *[On the assembly line] you don't fight for the simple fact that you see that you don't have anything to gain. . . . What's the point of fighting? . . . You have a little more power [in piecework].*
>
> Manuel, Andromex smock folder

As one enters the swinging doors to the Andromex shop floor, one's eye is immediately lost in a jittery mass of blue—chaos amid uniformity. First shift, close to a thousand workers are scattered across the factory's flat, low-ceilinged expanse, every one swathed in the blue smocks and light blue caps produced in the plant. There are no assembly lines, no conveyor belts, no overwhelming machines shaping and pacing production. Instead, workers sew, fold, or pack to their own feverish rhythms—pushing their products aside for others to transport to the next step in the process. All around the enormous room, piles of unfinished paper blankets, smocks, and caps are being carried or wheeled in towering, precarious-looking edifices from one frenetic, anonymous figure to the next.

Music blasts through the scene, a constant beat over the clatter of sewing machines. At intervals, loud whoops emerge in response to someone's entrance onto the shop floor without the required sterile smock or cap or to mark approval of a particularly favored song selection. If the music is especially inspiring, the commotion may develop into an impromptu salsa—a couple of paired blue smocks dancing in the aisle—sometimes a man and a woman, sometimes two men, sometimes two women. Always these outbursts delight and enliven, contributing to a sense of workers' unchallenged control of the social space of the shop floor.

And yet, despite the appearance that workers have free rein, the limits of this behavior are clearly and consensually established around the norm of high productivity. What's more, the contention over shop-floor control itself stabilizes production. It is precisely through struggles over material shortages, minimum production levels, and status that those hired become shop-floor subjects, recognized by management and by themselves as "Andromex workers." These myriad minor conflicts assume and create a masculine subject—a breadwinner always-already legitimately invested in both autonomy and high productivity.

In the following pages, we will enter one of the factory's ten, first-shift smock-assembly sections, in the plant's productive heart. When I first ask Gómez if I can work in production, he immediately grasps why working matters. He does not, however, consider allowing me to sew, where I would destroy his valuable materials and create bottlenecks in production. Hence, in short order I find myself standing at a folding table with a dozen other workers, involved but out of trouble. In the section, forty workers—twelve women and twenty-eight men—transform precut pieces into boxes of sterile paper smocks. They push themselves to control the process, to wring a few extra pieces from the hour, day, or week against which they clock themselves. A few stitch the smock's body, others add sleeves, collars, sashes, or cuffs. A half-dozen workers later, a recognizable object emerges, product of many hands, folded neatly in sterile cardboard boxes for shipment across the border. This process works relatively smoothly, judging from the plant's efficiency statistics. However, seen from up close, it appears to produce as many conflicts as it does smocks. Efficient it is, smooth it isn't. The struggle is constant, around the intractable work and—even more—around its social context. But it is this structured conflict that ultimately evokes the focused, masculinized workers who make Andromex tick.

PAY BY THE PIECE

There is something implacable about an assembly line. Unless you work in a team setting like Participex, no matter what you do, it keeps on coming. And even in team structures, the decision is not yours alone. Piecework is something else again. It provides scope for imagination, games, personal decisions. In Andromex, all this is framed as the possibility of control. As a result, the structure of production interpellates workers as potential masters, as those who might shape their own daily experience.

Within this framework of possibilities, workers take different routes. Some set themselves externally linked monetary goals and then push to meet them. Manuel sets the number of completed boxes per day that will cover household expenses for a stay-at-home wife and child. Santos sets the number of sleeves that will allow him to save for school. Gladis works to buy clothes from El Paso that she can sell on the shop floor, thus funding her children's education. Goals have other functions as well, however. Eduardo is more typical. He sets himself challenges, but says he has no idea how much his increased production will bring in financially. His goals are their own reward.

This self-imposed and self-referential structure makes sense here. The most compelling aspect of piecework is the possibility of organizing it as a personal trial, thus evading the boredom otherwise inherent in repeating the same process hundreds of times a day. The shop floor is full of stories of mastery. People change positions to learn new jobs and create new challenges. They set goals by the hour, by the day, by the week. They promise themselves breaks after having made a particular number. They work hard mornings for easy afternoons. Torturous Mondays are compensated by easy Fridays. Julia contrasts Andromex with her last maquila job: "I used to work in harnesses. I was so bored I used to go to the bathroom and sleep. Here I say, today I'm going to make so-many, and that way I don't get so bored."

Piecework makes production primary and sets it as a challenge. If assembly work elicits daydreams of escape, of sex and play, piecework elicits dreams of production—pitting the self against the material world. This might take on many meanings. In Andromex, these production practices are construed as trials of endurance, strength, and skill. Participating in these games, workers are interpellated as masculine producers, struggling to dominate their everyday world.[24]

MATERIAL SHORTAGES

Piecework frames workers' interaction with their product. It also shapes their social interactions on the shop floor. This is particularly evident around the problem of material shortages. Shortages create tensions with management around the question of who pays for work that would have been done if the materials had been available. Shortages also create tension around work speed between workers responsible for sequential operations. And they create tension around access to scarce materials between workers doing the same job. In Andromex, management generally does not compensate "downtime" (periods when work materials are unavailable), despite its formal obligation to do so. As a result, workers fight with each other, struggling over who gets raw materials when they get scarce. These conflicts elicit a combative, production-focused self, determined to get his rightful work at any cost.

Material shortages in Andromex do not stem from external problems such as inconsistent suppliers. Instead, they are generated within the production group itself when those in consecutive positions operate at differing speeds. Engineers are responsible for setting pace and pay rates for particular operations, and their miscalculations on a single job can throw off an entire production group. Group chiefs' mis-estimations of how many workers they need for a particular position has similar repercussions, as do even a couple of unmotivated or unskilled workers. Thus, the sewers at the beginning of the process feel ongoing pressure from the rest of the group, and the folders at its end are most subject to material shortages.

All these dynamics are made more acute by the hierarchies within management. Engineers are high status, and their assessments of timing are rarely challenged. Hence, it is group chiefs who are generally held responsible for downtime by their superiors. Group chiefs, on the other hand, are in an extremely vulnerable position in the plant. Their supervisory position moves them out of the range of what little union protection there is, and their lack of formal training means that they could not retain their current status by working elsewhere if they were fired. Thus, although willing to pay exorbitant overtime charges, as a rule they refuse to even informally recognize downtime, still less to bring it to managerial attention by paying it. This refusal to acknowledge downtime inevitably leads to conflicts with workers, who know they are owed money which they rarely see.

This structural situation causes constant problems for the folders located at the end of the smock production process. During my sojourn folding, "cuffs"—the final sewing operation—is the group's most serious bottleneck. Several cuff sewers have left recently, and among those who remain, the most skilled sewer spends much of the day joking around with friends elsewhere in the plant, producing exactly the required minimum, not a smock more. There is general agreement among workers that this is due to the job's inadequate pay rates. The group chief acknowledges this as well, although never publicly. Despite the consensus, plant engineers aren't about to allow their scientific assessments to be affected by the opinion of those in production, group chiefs included. As a result, the dozen folders who follow this position spend much of each day complaining to the group chief and quarreling among themselves over the inadequate material.

Six months before my arrival, the lack of payment for downtime had had more serious repercussions. The folders had collectively decided to work to rule, producing exactly the minimum for a week. Already the object of their collective exasperation, the group chief had been unable to shake them on her own. Nonetheless, they had been easily scared out of the action by lectures from the union and top managers. Javier complains: "Before, they [other workers] said to me, 'Hey Javier, they don't count our downtime,' and there I went to complain, and at the moment of the fight, they all wimped out."

The problem of unpaid downtime is particularly obvious in the mornings, when folders often wait up to an hour before they can start working. At one point, a subset of folders moves from blaming the group chief for not reimbursing the lost morning hour to blaming the folders of second shift for not leaving them material. They surmise that second shift folders are hiding their leftover material, and decide to respond in kind. The material handler, León, begins hiding boxes of unfolded smocks every afternoon, so that in the morning they can begin work immediately. The problem with this is that there is not enough space to hide material for all the folders, so only a small group of León's friends benefit. As Saúl, one of the lucky ones, gleefully recounts in an interview: "Early in the morning . . . Francisco, Miguel, and I . . . we always let them . . . fight over the [few available] smocks, and only a minute passes and León brings us the boxes we saved." Not surprisingly, the other folders become even more irritated by the problem when faced by this "solution."

Shortages caused by differing work speeds actually create more problems between workers than between workers and management. Sewers in cuffs complain that the providers don't bring already-assembled smocks early enough in the morning. Gladis in sleeves fights with the guys who follow her because they don't take their full lunch hour, then complain to the group chief that they don't have material from her. "Let them tell me themselves! They're men!" One of the folders quarrels with a woman sewing collars because during a break he uses her machine so that he'll have more to fold. "He'll leave me with pure defects," she complains.

The reigning drama for weeks on end is a fight among the folders for scarce material as the bottleneck in cuffs persists. During the workday, they lose valuable time standing by the sewers and claiming finished smocks as they emerge, instead of intermittently checking in to pick up a large bundle. Tensions emerge as unattended, unfolded smocks begin to disappear from supply carts. Suspicions revolve around three folders who tend to keep to themselves, but no one is ever caught in the act. By the time I leave, Manuel is spending his mealtimes hiding out trying to catch the thief who keeps stealing his accumulated material. Francisco and Miguel switch their full cart for the cart full of defective smocks during lunch, in hopes that the defective material will be stolen. Julia and Lucía form and dissolve a friendship in the crucible of the tensions. Javier and Carlos nearly come to blows with mutual accusations of robbery. The issue becomes so loaded among the folders that when Manuel jokingly grabs Saúl's material when he's not looking, his confession barely averts a fistfight, Saúl so quickly turns to accuse Carlos.

The issues around material shortages and downtime are real. Every glitch in the transformation from cut paper to smock costs a worker money down the line. However, the struggles around these issues have effects on the shop floor that go beyond depressing individual wage packets. Each conflict interpellates workers as legitimate and embattled defenders of the right to produce. As a result, they ultimately emerge as masculinized super-producers, accounting for the soaring efficiency indices of recent years.

STANDARDS

"Standards"—the minimum amount of production for each position above which incentive wages are paid—is another aspect of the Andromex piecework structure in which conflict is ongoing and formative. Significantly, standard levels themselves are rarely directly contested on the shop floor. As always in Andromex, the details around the primary problem, rather than the problem itself, become the subject of shop-floor contention. Thus, workers fight job allocation given differing standards; and they fight over their basic obligation to the plant: is the workday over when they've produced the standard, or do they have to work a full nine hours? The centrality of these conflicts varies by area.

In sewing, job allocation is the crux of conflict. Because cuff sewing is poorly paid compared to other positions, there are ongoing tussles with the group chief over who will do the job. Eduardo, who has the misfortune of being unusually good at it, is always angling to be moved to a better paid position. For a time he is moved to sashes, but to his frustration, as soon as a couple of his old co-workers in cuffs resign, he is moved back.

The group chief's right to move workers when necessary is basically accepted by workers. However, when she moves people to new or difficult positions, there is an informal understanding—rarely honored without hassles—that she will pay them the difference between previous and current earnings. In a typical example of this struggle, Gladis describes weeks of confrontations with her group chief over the consequences of being moved around without having her wages protected: "She pulled me off 261 [the first assembly position], and then she wasn't paying me my bonuses. . . . I told her, 'No, it isn't worth it to me!' She said, 'It's that I can't move you.' . . . I told her, 'Fine, then, but if you're going to move me here and there,' I told her, 'I need my bonus and my incentive.'"

Even in the absence of frequent position shifts, the overall fuzziness of job allocation rules provokes persistent confrontations—often between workers rather than between workers and supervisors. For instance, Gladis and her friend Marta, both long-term workers in the plant, are particularly irate at Ana, who was only recently hired but is proving extremely adept at working the system. By simultaneously "failing" to produce the standard in jobs she doesn't like and begging constantly to be moved, she has landed a lucrative position attaching sashes:

> *Marta:* Why is it fair that they have more consideration for a new person than for us, when we've been here so long? . . . Who's going to produce more for them?
>
> *Gladis:* Because you yourself have asked them for changes, no? "Move me over there" and they don't move you. And for them [the new workers], it's yes. She says, "Change me to over there," and they do!

Confrontations among workers occur not only around job allocation, but around production levels. Because workers depend on those who precede them for material, any decision to take it easy or to stop producing after reaching the standard places them in conflict with those who follow them in the process. Thus, the folders are constantly yelling at the one competent guy in cuffs who spends the greater part of his day playing around. In fact, one folder explains his preference for folding over sewing in precisely these terms: "I have more freedom. I can go here and there. If I want to get out production, I push myself, and if I don't want to get it out, I put my foot down and no more."

On the other hand, for the folders, pressures emerge in their vertical relationships around whether the standard or the workday defines their basic obligation to the plant. Manuel reports: "When I began on the line, I said to . . . the chief . . . 'If in nine hours, five and a half boxes, six boxes should come out, I'm going to make you nine. Once those nine boxes are out, the day is mine.' She was fine with that." Javier agrees: "If I'm fulfilling my responsibilities, if I make the standard, she can't say anything to me. She can point it out, but that's it." These assertions to the contrary, the group chief's behavior clearly indicates her disagreement with this framework, and confrontations are common. One day, when Javier goes wandering off after finishing his usual nine-box personal standard, she gives him a long public lecture. In retaliation, he produces exactly the five-and-a-half-box company standard, using every minute of the nine-hour workday, for the next several days. As he predicts, when he returns to his previous production level and habits, she refrains from yelling. Nonetheless, her displeasure is palpable.

Workers do not always win such confrontations, however. This is evident during a day of required Saturday overtime in which the informal rule is that everyone can leave once every member of the section has completed his/her individual standard. With that accomplished by 12:30, glances begin veering toward the door. However, the group chief has no intention of leaving without *her* standard, still unmet because of numerous absences, and this goal requires two more boxes per folder. As word of her intentions spreads through the folders' section, the entire group begins to whoop and yell. Without a word, she begins stalking between the tables, ominously silent and composed. The yells fade into uncertainty and the folding resumes. At 2:00, only an hour before the normal workday's end, the overall standard has been folded and the group is released. Complaints about the unfairness of her behavior continue for weeks, joining many others in the worker narrative of unfairness and resistance that sustains Andromex's compelling shop-floor life.

Sewers and folders are enmeshed in distinct, if often interrelated, struggles, and their quarrels are as likely to be with each other as with supervisors. Despite the appearance of chaos, the most significant impact of these confrontations is to make production a center of attention within which work-focused, masculinized subjects emerge. Over time, the practice of grandstanding evokes a shop floor full of legitimate fighters, struggling on the managerially defined terrain of production. As a result, the current, assertively masculine, mixed-gender Andromex workers remain—unlike their "unwomanly" female predecessors in the plant—securely within the managerial frame.

RESPECT

The possibility of fruitful struggle inherent in Andromex's production structure makes the texture of relationship itself a legitimate object of contention. In direct confrontations, both with each other and with management, workers repeatedly assert their basic human right to respectful treatment and autonomy. And in jokes and highly personal criticisms, they mark the equally human fallibility of their bosses. Workers also struggle over status among themselves, publicly competing over work pace and productivity. This jockeying for respect echoes practices of masculinity outside the plant, both in and out of jobs that are publicly marked as "men's work." Nonetheless, as in the ongoing conflicts discussed above, gender is rarely named at Andromex and women are full-fledged combatants.

These struggles over relationship often accompany and even impel the conflicts over the mechanics of production. When Javier asserts he can stop work early, when the folders demand that oft-promised downtime be paid, when Gladis and Marta insist that their seniority count for something, these challenges are as much about respect—about the right to control one's own work life—as they are about exhaustion and money. Some struggles skip the pragmatic medium entirely, and are explicitly directed at questions of respect and control. As Manuel says in an interview: "In life we're a chess piece that destiny moves here and there, but in the factory, you have a way to stand up for yourself and show those above that you're a person too."

These struggles to assert personhood take many forms. Workers often contest managerial attitudes in private discussions. There are frequent stories told on the shop floor about managerial attitudes toward workers: they think workers are "animals," "savages," and, the most common phrase, "machines." Elena, a woman with many years' tenure in the plant, explodes one day at lunch: "I keep this cup [raising a paper cup] because now it's useful to me, it holds my milk, but when it stops being useful to me, I'm going to throw it out. That's how they treat us!"

Her anger has practical consequences in production, as she is in constant conflict with her group chief over her level of production: "That bitch, she's at me with the standard, the standard. That way I'm *really* not going to do it. I don't let myself be pushed around." This attitude and the actual refusals to produce that accompany it have gained her a reputation among managers as "problematic." Other workers, however, including those who pride themselves on not getting into trouble, see her behavior as legitimate:

Gladis: She won't let the group chiefs push her around, because if they say "do this" and she doesn't want to, she doesn't do it. For them this makes her problematic.

Marta: The fact that one won't let oneself be pushed around is already a problem for them. . . . They want submissive people, people who won't defend themselves, but that's impossible.

This belief, that conflict around basic issues of control is legitimate and to be expected, is pervasive on the shop floor. Manuel provides a gendered gloss on this process: "It's rare really, the person who's man enough to stick it out, not to budge, to withstand it—better said, to withstand them."

Although group chiefs and managers complain about workers who "act up," in practice they accept a level of resistance impossible to imagine in the other maquilas I observed. Javier tells an extended story of being called into the office of the manager of "labor relations." The manager closed the door and began yelling and cursing at him. Javier recounts responding in kind: "'Look, if you're going to speak to me with your balls in your hand,' I told him, 'That's how I'm going to speak to you. I'm going to curse, I'm going to say any fucking thing that comes into my fucking head. . . . I don't give a fuck if you fire me. . . . They've fired me from better jobs.'" Instead of firing him, the manager eventually backed down and tried a more conciliatory tack, implicitly accepting Javier's analysis. "I told him, . . . 'Just because you wear a white smock, you think you're better than me?' What he has is his pride." Summarizing the plant common sense around worker/boss relations, Manuel comments: "You've got to find a way not to give in, at least to end up even, because they [the bosses] don't want to lose either."

As is evident in Javier's account, workers attempt to evoke respect not only through assertions of their own humanity, but also through descriptions of managers as similarly human. Thus, Gladis complains about a group chief who reported her to quality control: "She's there to receive reports from control, not to wander around gossiping . . . if I had gone to the union to complain about her, they'd have reprimanded her." Following this story, Marta and she continue by discussing why this particular chief is such an "old bitch" and conclude that her single status has left her "bitter." A joke moving through the group goes this way: "A guy is looking for a job. The interviewer asks him what he knows. 'Well, nothing,' he responds. 'That's too bad,' says the interviewer, 'I already have managers.'"

These assertions of self-worth vis-à-vis managers are accompanied by similar claims vis-à-vis other workers. Not making the standard is a daily social humiliation for those who can't keep up, and those who fail tend to leave before being fired because of the social discomfort. Among the most skilled, competition is the norm. In sewing, Santos calls me over every few days to tell me loudly how much higher his production is than everyone else's in his position, and everybody knows everyone else's average level of productivity. In folding, these contests are even more direct. Every morning, Carlos and Julia set their sights on folding more than each other, and all those nearby keep track of the outcome. Everyone in the group knows who cares most about being the fastest folder, and those not skilled enough to win competitions over speed can get their own back in other ways: León and Saúl gleefully recount exposing Javier's self-satisfaction by jokingly telling him he has been chosen as "operator of the month," then publicly teasing him about believing it.

Javier describes his first days in the plant: "I said, 'How is it possible that I'm only at the standard and they are at ten, eleven?' . . . So I busted my ass. I made seven. Then Manuel said to me, 'That's nothing,' and again I busted my ass. . . . To say you're no worse than the others. . . . Really, here we don't need bosses."

As Javier points out, the effect of all these struggles for respect is to increase production. In competition among workers over who can sew or fold the most, the impact is direct and unambiguous. However, even struggles with management which interfere with production in the short term serve to keep shop-floor attention on the work. This is as true for the struggle for respect as it is for the more direct tussles over pay and work conditions described earlier. Ultimately, all the refusals, foot dragging, assertions of pride, and rights claims are part of the constitution of new hires as Andromex workers, recognized and self-recognizing as would-be master-producers, willing to fight for the right to earn more through working more.

Although these productively combative shop-floor subjects are anomalous in the maquila industry, they make sense in the context of the plant's unusual history, production imperatives, and management. Even the ongoing, if mostly unnamed, enactment of masculinity is comprehensible as an intrinsic element of this package. As men entered the plant in the mid-eighties, they were exhorted to "be men."[25] In a hegemonic structure based on controlled conflict and the ongoing performance of resistance, that invitation has been enthusiastically accepted by male and female workers alike. The confrontative, productive Andromex shop floor is the result of this process.

Gender without Bodies

In making visible Andromex's masculinized narratives and practices, we can account for the plant's capacity to make men productive in "women's work." But given this, how can we explain their female coun-

terparts, who also appear to function successfully in this (always relatively) masculinized space? Why and how are women recognizable, to
themselves and others, within the historically masculinized category of
producer/breadwinner? Elsewhere we have seen workers addressed
within gendered categories that match those they inhabit outside the
plant, even when, in the case of Particimex, the *content* of these categories deviates from those outside. In Anarchomex, the subject of the
next chapter, workers are indeed addressed within the "wrong" categories, but there the address generates contention rather than consent.
In Andromex, however, this does not seem to be a problem. Women
respond when addressed within a masculinized category. This is made
possible, I argue, both by gender's diminished visibility within Andromex's production processes and by the way in which masculinity
functions more generally.

On first entering the shop floor, it is difficult to distinguish women
from men. Andromex's product is sterile: thus, makeup, long nails, jewelry, and beards are prohibited. Workers wear dark blue smocks but-
toned high and light blue caps that cover every strand of hair. Dress requirements are strictly enforced, and when women workers occasionally
sneak in with "just a bit" of makeup, quality control workers report
them with evident satisfaction. The notion that workers can't wear
makeup on the shop floor is so crucial that applicants are asked to re-
move makeup for a preliminary tour, even though secretaries enter the
shop floor with makeup on a regular basis. Although smocks and caps
are mandatory only on the shop floor, taking them on and off is time-
consuming, and break time is short. Thus, by practical convention, they
remain firmly in place even during brief workday meals.

Both men and women sporadically attempt to reinstate gendered
physical markings as elements of personal style. Caps, the most gender-
obscuring element of the uniform, are a favored resource in this project.
Female group chiefs and quality inspectors with special access wear
flowered caps taken from another Pharmaworld maquila or gauzy white
caps packed (but not sewn) in the plant.[26] Because everyone has the
blue caps, how they are worn becomes a marker as well. Most male
workers tighten them by putting a rubber band around the center and
turning it inside out. Some women tighten their caps with tape. More
conspicuously, some men wear green dust masks over mouth and nose
or pushed up like headbands; and some women wear two caps—one to
protect their bouncing, up-to-the-minute Juárez bangs, the other to
hold the long hair behind. Those with a real eye for fashion create this

latter style using caps of different colors. They spend the moments before work begins in front of the mirror, assembling and pinning the edifice into place. There is something desperate about these attempts, however, and the diminished presence of gendered bodies is a widely recognized fact of shop-floor life.

The absence of gender markers on the shop floor has a powerful impact on the texture of gendered interaction. A young man I met elsewhere had worked at Andromex briefly and left. "You couldn't tell who the pretty ones were," he complains. Some of the women in the plant suggest that without these markers there *are* no "pretty ones." "The guys are used to seeing us that way [in uniform]. . . . The day they see us gorgeous, I mean really gorgeous, they go out with us . . . it's that you change, no? Yes, you change. Makeup does wonders." Among workers I encountered throughout the maquilas, the common U.S. distinction between "real" beauty and facade has little currency. As the women just quoted suggest, to be decked out gorgeously is to *be* gorgeous. In a context where beauty is less than skin deep, there are no attractive women at Andromex.

Masculinity is as veiled as femininity by these uniforms. The plant manager, insistent at every level that gender doesn't matter, boasts about the plant's capacity to carry this off: "Imagine, we have men sewing—wearing caps! It's like being a woman . . . with the Mexican *machismo*!" Gendered bodies are not just unaccentuated; in contrast to the bodies in most other maquilas, they are actually hidden from view on the shop floor. The power of this concealment is evident in the uneasy atmosphere that prevails in the parking lot at the end of the day. The sight of abruptly re-gendered co-workers leaving in street clothes is a shock, somehow obscene, as if they had been stripped of clothes entirely. Eyes fall and smiles are uneasy.[27]

Gender is as unmarked in shop-floor geography as it is in individual bodies. Although workers in the plant glue, fold, package, and sew, providing plenty of opportunity for job gendering, tasks are not allocated that way. To the contrary, during first shift, the proportion of men and women in the smock area is even, exactly mirroring their respective proportions in the plant as a whole. This is less true within each smock section, where gender proportions vary widely in accord with group chief preferences. Thus, smock sections range from 30 percent women (as in my section) to 30 percent men. Nonetheless, these differences are matters of personal taste, not plant policy, and the shop floor is not arranged in gendered patterns. This is particularly remarkable to a new observer.

Once the swathing blueness is decoded, scores of men emerge into view, bent over sewing machines, whipping out smocks beside their female co-workers. The personnel manager is matter-of-fact: "Group chiefs do sometimes request women for particular jobs, but not in the smock section—of course not! That's sewing!" Sewing is hard work with high turnover—often as high as 20 percent monthly. Group chiefs, she implies, don't object to men sewing. To the contrary, they will take anyone they can get.[28]

Unlike in most maquilas, where gender is marked by uniform, position, and personal style, gender is obscured on Andromex's surface—reflected neither in shop-floor layout nor in worker costume. Thus, it has no tangible expression or anchor in the plant. Nonetheless, it continues to operate symbolically, in the larger masculinization of shop-floor practice. This disembodiment makes it possible for women and men to inhabit a single structure, and to be interpellated together within what are historically masculine categories.

This set of local idiosyncrasies operates on the field of gender itself, and is further amplified by the long-standing conflation of "man" and "person" in language and practice more generally.[29] This identification makes it possible for something to be framed as simultaneously masculine and "human." Thus, masculinity can operate implicitly, and thereby potentially ambiguously, constituting an activity as symbolically male without naming it as such. Femininity is another story. "Women's work" is always explicitly marked and its intrinsic femininity is frequently established with reference to the individual body.

In the maquila industry as a whole, the repetitive naming and physical allusions involved in construing a job as feminine are evident in the insistent description of workers as "women workers" and the frequent references to "small hands" and "slender fingers" made within this description. In Andromex, on the other hand, the mere practical invocation of the categories of producer and breadwinner on the shop floor makes any further specification of the work as masculine unnecessary. As a result, express trappings of masculinity are absent in production, making it possible for women to overlook the gendering implicit in the category of the Andromex worker and recognize themselves within its confines.

Set against the pointedly feminized background of the industry as a whole, Andromex's uniforms serve to obscure the gendering of individual workers, particularly women, allowing masculinity to operate in the plant in abstract form, unattached to either bodies or particular workers. This is not to say, of course, that women workers no longer remember or express individual gender identities. However, "women" go unaddressed by management. As a result, the individual expressions of femininity that do emerge in the plant follow no overall pattern and have no impact on production. Instead, in the work itself, women and men alike come to understand themselves within categories which are historically and culturally masculinized.

Some of the complexities of this process emerge during an interview with Gladis and Mari. Gladis describes an involved, and ultimately successful, struggle with her group chief over standards. As she reaches the end of her narrative, a tale of standing her ground that would have lost her both her job and her claim to appropriate femininity in most other maquilas, she makes a comment unusual for the plant. Marking the difference between her behavior and that of her male co-workers, she says: "They [men] can't stand being yelled at. For a woman, they yell at you, and, well, you just turn around and look at them. At least I'm like that. I don't like to fight." Here, we see a woman who routinely, and proficiently, engages in masculinized practices of ritualized conflict, renaming her actions in the context of her own feminine identity, without shifting her behavior in any significant way. Her personal sense of her own "intrinsic femininity" remains intact. Nonetheless, it coexists, apparently unproblematically, with the implicitly masculinized combative producer evoked in factory discourse.

Andromex's capacity to address both women and men as breadwinning producers is made possible by the convergence of a set of empirical contingencies with the latent structure of masculinity itself. A plant manager convinced of gender's irrelevance and a production process that conceals gender's physical markers together conspire to create masculinity as an abstraction, rather than as a personal characteristic. Given the symbolic slippage between the masculine specific and the human general, women workers in the plant are thereby able to respond to an address framed in these terms, joining their male counterparts as legitimate, productive shop-floor subjects.

Masculinity at Work

In "manufacturing" in the Mexican or U.S. interior, Andromex would pass unnoticed.[30] The struggles over work practices, the dramas around respect, the persistent, implicit backdrop of the idea of the family wage are all familiar.[31] What is remarkable is the appearance of these features here, in the periphery's heartland, in the center of an industry defined around feminine productivity. Transnational assembly generally assumes feminine subjects. Andromex does not. This is not because the global image of feminine assembly is either irrelevant or ignored in the plant. To the contrary, the symbolic masculinization of work operates in direct contrast to the explicitly feminized, "supplementary-wage-earner" jobs typical of most transnational assembly. Thus, the immediate causes of this unexpected outcome are contingent and local, but the background against which plant meanings are constructed is global. As such, the case deepens our understanding of how transnational tropes come to roost by demonstrating that, rather than being reproduced locally, they provide the raw material and background against which (occasionally contradictory) local meanings and practices are formed and become intelligible.

The edifice of transnational production is structured around an image of a particular sort of worker—a docile, young, single woman working for pin money, not basic sustenance. Because of this, shifts in the structure of work require, imply, and are impelled by a regendering of the worker managers see in their mind's eye when planning production. Thinking about women workers implies routinized work and low wages; thinking about routinized work and low wages brings women to mind. Shifting this paradigm requires a shift in both its elements. Thus, in Andromex, as men became a new prototype, work was restructured to be (relatively) autonomous and (relatively) well paid; just as minor increases in shop-floor autonomy and pay made men seem a natural new workforce. Although in Detroit or Mexico City Andromex would probably not be read as classic "men's work," against the background of the feminized maquila sector, it can be so construed.

Gender is an explicit element of the trope of feminine productivity which frames maquila production. Given that gender makes meaning through contrasts, this is a difficult context indeed in which to create a non-gendered workplace, as a workplace which is de-feminized is immediately relatively masculinized.[32] Thus, it should come as no surprise that, Gómez's claims to the contrary, he has not created a shop floor where gender doesn't matter; he has masculinized assembly instead. That he and other participants explicitly narrate the work's earlier feminization while ignoring its current masculinization does not mean that the current gendering is any less consequential. Instead, the varying emphases confirm once again the durability of masculinity's conflation with the general and femininity's association with the body, revealing the consequences of these differences at work.

A quick look at assembly plants around the globe might suggest that transnational assembly requires young women on the shop floor. The case of Andromex, however, with its highly productive, mixed-gender workforce, suggests other processes at work. One of the things that is distinctive, although by no means unique, about the arenas in which third-world workers assemble commodities for first-world use is the primacy of the image of productive femininity. Thus, these plants require a shop-floor narrative in which workers can make *gendered* sense and selves of their daily experiences in production. Andromex has succeeded in meeting this challenge, although it does so by contesting, rather than incorporating, the definition of assembly as feminine. Although Andromex workers look little like their counterparts in Panoptimex and Particimex, they become subjects against the backdrop of the same set of assumptions. The image of feminine assembly work still functions, but here it has become a source of fruitful contrast—a model to challenge rather than to emulate. Gender matters throughout transnational production; how it matters is a local affair.

Gendered Meanings in Contention

Anarchomex

The phrase "women on the global assembly line" is so resonant because it implies some of the most salient aspects of transnational production—the disproportionate number of women workers on the line and management's equally disproportionate level of shop-floor control. However, it misses a set of less obvious, but equally important, dynamics. In particular, the phrase obscures the flexibility and local specificity of gendered meanings at work. In the process, it makes it impossible to imagine that gendered meanings might themselves become an object of struggle, and thus that gendered meanings on the shop floor might work against, rather than in the service of, managerial control. Yet this is precisely the situation in Anarchomex..

Anarchomex is one of Autoworld's oldest outposts in Ciudad Juárez. Like Particimex, it produces harnesses—auto electrical systems—that will later be assembled into the company's cars and trucks elsewhere on the continent. In early 1992, after a decade of operation, managers idled half the plant, choosing to cut their losses rather than to continue to deal with the shop-floor chaos that emerged every time they ran the plant full-throttle. In order to make up for the lost production, they built another, smaller, factory nearby and moved the rest of the production there. By the time I entered the plant in February, first shift had fallen from its maximum of 1,300 to 996 workers, and when I left in April it was down to 770. The back half of the plant was ghostly, with sheeted lines gathering dust beneath the fluorescent lights—shadows of grander days.

Anarchomex is a failure. Yet plant managers are knowledgeable and experienced. What went wrong? Trips from the cacophonous shop floor up to distant managerial offices suggest an answer. Anarchomex managers do not know too little; on the contrary, their failure arises from investment in rigidly gendered frameworks which keep them from addressing their workers in recognizable terms. In Anarchomex, men make up 60 percent of the workforce. However, managers remain convinced that maquila work is feminine by definition. Thus, they implicitly impugn the masculinity of the men at work on the line and, in the process, inadvertently constitute gendered meanings as a terrain of contention. In response, male workers spend their days contesting such aspersions. They claim the work as masculine territory, both in language and practice, and they address their female counterparts as potential sexual partners rather than co-workers, implicitly negating managers' claims about the work's inherently feminine nature. These ongoing struggles over the gendering of maquila work and the meaning of masculinity absorb worker energy and attention during the workday and make it impossible for managers to incorporate workers in productive terms. As a result, the struggle over gendered meanings disrupts managerial control, and the operation of gender as a discursive structure is laid bare. Who workers are at the outset is not the problem. It is the content of legitimate masculinity, and who gets to decide just what that is, which is at issue in production. Here, gender is clearly operating on the shop floor, but the assumed feminine character of global assembly undermines production itself.

Distant Managers

Autoworld maquilas have high levels of discretion in choosing their basic strategy of shop-floor management. When I first spoke to Gianini, the head of Organizational Development at Autoworld's Juárez headquarters, about seeing a factory, he suggested two plants: his prized "new management" style factory in Santa María, and a "totally traditional" factory in Juárez. This traditional style—Gianini made clear his irritation—came straight from the plant manager.

Smith is in his mid-fifties. He has worked on the border for only six years, and his managerial style crystallized long before his arrival. After decades of work for Autoworld's U.S. parent in the Midwest, he is deeply set in his managerial ways. Accustomed to operating within long-standing regimes of hegemonic control, he continues to operate as if these consent-inducing and individualizing structures were firmly in place.[1] As a result, he shows little aptitude for dealing with the young workers—themselves fully aware of the absence of promotions, guarantees of fair treatment, and other aspects of due process—whom the maquila sector regularly attracts and then ejects. At one point he tells me an elaborate story about how workers who are promoted to "utility," a minor salary increase from entry level, go through an "informal ceremony" in which they exchange their blue smocks for yellow ones. In all my time on the shop floor, I never saw this occur. In fact, rather than eagerly taking the symbolic approval, many workers accept the pay increase but not the change of costume, believing that supervisors would otherwise demand more work of them. During our conversations, Smith describes other such formal processes—daily evaluations during the first two weeks, monthly evaluations during the first six months, weekly supervisory meetings—which similarly fail to materialize during my period in the plant. Nonetheless, Smith continues on his way, confident in the knowledge that the process is in place.

Not surprisingly, my tenure in the plant bears the imprint of Smith's managerial style. He initially allows me to enter and accedes to my working on the line with visible reluctance, evidently constrained by my contact with Gianini. Once I have arrived, however, he sends me off for others to deal with, stipulating only that I not expect to be put on the plant payroll, as that would be illegal. Shortly thereafter, I find myself in the plant secretary's office in the company of other new workers, signing official employment papers. I of course object, but the Mexican head of personnel is so insistent that these are Smith's orders that my protests quickly border on the insulting. Thus, the secretary blithely creates a Mexican social security number and birthplace for me, and for the month in which I actually work on the line I collect the roughly US$40 weekly of a new worker in the plant.[2] Although I have a series of friendly interviews with Smith later on, the incident strikes me as so embarrassing for him that I never tell him of my illegal status.[3]

Smith's long tenure in the industry makes him uncomfortable with new, "fancy" managerial practices, and in any case, his conviction that the work done here, as opposed to that done in Autoworld's U.S. plants, is "simple," makes him reluctant to embark on new strategies around production. When I ask him why they don't use the work teams currently functioning so successfully in Particimex, he looks uneasy. "My sense when I'm in Santa María is that I always see people who look like they have nothing to do." The high Santa María quality indices can't erase his discomfort at the sight of workers taking their ease during the workday. "Supervisors are disciplinarians," he adds, in describing what he expects of his own staff. "They make sure workers come to work every day, come back from lunch every day. . . . Their main job is to get people to work."

Even if Smith felt more open in theory to introducing newer labor control practices in his factory, his poor command of Spanish and his lack of respect for most Mexicans would make it difficult. Despite his claim to speaking "50 percent Spanish," he actually can speak, or even understand, very little; hence his communication with supervisors is difficult and that with workers is negligible. At one point he tells me a story, one I had already heard from several other non-Spanish-speaking U.S. managers at the border (among them Jones in Panoptimex), intended to define the Mexican attitude to personal responsibility. The phrase for "I dropped it" in Spanish is "it fell" (*se me cayó*), he explains, and this passive grammatical form is indicative of a serious problem in Mexican culture at large. Although such problematic attitudes are most common among workers, he sees them among his Mexican supervisors as well. "Some supervisors do a good job, but others are typical Mexican nationals," he comments. "The biggest problem we have with supervisors is to get him to accept problems in his line. It's a cultural problem. 'It's everyone's fault but mine.'" This abstract and disrespectful relationship to Mexicans makes it unlikely that he would consider using managerial practices that depend for their effectiveness on the intelligence, responsibility, and commitment of his Mexican staff.[4]

Despite Smith's general distance from and lack of respect for Mexicans, Autoworld policy requires that his managerial staff be Mexican, not American. In this context, what is most remarkable is the extent to which his immediate subordinates share his perspectives on labor control, if not on Mexicans in general. This group is comprised of Mexican men of Smith's generation and corporate history. Longtime employees of Autoworld, they too focus on workers as fixed inputs, rather than as subjects to be formed at work. In any case, they are above all anxious to distinguish themselves from Mexican workers and to ally themselves with U.S. management. And even if they were to disagree with Smith in a particular instance, they are unlikely to tell him so. Smith makes it entirely clear: this is his shop and countervailing opinions are not of interest.

These managerial perspectives have a series of ramifications for labor control practices. The entire plant is organized around manufacturing, collecting, and reporting production statistics. Smith himself does sometimes descend to the production floor, but when he does so, he is too busy checking production indices—or pointing them out to visitors on a portable whiteboard—to look directly at the workers themselves, still less to speak to them. This tendency to abstract away from those producing to the records of what they produce is imposed down through the factory hierarchy. Smith defines the supervisor's job: "A line is like a grocery store. The supervisor is the person in charge and in control. He buys inputs and sells a product and he has to balance his books." Everyone in the plant is first and foremost accountable to the numbers. Labor is just another input.

As a result, plant problems are dealt with by focusing on the nature of workers and not by examining the context in which they work. For instance, when I mention that since there are no places to sit and talk in the factory, women sit in the bathroom and chat, Smith responds, "Is that cultural?" Portes, the Mexican head of personnel, describes the constant quarrels on the shop floor as a case of workers' failing to grasp the function of the factory: "When you enter a new arena, you feel bad, people say things to you, you need help, but this is not a school, this is *industry*." Smith, discussing the control problems that led them to decide to idle half the plant, remarks, "Two thousand teenagers in one building. No one can manage that group. . . . No one can control two thousand teenagers." In none of these cases do managers consider changing factory structure; the assumption is that the causes of factory problems lie in intrinsic aspects of worker personality.

This attitude is even evident when the plant has to deliver bad news to workers. At one point during my tenure Autoworld hits a financial crisis, and the corporation's Detroit headquarters mandates various cost-cutting measures, all to be borne by workers. The assistant manager of personnel calls in all the workers line by line and tells them they will be furloughed for two weeks and that all promotions are off for the foreseeable future. Period. A few object; all look sullen. I ask whether he is worried about the impact of their responses on morale and production. "They're just kids," he says casually. "They'll be glad when the time comes."

Such analyses lead to strategies that deal with labor problems principally through hiring. As a result, the personnel department is constantly seeking what they define as "good workers." This search is particularly striking because it so often focuses on questions of style and morality rather than on issues of skill or even stability. One day I watch a hiring interview where a long-haired young man, asked about plans, responds, "I'll stay as long as I feel like it." To my surprise, this does not faze the interviewer. Instead she focuses on his hair. "Come back tomorrow with your hair cut and I'll hire you," she says. She explains to me after he leaves, "We don't allow long hair. I don't know if you'd noticed, but you can smell that these people don't clean themselves. They're dirty." In the brief interviews, she asks intimate questions about numbers of people, rooms, and beds in the house. "So who sleeps in *your* bed?" Each two-minute interview is structured around the assumption that getting good, moral workers—the right sort of people—is the key to success in production.

As one might expect, given the emphasis on the importance of "correct" hiring for successful labor control, managers in this factory present a highly developed set of demographic preferences as well. They make talismanic distinctions around age—under twenty workers are too "playful"—and gender, in which gender trumps age. Thus, "a sixteen-year-old woman is preferable to a twenty-two-year-old man." Their analyses of gender are unusually elaborated and true to the transnational narrative, although they differ among themselves in which elements of the trope they cite. Alone among Anarchomex managers, Smith focuses on the body, commenting, "If we had our choice, we'd be 75 to 80 percent female because of finger dexterity." The Mexican managers, on the other hand, are more willing to note workers' basic humanity, and in any case are active participants in the Juárez elite's anxious discussions of working-class men's faltering masculinity. Hence, they focus on more social issues. The personnel manager claims that problems with women are "easier to solve, their problems are individual," as opposed to men, who bring social problems such as graffiti. His assistant complains that men are likely to get drunk and take off "*San Lunes*" (St. Monday's day), whereas "85 percent [of women] are manageable." The most elaborated commentary comes from the production manager, who discusses the issue at length, "If we set her [a woman worker] to work doing a routinized job, she won't complain, she won't want to change, or rather, she will want to change, but she won't have the will to leave." He adds wistfully, "The subordinate should obey. It's harder with a man, he struggles more."[5]

This preference for women workers is reflected in all the plant's job advertisements, which continue to ask for "*operadoras*"—female line workers—even though the woman who places the ads acknowledges, with gentle understatement, "We still get men applying, because now they know we can make exceptions." This reality is reflected in the assistant personnel manager's sarcastic comment that hiring criteria begin with being female, single, eighteen to thirty years old, and having lived in the city for at least a year, but end with "having at least ten fingers."

As this comment indicates, despite managerial preferences, the exigencies of offshore production within a tight labor market for women workers ensure that the actual workforce is consistently quite far from its model. Autoworld decisions are made far away, and its Mexican outposts are often asked to crank up production on short notice. Managers in Anarchomex and Particimex alike complain about the problems caused by headquarters' sudden demands for new shipments of a particular model, after the boards set up for its production have long since been dismantled in response to prior corporate plans. Combined with the plant's large size, these production patterns frequently force Anarchomex managers to hire large numbers of workers within short time periods. This makes it impossible for those hiring to hold out for the wished-for 80 percent female workers.

In addition, although maquila jobs are understood by workers, as by managers, to be women's jobs in the aggregate, within this aggregate, workers distinguish jobs as more or less masculine or feminine. Jobs in electronics are marked as feminine,[6] whereas those which are performed standing are understood to be relatively masculine. A manager in Autoworld's central Juárez office expresses this clearly: "Harnesses has more movement, it's done standing, the work is more aggressive. Electronics is more manual labor. Women like that work more." Local women workers, equally embedded in these narratives, tend to look elsewhere, for instance Panoptimex, before considering Anarchomex. The combination of these two processes ensures that, whether they're hiring under the pressure of full capacity or not, 60 to 65 percent of Anarchomex workers are male and 30 to 40 percent are under twenty. This predominance of available male workers does not lead Anarchomex managers to modify their notion of an ideal workforce; in fact, the situation only reinforces managers' sense that the right worker mix would fix all their shop-floor control problems.

The tenacity with which Anarchomex managers hold to this gendered model of the ideal worker is due in part to their assumption that the "right" workers can be found but not formed, but it has other roots as well. The most obvious of these is their participation, along with their colleagues in other Juárez maquilas, in transnational managerial conversations where the status of young women as paradigmatic export-processing workers remains unquestioned. Nonetheless, we have seen that maquila managers in fact do very different things with this "common sense." In the context of their glaring inability to actually fulfill the image, one might have expected that managers in Anarchomex would shift strategies. This has not been the case.

One of the central dynamics operating here is that these men define masculinity in paradigmatically patriarchal terms, and patriarchs are not who they imagine working in their plant. To the contrary, only a young woman would appropriately subject herself to the routinized, boring, low-wage work conditions they see as intrinsic to maquila production. They strongly believe that men should be "breadwinners," with all the familial authority that such a situation implies. What's more, they themselves, Mexican and American alike, enact masculinity as a position of command and responsibility, and they expect other men to behave similarly. For their workers, however, performance of this sort of masculinity is virtually impossible. The jobs at Anarchomex provide no space to exercise such qualities on the shop floor and do not pay enough to support such behavior at home. This is not something that these managers are comfortable thinking through, however, particularly the Mexicans, who see themselves as part of a responsible local elite, legitimately concerned about working-class masculinity. Thus, they frame the problem this way: Line jobs are women's jobs. If men take the jobs anyway, well, that is their responsibility, isn't it? In accepting the job, they accept women's work, and in so doing, they become exemplars of the problem of the decline of working-class masculinity. There's nothing Anarchomex managers can do about that.

This set of beliefs has different logics for Mexican and U.S. managers. Smith takes maquila wages at face value. Raising salaries is always a mistake; it only creates "bidding wars" among maquilas over workers. The Mexican personnel manager, typically, is more ambivalent about wages. "We sacrifice a lot for peanuts," he says, discussing the decision to save money on worker salaries. Despite these differences in the evaluation of the situation, they both take low maquila wages for granted, and their assessments follow upon this fact of life.

Given the unshakable fact of non-breadwinner wages, men who engage in such work are evidently impaired.[7] Marcos, the top quality manager, articulates this most clearly when he comments, "I'm twenty years old. I know that with this job I can't support a family. *Obviously,* I'm going to look for something better." He is not alone. The production manager argues that women make better maquila workers, because (real) men have "more ideas about self-improvement. It's the culture here of Mexico." In one way or another, every high-level manager in the plant I interviewed, when asked why the factory still advertised only for women, made clear his view that a man who appropriately understood his familial responsibilities wouldn't choose maquila work.

The consequence of these beliefs comes through clearly in the disparaging terms in which managers discuss male workers. As usual, the Mexicans' analysis closely tracks the unease among Juárez elites. Thus, the assistant personnel manager implies that men and women are increasingly similar among the working class. "Young men don't need much money, they live with their families. And now the man tells the woman that she needs to work." The personnel manager comments sympathetically that (working-class) "women here don't want husbands anymore." Working-class men in Juárez have lost their rightful familial place; hence they are willing to accept, and it is reasonable to offer them, emasculating jobs such as those in Anarchomex.

Smith, as usual, sees workers from a greater distance. He is less concerned with explaining this inappropriate willingness than with describing it. "I'm not sure about the Mexican male anymore. In the early days, maquilas, that was women's work. Now it's just a part of survival." Clarifying his sense that men become feminized in accepting Anarchomex jobs, he returns to his focus on workers as bodies: "Maybe part of the explanation is that the Mexican man is smaller in features, smaller in stature and fingers, so maybe here it doesn't make much difference."

Smith and his staff's basic gendered assumptions make them unwilling to accept the fact that they employ a primarily male workforce at non-breadwinner wages.[8] Thus, their shop-floor rhetorics and practices ignore the presence and belittle the experience of the men who in fact make up the greater part of their labor force. This keeps them from speaking effectively to the majority of those on the shop floor and thus ultimately undermines their control in production. These are not "mistakes" on their part. They are highly structured decisions—decisions based on what they are capable of seeing, given their own sense of masculinity, national identity, and corporate location. Thus, gender intervenes here not through the fixed selves of those hired, but through the fixed ideas of those who hire them.

In Production: Meaningless Labors

Against the background of these managerial frameworks, production in Anarchomex is a chaotic affair. The factory itself is an enormous barnlike structure—dingy, old, and confusing. Exposed fluorescent lights hang from cavernous, unfinished ceilings. Walls and floors are a regulation dark gray. On the right side of the building, huge boards circulate on raised platforms. Workers stand on the platforms, following the boards as they go. On the left, smaller boards revolve at a brisker pace, interspersed with splicing stations draped with wires of every imaginable color and length. At each splicing station, a single worker stands hunched over mysterious chemicals, soldering the wires to be used in the rest of the process. Throughout the building, apparently unoccupied workers can be seen wandering the factory floor—often chatting casually with those at work. A popular local radio station blares from speakers in the ceiling, silenced only when managerial visitors appear.

Despite concerns about hiring women workers for assembly jobs, once a mixed workforce arrives, managers make no effort to ensure the allocation of particular jobs to women. On the contrary, on the line, gender distinctions are downplayed. Direct production workers—men and women both—are all located indistinguishably at the bottom. Off-line jobs are another story. Only men are hired as material handlers, ensuring that the sole entry-level jobs requiring or even permitting mobility are entirely male. Supervisors and their assistants ("technicians") are also men, although there were reports in the plant of a woman supervisor who had been hounded out by male workers who wouldn't listen to her. Support workers, chosen by supervisors, are generally male as well, although this is complicated by the fact that women asked by supervisors to be supports tend to refuse. Thus, although women are much sought after in hiring, on the shop floor, supervisory practices on the line do not recognize gender, and outside direct production, managerial practices reserve positions of mobility and authority for men.

As in Particimex, the great majority of workers are on the assembly lines—more experienced on the larger lines, less so on the smaller ones. They stand, following the moving boards through their stations, then returning to their initial location to catch the next one in its rounds. Behind them hang long colored wires and baskets of small plastic components. They turn to grasp their particular set of wires, perhaps a red, two oranges, and a yellow, then turn to plug them into the appropriate slot on the revolving board, bending and reaching to rout the wires as they walk alongside the moving board. At the end of each "station" the last insertion beeps and a number lights above the board, telling them their job is completed. On the smaller lines, workers often reverse the order of insertions, plugging in the final cable first, as this means that every insertion elicits a satisfying beep.

During the first days, weeks, even months of work, the process is challenging and mesmerizing. José describes this period: "At first I said, this is *hard*, but I've got to do it. But then after like a week, man, I was so happy there! . . . At first I said to my brother and my sister, 'Yes, I've put myself in hell there!' But afterward, nahhh, what the hell?" During the month I spend on the line I am alternately exhilarated and traumatized by my daily ability or inability to keep up. Throughout the entire period I have nightmares in which, just as I hear the "click" that means that the wire is now engaged and can only be removed by a support person, I realize it is the orange not the green wire that belongs in this spot. Nine hours of push, click, pull, *damn!* repeating throughout the night.

The obsessive quality of the work diminishes quickly, however. Whether it's the five-minute cycle time of the big lines or the one- to two-minute cycles of the smaller lines, the work eventually becomes unbearably predictable. By the time I meet José, a mere six months after he and the rest of his line were hired, the entire group is busy switching stations to stave off the overwhelming boredom, and he is threatening to quit because no one is willing to move to his particular location. When Miguel, a support worker who's been in the factory eight years, tells me he is planning to leave, he explains his decision in a lengthy digression about those aspects of factory structure that ensure that he will see the same people, day after day, thus continually foreclosing the possibility of novelty in his social life. The obstacles to using the work itself to generate interest are too self-evident to merit discussion.

Like most of the other Juárez maquilas, the uninspiring nature of the work is significant because the work pays poorly even in local terms, so the money itself is not sufficient to instill loyalty to the job. Wages— not coincidentally like those in Panoptimex[9]—are close to $40 a week, raised to $50 by various benefits. This is low enough that it provides no real possibility of maintaining a family.[10] The few workers who support families independently work several jobs, and Anarchomex matters in large part for the access it provides to state health and housing systems. Most workers live with their parents, siblings, and/or members of their extended families. Thus, many use the money for personal expenses above and beyond food and shelter or understand it principally as a ticket to some level of symbolic independence from, and a way of expressing appreciation to, their parents. Thus Susana says she works "to dress myself," and Margo, "so as not to be asking [for money]." The money matters, of course, but in many cases it is not crucial to daily survival. Combined with the fact that similar jobs are available elsewhere, in most cases losing the job would not set off a severe financial crisis.

At the same time, there are no incentives for the quality of production, and only the most minor rewards for seniority (about $3 monthly for every year worked). Promotions—rare in any period—have been halted for economic reasons during my stay in the factory. Even a cursory look around the factory reveals few workers over twenty-five, even fewer over thirty. In line with the salary and hiring structures, most workers assume that once they have children they will need to seek either better paying (for the men) or more flexible (for the women) jobs. The few workers who nurse illusions of advancement within the plant either leave quickly, disappointed, or are the subject of ongoing teasing by their co-workers. Thus, neither pay nor expectations of promotion are viable inducements at work.

The problems caused by the combined absence of intrinsic interest and material incentives in the work are not helped by the half-hearted efforts at generating factory loyalty and reforming personal habits that take place during the week-long induction period. The "training program" is full of motivational films about quality and gifts of knick-knacks emblazoned with the company name. The obvious skepticism of new workers is reflected in the unconvinced attitude of the trainer himself, however, who seems embarrassed in the face of the exercises he asks the group to do. Mostly the week passes in presentations of rules directed at making us better people: the plant nurse discusses "personal hygiene"; the head of safety shows gory pictures intended to convince us not to wear jewelry or run on the shop floor; the "social worker" advises against betting and playing and selling and cursing on the shop floor. The capstone of the experience is a full day organized around a video designed to foster "excellence" both at home and at work. Upon hearing that we are scheduled to do this training, the "social worker" laughs, "Bring your pillows!" she advises. During lunch at the end of the week, one of my new co-workers comments matter-of-factly, "Excellence is important for the bosses, not for one of us."

The distance workers feel from management is enhanced by the physical layout of the factory. There is no location from which a supervisor can see his entire line at once, still less an omniscient vantage point from which the entire workforce is visible. Everything on the shop floor obstructs the view of everything else. Supervisors are not around anyhow. They are notable for their absence on the shop floor, spending much of their day doing paper work, keeping track of a half-dozen indices. Even "technicians," the promoted workers who do the bulk of hands-on supervision, are ultimately judged by the numbers. No one is there by the production line, hanging over workers' shoulders and watching them work. It is numbers that supervisors pore over, not bodies.

The impersonal nature of supervisor/worker relationships is echoed in the realm of sexuality, removing another arena where personal, supervisory power might have been exercised. Autoworld has strict policies regarding sexual harassment throughout its Mexican operations. Supervisors are actually fired if they are discovered having affairs with their workers and refuse to call them off.[11] Portes boasts, "We're more advanced here," and later elaborates, "I have only little girls here, I have to protect them." Even more muted instances of these sorts of interactions are frowned upon. For instance, quality checker is a relatively cushy job, and supervisors often allocate it to the prettiest girl on the line. However, Smith makes clear that he disapproves of this practice, and workers explicitly objected when an attractive young woman was chosen for this job on my line, noting acerbically that several women with higher educational levels had been passed over.

The few labor control mechanisms that do exist are of a punitive nature. There is no union, and the personnel office plays little part in workers' daily experience. As in most maquilas, absenteeism is highly penalized by the pay structure, and workers lose a third of the week's salary for missing a single day of work. Technicians are constantly coming by and scolding people for producing defects, for sitting down, for disappearing from their posts. However, as their title indicates, technicians' primary focus is on technical and not personnel issues. Thus, their labor control method of last (if frequent) resort is to call meetings in which they bring workers into a small room and tell them about their line's numbers in mind-numbing detail—numbers of defects, of harnesses unmade, of extra workers per line—and angrily exhort them to improve. The factory has made a perfunctory effort to remedy this situation through appointing quality checkers, whose job is to get workers to sign acknowledgments of their mistakes. However, most workers have a deal with the checker that she can sign off for them, and when she tells them they simply nod brusquely and keep working.

In this context, it is workers who keep each other in check on a daily basis. Assembly is done standing by a moving line. Workers are mobile, following the boards as they go. If experienced workers want to take a break, they can work ahead, intruding on the previous workstation and reappearing just in time to finish a subsequent board, by now already moving through an adjacent worker's territory. However, in most workstations, part of the assigned task is contingent upon the completion of previous jobs and is difficult to do once later stages have been finished. As a result, this work rhythm—or even a real inability to keep up— disrupts the work of those nearby. Those who are often behind, for whatever reason, soon feel the wrath of their co-workers. Thus, the limits on work pace are social and lateral, depending on the tolerance of co-workers and the thick-skinnedness of the worker in question. This peer monitoring constitutes co-workers as the central arbiters of success at work. Ultimately, this not only enforces speed but undermines production quality, as defects are a problem for absent supervisors, but not for aggressively present co-workers.

This process goes beyond undermining efficiency. Workers' shop-floor autonomy occasionally generates active, (minimally) collective resistance as well. When workers are called in and told about enforced vacations, a technician queries, "Is that legal?" His comment is immediately followed by disgusted snorting noises, emerging from around the room. Despite the prompt public silence that greets the supervisor's "I don't want backtalk," disgruntled discussion continues on the line for the rest of the day. Several young women go so far as to have me drive them to another maquila which they had heard was hiring. On the small harness line where I train, Sergio repeatedly turns the line's speed down. He is openly supported in this by his co-workers. The technician lets the situation continue, unremarked, quietly recalibrating the line on a regular basis. The most effective instance of this sort of intermittent resistance occurs shortly before my arrival on the same line in response to a particularly nasty supervisor. José tells me the story. "So, we finally got tired of it. We wanted to unite, all of us, no? To talk to the manager. In fact, the line was walking and yes we came together and yes we were going to go. And no, lots cracked and returned to their places again. We tried three times. The ones who didn't turn back, who stayed ahead, were two *güeras* (blond women). But when they saw everyone else . . ." He shrugs. Eventually, despite the line's inability to stick together for long enough to reach the door, their ongoing disquiet became obvious and the supervisor was moved. None of these incidents change the conditions of work in any fundamental way. Most have no discernible impact at all. So I do not by any means intend to exaggerate their importance. Nonetheless, they indicate the potential for resistance that lies latent in the autonomous social world of the shop floor. Once workers sideline managers to become each others' shop-floor interlocutors, the conditions of control shift and new forms of resistance become possible, although they are by no means assured.[12]

On the Anarchomex shop floor, co-workers are the central authorities for each other, both in the labor process and outside it. Managers and supervisors, convinced that they have the wrong workers at the outset, spend little time in production. In those infrequent moments when they are actually on hand, they are more likely to yell than to persuade.[13] These practices leave workers' sense of self—whether gendered or otherwise—relatively untouched. In periods of heavy production, when supervisory yelling-resources are stretched thin, workers have little internal motivation to produce quality harnesses. At the same time, by relying on social pressure between workers around the assembly line to enforce speed, labor control practices effectively locate the essential social dynamics in production between workers and not between workers and management. As a result, shop-floor subjectivities are evoked among workers, effectively foreclosing managerial ability to set their terms at the outset, or to be in a position to legitimate them as a means of control later on.

Gender in Play

Anarchomex's ineffective, number-focused labor control strategies are impelled in part by gendered meanings—by managers' ongoing unwillingness to waste energy on inherently problematic workers. They also work themselves out on a gendered terrain. Managers' dismissive attitude toward men highlights gender and makes masculinity an ongoing subject of contention in production. Within this context, the subjects who emerge on the shop floor are explicitly gendered, and the terms of that gendering are as explicitly oppositional. This is not to say that Anarchomex managers would necessarily have been successful without gendered impediments. The problems described above suggest they might well have been ineffective in any case. However, that is not what occurred. Just as successful labor control operates on and through shop-floor subjects, so does its absence, and in Anarchomex, those recalcitrant subjects are gendered.

In this fraught context, both male and female workers respond to the absence of direct supervision by constituting shop-floor subjectivities which are beyond the reach of managerial legitimation. They enter this process from quite different vantage points, however. Male workers enter on the defensive—their masculinity questioned outside the plant by popular images of feminine maquila workers and inside by the very managers who hired them. Female workers encounter no such challenges to their femininity from their bosses, but their status as workers is under siege by their male co-workers, who address them as sexual rather than productive subjects. In this context, male workers defiantly assert the manliness of the work—representing it as inherently masculine and themselves as paradigmatic harness workers. At the same time, female workers choose the pleasures of their male co-workers' flirtatious if constraining address over managers' more distant and unrewarding naming. In Anarchomex, gendered meanings emerge as a shop-floor battleground, and male workers unequivocally control the field.[14]

MAKING WORK MANLY

Male workers' definition of harness work as masculine is a literally never-ending struggle, and in waging it, they employ a variety of tactics: feigning ignorance that others define harness assembly as feminine; describing the work and factory through masculine tropes; portraying female sexuality as inherently disruptive on the shop floor. Managers are the most problematic opponents in this symbolic struggle, so male workers are particularly disturbed by my suggestions that management prefers female workers. In every interview I do with a man, my allusion to the managerial preference for women is met with an incredulous, "They say they prefer women?" even though each one of them has, in fact, responded to an ad or sign that specifically requested women workers. Miguel says off-handedly, "There in the factories they hire all women, but then they hire all men," and then quickly changes the subject. Roberto responds by offering an alternate explanation for women's presence. Blithely ignoring the fact that half those on his own line are women, he explains that the reason there are so many women here is because here there are easy splicing jobs, so women can do *them*. At the end of a long interview, José admits, "The ad did say only women over eighteen years old," but then goes on emphatically, "Then I went, and it's that *no*, that is they said only women, but it wasn't true. *Look, Leslie, that wasn't meant seriously.*"

In these interviews, male workers frequently redescribe the work or the factory through highly symbolic, masculine images. They define the work as easy when emphasizing the other, gruelingly masculine jobs they have done, but as challenging when affirming the truly masculine nature of *this* work. Thus, as we sit down for an interview, Sergio, the fastest worker on the small harness line where I work, launches into a long unprompted speech. He elaborates on the unique challenges of his station, claims having learned to do it on his own, and insists to an invisible audience that therefore, "nobody can tell me anything about it." On the big line, Mario and Güero tell me every time I come by that they could work twice as fast as the line's current pace if they so desired. On the shop floor, male workers often and conspicuously employ the term *"jale"*—an expression otherwise used for masculinized manual labor— or even more assertively, *"estoy jalando"*—I am laboring—to describe harness assembly or work in the plant.

The sheer size of the factory and the harnesses produced are also repeatedly and symbolically emphasized. José describes his emotions upon first applying for the job after a long period working at another maquila that he labels "easy women's work." "They told me, Christ, you can't keep up. I mean they really drive you. And I believed them, because it was Anarchomex, those were the *biggest* harnesses, everyone said, in all of Juárez." Sergio previously worked at TVA, like Anarchomex one of the oldest and largest maquilas in Juárez, but one that has continued to employ a predominantly female workforce. He comments, "It does have a rep, because TVA is big, but it's not big, I would call Anarchomex *really* big."

Many of these comments assert the essential masculinity of the work through explicit distinctions between *their* relationship to the work and the relationship they claim to be typical of their female co-workers. Thus Sergio, trying to decide if he is willing to take on the challenge of a support position, tries to explain why his reluctance suggests that a woman certainly wouldn't or shouldn't take on such a task: "I say and think they're slower. That is they do work fast, but . . . They put you there to be a support, and *there* you can't fool anybody, *there* you're going to be put to the test. . . . I, for my part, *still* don't want to be a support. Although I knew they wanted me to be. . . . Women aren't slow, but it seems to me they can't do it." On the big line, Mario and Güero work side by side. All day long they carp about the inefficiency of the women nearby. "Guys are faster than girls," Mario asserts. Lupe is a repeated target, accused of laziness for her tendency to work fast and then sit down between boards. "I'd never sit down," says Mario disdainfully, typically noting her sitting, but not the speed that makes it possible. On my last day at Anarchomex, Lupe asks me to take over for a couple of boards as we chat. "Put *that* in your book," says Miguel. "Lupe got you to work so that she could just goof off." In fact, Mario and Güero work in a rhythm similar to Lupe's, although for different reasons. In order to go off and chat with women on other lines, they consistently work ahead of their stations, crowding Margo, who works in the station just before theirs. This allows them to disappear for five minutes and return in time to catch the next board. "They keep doing it," she complains in frustration, "even though I ask them politely." They take no notice. Working faster than their nearby female co-workers in order to go flirt with women elsewhere in the factory—this is what it is all about.

The men's critiques are most vigorous when they describe how their female co-workers' sexuality wreaks havoc in production. Commenting critically on two female co-workers whose flirting is unacceptably assertive, José speaks in the voice of a supervisor, "If the line were faster and there was more pressure, I can assure you they wouldn't have time to go around grabbing like that." Similarly, when I express my surprise to several workers at management's sending a woman home for wearing a mini-skirt, Miguel comments, "Girls shouldn't wear minis, it's distracting." And Roberto offers, "They shouldn't wear minis. The point at work is to be on the ball, it's impossible that way."

Women workers assert a distinct relationship to the work. They make meanings that sidestep and even ignore the actual experience of labor—focusing instead on the social experience of the shop floor. When a group of workers on the small line are promoted to utilities, only the men turn in their old blue smocks for the yellow ones symbolizing their new position. The women prefer not to call attention to the change. They would rather affirm their similarities with their friends than their productive capacities. For similar reasons, Ingrid, whose years of seniority make her a natural choice for a support person, lasts a matter of months in the position. "I'm one of those people who is very hysterical sometimes," she explains. "A support person who offended everyone. That is, I have a very strong character." The fact is that support people always end up offending people, it is part of the job. In a man, this seems normal. For a woman, experiencing and seeing herself experienced in this role is untenable.

Despite women's lack of interest in claiming the work, they respond to men's suggestions that they really aren't serious workers through a stubborn dismissiveness. They don't create identity around the work, but wages are something else again. This insistence on the right to work in the face of male denials can be seen most clearly in the perspectives of Susana and Raúl, a couple who has recently moved in together. Raúl comments: "It isn't necessary for the woman to work. It's not her obligation. . . . Some women are working just to buy nice clothes. . . . In my case, I would have to work because I have to work, in order to depend on myself, I like to depend on myself." However, Susana responds to the idea that she quit work and allow Raúl to support her by saying: "I don't like to just be sitting around. You feel like an idiot, useless, that you can't . . . It's not for me. As soon as he's supporting you, you feel bad." Women make little effort to claim a privileged relationship to the physical work of the factory, but neither are they willing to cede their status as legitimate wage earners to their male co-workers.

In the face of managerial denial, the masculinization of harness assembly is an ongoing project for male workers, and it compels the bulk of their attention and energy on the shop floor. The strategies through which they make their claims are varied and creative, but their tactics share an implicit interlocutor—managers—and an explicit other—women workers. Managers generally dismiss and ignore these claims, but women workers deal with them on an ongoing basis. With little at stake, women in Anarchomex cede any claims to the work itself, insisting only that work in general is a legitimate occupation. As a result, gendered meanings interfere with production for everyone on the Anarchomex shop floor. Only managers think harness assembly is important, but they have long since ceased to address their actual shop-floor audience.

SEXING THE SELF

In the context of managerial disrespect, male workers go beyond marking harness assembly as masculine. They also use their interactions with female co-workers as an arena in which to perform an alternate, legitimate masculinity. Thus, they constantly proposition, hassle, and court women workers, articulating terms for shop-floor femininities that are both highly sexualized and narrowly constrained. Women workers, who experience no such managerial depreciation of themselves as women, turn to this social context for meaning and pleasure, rather than as an opportunity to rebut an aspersion on their character. In this context, the shop floor emerges not as an arena of harness production, but of male-dominated sexual play. The interactions prescribed here by male workers are as clear-cut as managers would have hoped production norms to be: men initiate; women respond. For women, stepping outside these bounds is aggressively sanctioned. Nonetheless, within these ritualized limits, gendered performances are pleasurable, compelling, and primary for men and women alike, distracting them from production and undermining managerial ability to address those aspects of worker subjectivity of most immediate concern on the plant floor.

These processes have given daily life in Anarchomex a distinctively playful, sexualized social texture. An applicant tells me that he wants to work in harnesses because it has a reputation for being "less serious." Ernesto says he came because his brothers told him that "there it's cool, with a lot of teasing and fooling around." Susana explains that, before applying for a job at the plant, she borrowed her sister's uniform to slip onto the shop floor undetected and see if she'd have fun working there. "I came with the intention to work, and, yes, no? Enjoy myself." Other workers commented that they'd come to the plant after being told it had a lot of *ambiente* (atmosphere). And indeed workers do spend the day at play as well as at work. The shop floor is full of catcalls. It is impossible to walk from one line to another without a whistle, a tease, a kiss, "Eh, *güerita*!" At any given moment on the line someone is always visiting—chatting, occasionally "helping," sometimes with disastrous results for the quality of the work. On the small line I trained on, adjacent workers often combine their two stations and work on the same board so they can talk more easily. In the bathrooms, there are always a couple of women sitting in the shower stalls gossiping or grouped around the mirrors comparing lipstick shades and the durability of the arches in their bangs. Before moving in with her boyfriend, Susana used to get to work at 5:20 every morning, a full forty minutes early, in order to chat and gossip with her friends. She is not unusual. Many workers arrive early, frequently leaving their homes by 4:30 A.M. in order to socialize before work. They are tired all day on the line, but it's worth it.

Workers see no conflict between the idea of the factory as a center of social life and as a place of work. Susana tells me: "Having a boyfriend looks worse at school. There you're studying, you go there to study, not to have a boyfriend. Here in the factory it's different. You go to work, but at the same time you go to find friends or to find a boyfriend. It's different at school." Bathroom graffiti tells a similar story—covering the stalls, it focuses entirely upon sexual and romantic attachments and rivalries between workers. Complaints about pay or speed-ups or generic supervisory hassling, even personal insults directed at technicians and supervisors, are notable for their absence. By the same token, workers discussing whether they like the work focus almost entirely on their ability to make friends on a particular line, to "*cotorrear*" (to banter/ flirt), to find or create the companionship that forestalls the otherwise corrosive boredom and depression that the work evokes. In the absence of a managerially generated framework, workers must create their own meanings at work.

Within this context, male voices assert their presence, setting the tone for new workers as soon as they enter the factory—marking it as a masculine space. New workers don orange "training" smocks, in contrast to the navy blue smocks required for ordinary workers. As they walk down the long aisles between the lines, the low-pitched catcalls resonate around them, "Carrots, carrots!" But soon the women among the newcomers notice a different call. "Carrot, come! Come here! Here's your bunny rabbit!" Whistles and kissing sounds follow the new worker as she walks past line after line to her station. Within a couple of days she is angling for the navy smock used by other workers, an escape from the heightened visibility of the brilliant newcomers' uniform.

The new smock only changes the intensity of the erotic hazing, however. Although the whispers and calls diminish, soften and personalize with the new uniform, the male voices never stop. Sexuality—for both young men and young women in the plant—is a primary entertainment, occupation, preoccupation; and in the game of flirtation, men act and women respond. Male workers leave their posts to go flirt with prospective girlfriends. Women workers turn their backs on harness boards to chat with suitors. Men call out or visit, women smile and chat in response, either enthusiastically or with polite distance. But women ignore advances at their peril. The specter of teasing or ostracism is far more alarming than that of an irate supervisor yelling as the mistakes roll in.

On my line, a young woman in the adjoining station has a steady stream of suitors. They stand near her on the platform, obstructing everyone and everything. There are grumbles, but they are muted, it's all in the day's work. One day after one of her usual giggling conversations, she reports that a particularly serious young man has asked her to marry him. "I told him not to be silly," she says calmly, working away. When some young men from engineering are sent to check me out during my training period, my irritated response at their disingenuousness earns me a gentle reproof from my trainer José. "Don't be so angry. You'll offend them." My station partner Lupe keeps count of our suitors, and when a young man comes and stands hang-dog, she offers to cover for me so that I can talk to him. When I neglect to take the opportunity, she is more explicit. "If you act like that, no matter how pretty you are, sooner than you know, no one will pay any attention to you." In fact, being labeled "stuck up" is a constant threat for young women in the plant, and it is often a source of worried self-examination by shyer young women on the line.

There is broad agreement in the factory on the appropriate roles for men and women in these games of flirtation. In response to my comment that supervisors in other factories catcall women, Sergio responds, "I think that's how we [men] *all* are. I mean, I find myself among them, because all of a sudden there's 'Hey babe' and 'Hey beautiful.'" Susana echoes his comments from the other side, "Just imagine if I called out to a guy, 'Carrot, here's your bunny rabbit!' How bad I'd feel! It makes me ashamed. But it doesn't make men ashamed. For them, it feels natural." Men's catcalling within the factory is repeatedly described as a "normal" attribute of maleness—so normal that men who do not participate are forced into convoluted-sounding explanations of what they attempt to cast as their more gentlemanly behavior. Nonetheless, both men and women agree that catcalls from women to men, or even a woman seeking out a man to talk, are not appropriate. In uncomfortable conversation with me, Miguel comments, "A girl, she has her rights too, but the fact is, it looks bad."[15] Marisela elaborates, "It's always the man who talks to a woman. You cheapen yourself, no? Here, what we think is that one cheapens oneself talking to a guy." These opposing sets of rules for men and women are once again particularly evident in Susana's and Raúl's differing reflections on the subject. When I comment in an interview that having an established partner in the factory must take away the freedom to flirt, Raúl objects: "Yes I can, yes we *can* flirt. You get bored if you don't flirt. And let's say that you're married and there's your wife. Pretty unlikely, you're not going to do anything because there's your wife. No way!" On the other hand, in response to a similar comment, Susana agrees: "It's better that you get a boyfriend outside the plant, who isn't always there, because you have problems. Let's say you're talking with a [male] friend, and they go tell him and . . . Better that you work in one place and have your boyfriend in another."

The consensus on flirting norms within the plant is all the more striking against the backdrop of the actual diversity of sexual practices among these women outside it. Lupe says that she'd never had sexual relations with a man until she married. However, when I ask Marisela how she feels as a single mother in the plant, she comments dryly, "There are no more virgins in the maquilas." What is striking is that despite Lupe and Marisela's disagreement about private sexual behavior, their prescriptions for appropriate public behavior for women in the plant are identical. *Cotorreo* is fine, even required, but it must be in response to a man, not initiated by a woman.

Male workers are particularly assertive in noting women's transgressions of these rules on the shop floor. On the smaller line where I trained, men and women have far more egalitarian relationships on a daily basis than those on the larger line, where workers have more varied seniority and experiences in the factory. The group entered together, six months ago, and worked together through the tenure of an unusually nasty and abusive supervisor. Women here are markedly more assertive in teasing and flirting games than on the larger lines. Despite— or perhaps because of—the relative similarity of men and women's shop-floor behavior on the line, in private interviews men from this line are particularly insistent in their critiques of the sexualized play of their female co-workers. Thus Ernesto comments when I ask about men's catcalling, "Some women do it too, they're brazen. It's 'Hey *papacito*!'" Several others comment on two women on the line who are married but "act like they're single." José elaborates: "There are girls that are beyond the limit, they're too much. There on the line there are at least two who say things." He pauses. "Let's just say it, they almost seem like women from outside, from the street, let's say. . . . Sometimes it's *cotorreo*, but lots of times it goes beyond that."

Public breaches are quickly sanctioned by women as well as by men. The women's bathroom is full of graffiti accusing particular women— identified by name and line number—of seeking out men sexually or of stealing others' boyfriends within the factory. Reports of men's graffiti are similar. The few notes on the bathroom walls expressing less acceptable desires and attitudes are left unsigned: "Beto, the one in quality, is like a mango," comments an anonymous writer. "I'm a whore, what of it?" writes another, similarly unidentified.

It would be all too easy to see gender relations on the Anarchomex shop floor as a simple reflection of those outside, for in many ways, Anarchomex's gendered practices feel like those of a Juárez street corner. The catcalls and expectations of willing acceptance, the rule-bound, unequal, and mutual flirting, are relentlessly familiar—if somewhat more intense than the external norm. This "natural" appearance—the texture of an unreconstructed locale—is an illusion, however. Whatever the logic outside, the gender dynamics internally both implicitly and explicitly respond to internal conditions. There is nothing casual about male workers' attitude toward their female counterparts in the plant. On the contrary, their determined sabotage of women workers in production and their intense insistence that women's sexuality is a liability at work are both ultimately directed toward rectifying their embattled situation at work. Heterosexuality in Anarchomex is an arena where men can reclaim a piece of what they have lost elsewhere.

Gendered Meanings as a Fulcrum of Struggle

In Anarchomex, gender itself becomes an object of shop-floor contention. Patriarchal managers define maquila work as inappropriate for real men, thus ignoring or insulting male workers. In response, these workers struggle to redefine the work, as well as the social space of production, as masculine. In making claims to the shop floor, they define their female co-workers as potential girlfriends, thus directly contesting managerial definitions of women as iconic maquila workers. This process undermines managerial control. Male workers are too involved in fighting over masculinity and female workers in responding to their male counterparts to attend to supervisors' criticisms or praises. Managers thus lose all purchase on shop-floor selves.

One might interpret Anarchomex as evidence that men simply cannot be incorporated into transnational production. However, the success of Andromex suggests that this is not the case. In Andromex, managers successfully fill feminized jobs with men by making small but symbolically significant changes in shop-floor practices and rhetorics, thus making it possible for them to address men as "men" in maquila work. In Anarchomex, managers make no effort to address men as "men" at all. Hence, they insult and alienate male workers, thereby failing to integrate men into production and ultimately enacting a classic self-fulfilling prophecy. Despite managerial convictions that men—their accumulated habits of being—are the problem, the problem is actually closer at hand. The issue is not who men "are," but who they become on the shop floor.

Workers, whether female or male, do not enter the shop floor with their gendered selves set in stone. To the contrary, gendered subjectivities are made on the job. In Anarchomex, managers' conviction that men are always-already inappropriate harness workers brings gendered meanings into contention, thus creating the recalcitrant workers they fear they acquired at the outset. Despite the belief, shared by both transnational managers and their critics, that fixed gendered subjectivities are at work in global production, it is gendered tropes and meanings that are in operation, and the subjects who emerge in that process are not imported, they are made in place.

8

Why Femininity(ies)?

Why is transnational production gendered? And why does it produce such varied gendered subjects? In the previous five chapters, I have aimed to systematically undermine the fixed image of the naturally exploitable woman. That figure, as we have seen, turned out to be a figment of the imagination, but not a fleeting one, implicated, as it was, in the shaping of subjects on a multitude of transnational shop floors. In these final pages, we turn from process to cause: asking *why* gender matters so much and *why* it takes the variegated forms it does. This exploration takes us back to the nature of gender itself, and to the importance of subjectivities in shaping economic processes that otherwise appear self-generated. Answering these questions should give us some purchase on how to think about the possibility of change. In grasping the reasons for gender's persistent variability, we can better see the moments where distinct choices might shift the constraints that structure daily life.

Tenacious Categories

When transnational production began to boom in the mid-sixties, one might have expected that gender would be a comparatively insignificant element in its structuring. After all, the raison d'être of the increasingly far-flung web of global production was the dramatic variation in wages across national boundaries. Given the magnitude of wage differentials, the search for even cheaper labor—that is, the demand not for third-world workers but for third-world *women* workers—would seem to be overkill. Once these newly available workers appeared—already constrained by a multitude of state practices and racial markings—why add gender to the mix? What is it about the notion of "cheap labor" which is so ineluctably feminized? Here we need to step back, to locate the trope of productive femininity within the field of the other, overlapping, gendered meanings within which it emerged. Rather than taking the image for granted, assuming its intrinsic logic or natural appeal, we need to trace the social conjunctures which give it such stability.

Gender's defining characteristic is its structure—the two, unequal, othered categories into which it divides human bodies and the universe as a whole.[1] Seen in this light, duality and inequality are essential aspects of gender, but masculine power and predominance are not.[2] Nonetheless, male domination is an endemic historical fact, and despite the temptation to optimism on the grounds that masculine power is "merely" a historical artifact, its accidental, social, necessarily repetitive "origin" does not seem to undermine its staying power. Given this, understanding male domination in any given moment requires not philosophical definition, but historical and geographic "genealogy,"[3] an account of the accrued accidents and discursive intersections which lie behind its current shape. Such a framework—focusing our attention as it does on masculine power's conjunctural but consequential repetitions—allows us to begin to sketch the fields of meaningful practices and practiced meanings within which the trope of productive femininity has garnered such fact-like status. As we have seen, gendered meanings tend to vary across local arenas; nonetheless this variation operates with reference to discourses which can be immensely durable across time and space.

"Productive femininity" has deep historical roots, as it is just one offshoot of capitalists' ongoing search for, and creation of, the prize of "cheap labor." The use of women workers in this capacity has been well documented—both during early industrialization and since, whenever purportedly unskilled, labor-intensive production has made low wages and coercive forms of labor control important for profits.[4] In this context, the notion of a feminized "cheap labor" has functioned as both cause and consequence, simultaneously describing and inciting women's exploitation. In fact, women's hiring in labor-intensive industries is often explained, even by critics, through their role as cheap labor, as if this were not the very issue requiring explanation.[5] Such adjectival phrases serve to obscure the process through which a particular demographic group becomes appropriate to a particular type of work. "Cheapened labor" would imply quite a different process, one more adequate to empirical reality. The use of the term is of course not only an analytic problem; it also has social and political consequences, reifying the links between women and labor-intensive production over the course of several centuries. The notion of the "cheap, docile, and dexterous" third-world woman worker that I have summarized through the term "productive femininity" is merely the most recent incarnation of a much older discourse.[6] Thus, its somewhat surprising endurance in the context of cross-border production, and its even more puzzling resilience in the almost half-male maquila industry, can in part be accounted for by the longevity of the concept of cheap labor and of women's association with it.

This tenacity is a geographical as well as a historical product. The notion of cheap, docile, dexterous femininity operates not only outside Juárez, but beyond Mexico's national borders and the maquila industry as well.[7] In the early sixties, improvements in transportation and communication made far-flung manufacturing systems increasingly feasible and markedly sharpened the competition over access to low-wage workers.[8] As a result, states throughout the third world began advertising their workforces—lauding their feminine cheapness, malleability, trainability and dexterity.[9] Thus, the icon, at least in this recent incarnation, originated in statements that were always intended for export, and the trope has been reinforced in transnational conversations ever since. Maquila managers are not mere onlookers in these discussions; they are active participants. Ambitious workers in global structures, they travel routinely, not only back and forth to meetings at corporate headquarters, but in long-term moves from a plant in Singapore or Detroit to one in Mexico, or vice versa. Whatever is happening on the ground in Juárez, the rhetoric of productive femininity is fed by these ongoing conversations. Thus, part of the trope's surprising resilience in public discussion in Juárez can be accounted for by its extensive geographic scope, and therefore by the multitude of semi-autonomous strategies and frameworks which converge upon it simultaneously from outside, fortifying and amplifying it from around the globe.

The rhetoric of cheap labor itself operates on a still larger field of practices and images of femininity—a field which clusters around women's position in the family. Women's purported willingness to accept low wages and reputed shop-floor malleability are both contingent on the existence of a "breadwinner" at home who calls the shots.[10] This structure, of course, is in turn contingent on the institution of hetero-sexuality itself.[11] Thus, the image of women's homegrown docility—whether enforced or inherent—has an extensive social root-structure, and it is only in the context of these other social and sexual relationships that the notion of the cheap, docile, and dexterous woman worker makes sense at all.[12] Hence, the rhetoric of productive femininity im-plicitly cites and refers to all these other, even more basic, symbolizing practices and enacted images. Its otherwise puzzling durability in the industry can be accounted for by tracing its location among other gen-dered tropes and practices—its ongoing nourishment from outside, its historical resonance, and its links to other foundational practices and images of femininity.

This accounts for the trope's ongoing presence, but its remarkable *salience* among many competing images of work and workers requires further explanation. Again, the causes lie in the meanings which have accrued to femininity and masculinity over expanses of time and space which extend well beyond Juárez in the last few decades. One of the fundamental contemporary structures of male power is the conflation, in both language and practice, of the masculine and the general—evident in the casual use of the "generic he." In the field of work, the equivalence of the male and the archetypal instance emerges in the term "worker" itself—"man worker" would be simultaneously redundant and grammatically incorrect, whereas "woman worker" is both intelli-gible and informative. As in other social spheres, such phrases go beyond mere rhetoric, expressing masculinity's capacity to literally "go with-out saying." "Woman," on the other hand, stands in for specificity—both for the fact of individual embodiment and for the very presence of gender at all. Masculinity can of course be highlighted, but the pres-ence of men in and of themselves does not necessarily bring gender into play. I am, again, not arguing here that this is a necessary aspect of gen-der in theory. Nonetheless, this particular duality was produced in west-ern writing, thought, and practice between the late seventeenth and early nineteenth centuries, and thus comes to us today with the conclu-sive stamp of received truth.[13] Hence, it has been remarkably tenacious in practice.

Not surprisingly in this context, the feminization of transnational labor is a process of marking which makes explicit reference to the fe-male body. Hence, managers' frequent claim that the work requires "slender" or "nimble" fingers—a standard metonymy for women workers not only in the maquilas, but in labor-intensive production more broadly. This pointed and embodied feminization makes men's entrance into maquila work extremely challenging—both for managers to envision and for male workers themselves to experience. It is for this reason that the feminization of maquila work is not only more persistent than one might expect, but more salient as well. One consequence of the fact that maquila work feminization operates through bodily marking is that undoing it requires explicit contradiction. For men to be able to engage in the work comfortably, local discourses must expressly reject this feminine image—as management has in Andromex. Otherwise, working on the line in a maquila remains a form of gender transgression for men, no matter how many men actually engage in the work. Despite the hundreds of mixed-gender plants operating in Juárez, productive femininity remains a conspicuous structure of meaning, practice, and individual subjectivity at work.

The salience of gender in transnational discussions and its consequent role in structuring the Juárez labor market does not by any means ensure its exact reproduction on maquila shop floors, however. To the contrary, these long-standing images provide a framework within which specific managerial ambitions, intentions, and constraints shape an image of appropriately gendered subjects on individual shop floors. Within broad parameters, the gendered meanings which emerge on each shop floor are distinctive. Shop-floor discourses evoke gendered subjects, but not necessarily, or even typically, those described by the trope of productive femininity.

This coincidence of a constant set of gender discourses at the level of the labor market and a variable set of discourses on the shop floors within that market's bounds is due once again to the character of gender itself. What counts as "feminine" or "masculine" not only moves with large-scale shifts in other social, cultural, and economic structures, but also metamorphoses within these larger parameters, in accord with local structures, practices, and intentions. What's more, larger gendered meaning structures are often out of sync with each other and move at varying speeds.[14] Those meanings which hold across greater swathes of space or time tend to shift more slowly, even as local frameworks fluctuate.[15] Thus, contrasting and more or less fragile meanings can coexist within a single social space. In the panorama I have painted throughout the book we can discern many such overlapping sets of gendered meanings. Several clusters stand out: the resilient trope of productive femininity, articulated by transnational managers in Juárez but operating far beyond its borders; the more limited image of femininity-on-the-loose enunciated by native Juárez elites; and those four less-enduring formations which emerged in the plants themselves. It is in the first of these—the trope of productive femininity—with its large geographical and historical extension and its links to other, even more enduring, tropes, that we find the key to gender's tenacious prominence in the maquila industry. The highly individualized shop-floor discourses reveal the extreme local variability with which this trope can be brought into play.

Thus, gender itself is revealed here as an interlocking, always emergent set of meaning structures intent on establishing difference in relation to sexed bodies. These discourses—enacted in both language and practice—extend over vastly differing expanses of space, time, and social life.[16] Those with the broadest sweep, longest history, or deepest social embedding tend to be disproportionately durable and authoritative where they circulate, but they all potentially matter. What's more, the tenacious historical association of femininity with specificity and embodiment has meant that in arenas marked as feminine, gendered meanings tend to be especially sticky. Nonetheless, particular discourses do not alight on a given social space from on high. Rather, they are called upon, distorted, and enacted—often in contradictory pairings—by local actors with their own idiosyncratic desires, intentions, and strategies. Thus, gender's on-the-ground shape and consequences can never be known in advance. These processes are on brilliant display in the Juárez maquilas, where the idea of femininity structured the industry's very birth.

In this context, the three plants in Juárez illustrate just how different gendered meanings can be, even when evoked within the trope of productive femininity, and even when enacted within a single cultural context and population. Women in the three plants run the gamut from productive sexual objects to disembodied, masculinized producers, while their male co-workers similarly vary widely, from shamed "women" to masculine breadwinners. And in Particimex, shop-floor femininities actively contradict those enacted outside the plant. We can explain the ongoing relevance and centrality of gendered categories, but we have yet to account theoretically for the production of these variable meanings. The nature of gender itself, the distinction between rigid categories and malleable content, explains what makes the level of heterogeneity we see in the Juárez maquilas possible. However, possibility isn't fulfillment. Why do gendered meanings and subjectivities multiply across shop floors in the Juárez maquila industry?

Subjectivities as Economic Agents

The Juárez maquilas operate in a discursive field which assumes workers to be both female and "feminine." In the early eighties, as these paradigmatic workers became scarce, some maquilas closed shop, some imported women from elsewhere, still others brought men into feminized jobs, with varying levels of success. This multiplicity of responses was due to material differences between plants (the greater importance of skilled labor at Andromex, for example), but it also reflected differences in managerial outlooks. Solutions require that someone perceive a problem and define what counts as a possible resolution. This is accomplished by socially situated subjects, and it is in large part the variation in their perspectives that accounts for the multifarious gendered meanings which eventually emerged in the plants. Until now, I have focused on the impact of worker subjectivities on production. In these last pages, I will turn to those subjects who set a shop floor in motion—managers.[17]

Managers' descriptions of their own practices tend to veer between two poles—focusing either on the external structures which take decisions out of their hands or on the impact of their own extraordinary prescience (or, less frequently, on their own mistakes).[18] Their own accounts notwithstanding, they are neither automatons who blindly respond to structural imperatives nor isolated, objective decision makers who weigh alternatives and make strategic choices. On the contrary, they operate from highly particular vantage points, and from within a variety of overlapping structures of meaning. Their decision-making processes are constrained and enabled by larger corporate, national, and gendered logics and beliefs and are made from specific locations. These social prisms unevenly highlight and obscure the choices they perceive.[19]

Their claims that they are situated within constraints and possibilities not of their own making are, of course, correct. Corporate hierarchies and rules, governmental regulations, material prices and availabilities, and labor market demographics are all instances of external (if sometimes movable) conditions and structures. However, it is managerial subjectivity that determines what constitutes a relevant condition in decision making. This is particularly obvious in transnational outposts such as the maquilas, where production takes place far from "the market," and local managers respond instead to a variety of demands from distant superiors. The fact that these conversations are generally couched in a rhetoric of "efficiency" and directed at the need to "com-

pete" in the contemporary "global marketplace" is, as such, no indication of the power of the market, only of the fact that the participants
think in these terms. All managerial decisions come from a particular
location and are made through a particular lens, whatever the pressures
brought to bear by external forces.[20]

This, of course, is not to recommend interpreting managerial strategies as mere expressions of individual psychology and idiosyncrasies.
Like the workers they hire and supervise, managers are embedded in
meaningful practices and rhetorics. The arena within which they are interpellated is less spatially defined—and thus less easily recognized—
than is the shop floor. However, managers too have subjectivities which
are evoked within external meanings, subjectivities that then frame and
impel their labor control strategies. Like the workers they supervise,
they are located within gender, nation, and corporation, and the ambitious, driven selves which emerge are inflected by their particular location within these structures. Thus, what concerns us here is neither
psyche nor context, but the impact of the situated selves which are produced when self and social meet.[21]

In the following pages, we will revisit the shop floors, looking for evidence of the symbolizing practices, structures of meaning, and situated
intentions which shape managerial decisions. I will focus particularly on
how gender,[22] nationality, corporate allegiance, and ambition converge
to produce a particular self, and thus to shape a concomitant sense of
who might be an appropriate worker and how s/he should behave. A
comparison of Anarchomex and Particimex provides a rich lode for beginning this exploration. The two maquilas are engaged in the same
production process, are both part of Autoworld, and report to the same
Juárez office, yet the genders evoked on their shop floors are radically
divergent. A look at managerial subjectivities in the two plants helps us
account for these differences.

The gendered subjects who emerge in Anarchomex are anything
but productive, and more closely resemble those of an unusually tense
Juárez dance floor than they do those described in the trope of productive femininity. The majority of workers are men—deeply involved
in contesting managers' emasculating frameworks through hassling,
courting, and otherwise dominating their female co-workers. The
women in the plant, in turn, respond primarily to the persistent voices
of male workers, for the most part disregarding more distant, supervisory, commentaries. This situation can be traced directly to the way
managers construe self and other.

The plant manager at Anarchomex is a late-career, superficially transplanted midwesterner who treats his current location outside the United States as alternately irrelevant or mildly irritating. Despite this attitude, he has succeeded in gathering a set of middle-aged Mexican men to work directly below him whose ideas about production and masculinity are remarkably similar to his. These men, whose corporate selves have been formed by years in the auto industry, believe that production requires the "right" inputs—and that workers are simply that. In view of the unquestionable given of low wages in the maquila sector, the "right" workers are not financially responsible for their families; thus, with customary gendered slippage, the "right" workers are female. At the same time, these men are deeply committed to enacting, and in theory propagating, a masculinity linked to being the head of the family—both being the breadwinner and carrying a certain innate authority. This set of beliefs and commitments places them in a quandary, for the majority of workers willing to work in Anarchomex are male. In response to the situation, managers focus their attention on production statistics and dreams of "better" hiring. Defensive male workers respond by commanding the attention of female co-workers, effectively commandeering the shop floor. Thus, managers' profound distance from their workers and their entrenched, patriarchal versions of personal masculinity ultimately set the stage for sexualized and contentious shop-floor genders—a far cry from the focused, pliant hands plant managers continue to fantasize in their place.

Lest these labor control decisions appear foreordained, we now turn to Particimex, where a differently located group of managers makes distinct disciplinary decisions within the same production process—with clear differences in the gendered subjects produced on the shop floor. Most of the workers in Particimex are women, and like their male co-workers, they are highly productive. As in Anarchomex, these useful subjects are evoked in contrast to, rather than in consonance with, the discourse of productive femininity. Here, however, the contrasts are defined by management, not by workers, with sharply divergent results. Again, a look at the way managers understand themselves, their jobs, and their workers accounts for these differences.

The Particimex managers are young Mexican men looking to move up in a hurry. Located in a small agricultural city south of Juárez, they are intent on distinguishing themselves from their rural workers, while simultaneously parlaying their insiders' understanding of "their countrymen" into a ticket out of the periphery. As a result of this positioning, they eagerly accepted the idea—previously rejected by their colleagues at Anarchomex—of instituting a pioneering structure of shop-floor management built around "teamwork," "equality," and "worker responsibility." In so doing, they have developed a narrative about their relationship to "Mexican traditions" which emphasizes both their ability to understand "traditional" women workers and their capacity to make them "modern." These U.S.-focused meaning structures and the positionings of self they engender constitute an unusual set of managerial subjectivities, where a non-authoritarian style of masculinity is made possible by its putative global/first-world character. These nationality-inflected, ambitious masculinities in turn make participatory management strategies conceivable. Thus, they evoke gendered shop-floor selves which invert the trope of productive femininity, while still markedly diverging from those enacted in Anarchomex.

One might argue, of course, that these differences don't respond to managerial subjectivities. After all, the demographics of the labor force facing the two plants are radically different. However, demographics too must be understood and addressed. Hiring decisions are made by managers; such decisions do not emerge in automatic response to labor market changes. This becomes particularly clear if we shift the comparison from Anarchomex and Particimex to the two other Juárez maquilas described in the book, each of which has a labor force comparable to one of these plants.

Like the workforce at Anarchomex, Andromex's workforce is in large part male[23]—yet the gendered subjects evoked on the two shop floors have little in common. In Andromex, all workers, men and women alike, express an implicitly masculine sense of self at work. On the shop floor, they are interpellated as legitimately and productively contentious breadwinners and producers—striking departures from the recalcitrant shirkers that populate Anarchomex or the docile supplementary earners that fill managerial imaginations. These shop-floor subjects are anomalies in the maquila industry, and their existence can only be explained if we recognize the distinctive prism through which the powerful plant manager views his choices.

Andromex's plant manager is a Juárez native, comfortable in the city and intent on running "his factory," not on moving up and out. He is remarkably multifaceted—fluently performing both the muted, organizational masculinity of the American bosses he golfs with and the stylized, northern-Mexican masculinity of the guys on his shop floor. He is a true border-crosser in other ways as well, sharing both transnational maquila managers' concerns about labor and local elites' anxieties about working-class male displacement. Thus, after a wildcat strike demonstrated the unreliability of women workers' famed docility, he was among the few managers who explicitly opened his plant to men. He went on to develop a structure of labor control focused on combative negotiation rather than command. This structure recognizes all workers as legitimate contenders over their livelihood, interpellating men and women alike within a structure of subjectivity which repeatedly references the images of young, working-class masculinity in play outside the plant. A border-crosser at home where he is, a Mexican man identified with the masculinity of his male workers, he can see his way to making production choices that his counterparts in Anarchomex find untenable.

Panoptimex provides a similarly telling example when contrasted with Particimex. Young women make up the overwhelming majority of line workers in both maquilas, and in both cases, managers have gone to great lengths to secure young women's presence. Nonetheless, the plants' disciplinary styles, and the subjectivities these styles evoke, are entirely distinct. Panoptimex's workers emerge in production as sexual objects—dependent on supervisors and managers for legitimation of both erotic desirability and shop-floor efficiency.[24] The femininities at work in the two plants are equally productive, but operate through opposed logics. Whereas Particimex femininities are assertive, posed in explicit contrast to the doctrine of productive femininity, Panoptimex femininities are passive, understood as embodiments of the iconic transnational assembly worker. Again, a look at the frameworks through which managers understand and experience their workers reveals the logic of their labor control choices.

Panoptimex produces TVs, and the visual rhetoric of the industry saturates the conversation of the ambitious, mobile, transnationally located men who run the plant. The results of these visual practices of attention are evident throughout the arena of production—not only in TVs produced, but in the subjectivities of workers and managers alike. The shop floor is intended, from its architectural design to the uniforms of its occupants, to enable over-sight and to "look right." This focus on the visual extends to the look of workers, compelling management's unusual, ultimately successful, efforts to fill the lines with young women who will have the right look. As a result, on the shop floor, mobile men watch stationary young women, producing a panoptic system where the pleasures and imbalances of sexual objectification become productive, and where both managers and workers are constituted as sexual subjects in the workplace. Here, managerial masculinity is shaped, within both corporate discourses and shop-floor architecture, around the male gaze. The working femininities that emerge within this context are as productive as those which emerge in Particimex, but their content is radically distinct.

The varied content of workers' gendered subjectivities in the maquila industry is enabled by the structure of gender itself and produced by a variety of material, institutional, and cultural pressures. Nonetheless, these pressures do not impose themselves directly on production; they are filtered through the experiences and understandings of the managers who ultimately make decisions about hiring and labor control. Managers choose where and how to produce based on their understanding of what is possible, legitimate, reasonable, and appropriate. This is particularly clear in their decisions about labor. Their sense of themselves and of "others," their understanding of what is basically human and what varies across "differences" of gender, nationality, race, and class, come into play in every assessment of who can be asked to do what and under what conditions. Thus, it is in understanding managers' frameworks—their location within structures of gender, nation, and corporation, and the perspectives that emerge from that placement— that we can begin to account for the abundance of the gendered meanings we find in the Juárez maquila industry.

A generation of feminist theorists have tackled the complexity of "situated knowledges,"[25] arguing that different truths are seen from different social locations. This is as true in production as in any other social arena, and the "truths" managers see are constitutive of the actions they take on the shop floor. These actions matter. If the socially situated selves through which managers perceive the world shape the production process and its outcomes in global factories, then the contours of the possible are in part set through these subjective processes. Even in highly competitive and closely monitored transnational workplaces, significant aspects of shop-floor control are determined locally, in the often unspoken common sense of individual plants. Many of the specifics are established through local managers' sense of workers as a particular sort of other, and of what can or should be asked of them given this imaginary relationship. Thus, a significant amount of invisible, often unconscious, decision making occurs locally. Assuming that everything is determined by larger structural imperatives or first-world corporate control misses these determinants.

Subjects emerge from economic processes, but they also set these processes in motion and shape their course. Understanding this provides us with new ways of thinking about local structures and suggests new forms of investigation. Once we grasp the causal impact of subjectivities, it becomes evident that we must "study up" as well as "down,"[26] putting the same imaginative and empathetic work into understanding managers' perspectives as we put into understanding those of workers. Only in doing this work can we begin to comprehend the multiple and contingent intentions which shape the path of transnational production. If we wish to delineate the ways in which global capital shapes our lives, the subjectivities of its agents, as well as of its "victims," must form part of our field of investigation.

New Ways of Seeing

When Fuentes and Ehrenreich wrote in the early eighties, they were propelled by a sense of urgency. Many early feminists had assumed that as women entered paid work, male power would erode.[27] However, the maquilas and other transnational assembly plants appeared to have achieved the perfect, diabolical, marriage of patriarchy and capitalism. Women's patriarchal oppression enabled their capitalist exploitation and their consequent exploitation in turn supported patriarchy at home. The situation called for revelation and condemnation.

There are many kinds of theory. Fuentes and Ehrenreich were part of an extended historical "moment" in which theory was expected to provide answers, the more general the better. Marxism is the paradigmatic example of such a productively totalizing theory, and the kind of answers it provided inspired formal emulation by feminists of all stripes,[28] in addition, of course, to radically changing the world. The world and theory have both changed, however, and the theory embedded in the present analysis is of a different character. Here, I offer specific queries, not general answers. Statements of the form, "women are X" or even "in transnational production, women are X" seem to me, at this juncture, to be deceptively comprehensive and assured. Thus, my intentions are more modest, although not, I believe, less useful to an ongoing project of transformation.

My purposes thus are threefold, but intertwined. I have argued here that understanding the dynamics of a global factory requires an eye for gender and subjectivity, but not assumptions about the content and significance of the femininities or masculinities one might find there.

Thus, my first hope is that the analysis offered here points to the kinds of questions activists—and here I refer to plant "insiders" as well as "outsiders"—might ask as they try to grasp the gendered selves in operation on a given shop floor in order to change it. Second, I hope the narrative will make it more possible for us, both individually and collectively, to see the gaps, cracks, and fissures in gendered subjectivities we might otherwise experience as seamless, and to become cognizant of their implications for larger structures of domination. And finally, I hope the work provides lenses which enable us to see the dizzying duality of contemporary global production, in which meanings and subjectivities constitute structures which in turn shape us all, whatever our role in creating them.

Over the course of the narrative, I have argued that economic processes operate via the formation of new subjects. If this is indeed the case, then figuring out who has been brought to life on a given shop floor becomes an indispensable political project. In the case of transnational production, where gender is such a salient and generative element, delineating the gendered meanings which are at work on an individual shop floor is a vital step in both understanding managerial structures of control and speaking to the local feminine or masculine selves they evoke.

It is all too easy to assume that women are willing to accept exploitative labor conditions because of habitual docility, or even in response to external economic pressures. However, there is tremendous variation across workplaces in the willingness of women culled from a single impoverished population to accept such treatment. Thus, the causes of these differences lie within the plants, not outside them. Assuming that women workers all experience themselves at work primarily through the category of "docile daughters" or "impoverished mothers" misses a wide range of possible variation in work experience and selfhood. Understanding the selves management addresses and evokes makes it possible to speak directly to the subjects actually working. It also makes a particular version of consciousness-raising available as an organizing tool, as activists themselves can come to see and make visible the processes through which gendered "manageability" is generated under exploitative conditions.

Concientización, the consciousness-raising-like popular education tool developed by Paolo Freire[29] in the seventies, is of course already widely used by Latin American grassroots organizers. In the maquilas, it was first used explicitly by COMO in the late seventies and early eighties,[30] and it continues to influence the organizing being done by the Comité Fronterizo de Obreras (Border Committee of Women Workers) across the industry.[31] My intention here is not therefore to suggest a new methodology, but to offer a new focus for its content. One of the great strengths of the feminist labor organizing of recent years has been its insistence that women workers have been misrecognized by unions, and that organizers must be willing to cross traditional boundaries separating home, community, and work in order to speak effectively to women's concerns.[32] However, implicit in these new frameworks are a set of assumptions about who women are and what matters to them. In this paradigm, women workers as a group are generally framed as dedicated "mothers"—whether of children or community.[33] As we have seen in the foregoing pages, however, who "women" are on a given shop floor is a variable business. In these new frameworks, women workers are once again at risk of misrecognition. Building on the insights of these new organizers, I am suggesting here that another boundary be broken, and that what femininity comes to mean in a given factory be made a subject of investigation. Here, gender's emergence at work, rather than its experience in the home, would become a direct object of discussion.

Despite its manifestly social nature, the gendered self is experienced, and thus treated, as private. As a result, being addressed in gendered terms in a public setting is simultaneously powerful and unspeakable. On the shop floor, gendered interpellation is both an effective element of routine managerial control and one that is difficult to name collectively when attempting to challenge this structure. Insofar as organizers focus explicitly on the gendered selves experienced on the shop floor, they bring previously invisible processes of control to light. Making this process a part of collective awareness thus makes new kinds of interventions and organizing possible, as workers can begin to look at how their most intimate selves are incorporated into managerial strategies.

Panoptimex provides us with one example of how such an approach might look. Shop-floor control in Panoptimex is generated through processes of objectification which are simultaneously sexualized and productive. This interpellatory structure is both powerful and pleasurable, and women workers come to see themselves through a masculine, super-visory gaze. The workforce's flirtatious gestures and decorated bodies appear as instances of natural adolescent femininity, both to an outsider and to the women themselves. Nonetheless, time spent on the

shop floor attending to managerial addresses suggests a more local process of production at work—as women in the plant matter-of-factly
recount the emergence of their embodied self-consciousness. There is
nothing "technical" about the critical awareness required to see this,
but it does require an eye for gendered categories and managerial processes of naming. With these lenses, and in the context of shared discussion, it would become possible to make the processes through which
the workforce's collective malleability is evoked and enforced visible.
This could then provide a ground for more traditional labor organizing—focusing for instance on authentic collective representation or on
supervisor abuses—as well as enabling women workers to contest shop-
floor sexualization itself.[34]

Anarchomex provides a very different example of how an understanding of gender as discourse might matter. On the Anarchomex shop
floor, gendered meanings are a center of contention. However, the
assumptions embedded in managers' insistence that all workers are
"feminine" remain invisible. As a result, male workers' primary energy
is dedicated to undermining the legitimacy of their female co-workers'
prized presence at work. Neither they nor their female co-workers ever
directly contest the assumption that maquila work is, by definition,
simple, boring, and poorly paid. Yet this is the underlying meaning of
managers' definition of the work as essentially feminine. Bringing this
process to conscious awareness—discussing how the feminized trope of
cheap labor ultimately shapes maquila work—would make it possible to
redirect the energy of defensive male workers and give them grounds for
working with rather than against their female co-workers. Again, this
process does not require complex intellectual terminologies. Rather, it
requires an understanding that gendered meanings are flexible and variable; and that they shape not only people but definitions of work and
fair labor conditions.

Feminist labor activists are increasingly involved in organizing
throughout the maquila sector.[35] Much of their success is due to their
focus on women, in sharp contrast to earlier organizers who—literally—addressed maquila workers as men, even in the face of the huge
preponderance of women who then populated the plants.[36] However,
even now, workers frequently disregard organizers' appeals. The reasons
for this situation are multiple, of course, including workers' legitimate
fear of employer blacklists and young workers' assumption that maquila
work is only a brief, hopefully entertaining, stop on the way to something more permanent. Nonetheless, too often, organizers' language

resembles that of the analysts of the early eighties, discussing shop-floor exploitation as if it operated without touching the selves at work.[37] In so doing, organizers bypass workers' own accounts of work as a social world and arena of personal evolution and hence fail to address the actual experience of the shop floor. Asking who "women"—or for that matter "men"—become on individual maquila shop floors and tracing how they came to be makes other interventions possible. Specifically, it becomes possible for organizers to speak to the subjects actually at work and to reveal the processes through which they are evoked in the service of managerial control.

These issues are relevant to lives lived far from the maquilas, as well as within them. All of us inhabit, and are interpellated by, multiple gendered meaning structures. Of course there are elements of gendered selfhood which we carry with us between arenas, and certain aspects of "femininity" or "masculinity" hold sway over great swathes of social space. Nonetheless, attending to differences suggests more variation than we generally experience or even recognize. It is now broadly acknowledged that gendered meanings vary across "cultures" or historical "periods." But the cases I have discussed here reveal that gendered meanings and the subjects they evoke shift across far less extensive expanses of space and time—for instance across different workplaces or between home and work within a "single" cultural context. This suggests that a specific individual may transverse dramatically different structures of meaning over the course of a single day. Insofar as people respond appropriately to these addresses, they necessarily express locally gendered forms of selfhood. That these processes are obscured both internally and externally by narrated experiences of continuous selfhood makes them no less significant. Of course, these ongoing fluctuations do not suggest that "femininity" and "masculinity" are less constraining than we had imagined; after all, they are always at work. However, their discursive form and the myriad contradictions in their embodiment across space and time do provide opportunities for bringing gendered forms into awareness and collective discussion.

To take an example close to home, as a sociologist at the University of Chicago, I move at work within various forms of address. In most university contexts, I am interpellated in a highly abstract structure of masculinity in which, like the women of Andromex, I emerge as disembodied and putatively ungendered. However, as a teacher of feminist theory, I am re-marked as an explicit symbol and embodiment of both femaleness and femininity within that masculinized context. Although

I only rarely experience my shifting comportment as I move between these arenas, with attention I can bring it to consciousness, and thereby make decisions about how I inhabit these structures. Important aspects of my gendered self and desires remain outside my control, of course, but in posing these enactments as decisions, I remind myself and others of gender's fundamentally social and changeable character.

Bringing gender's social character to consciousness is consequential not only in itself, but because of its links with structures of domination that go beyond the constitution of selfhood. In this historical moment, gendered meanings and subjectivities are connected both directly and necessarily with male power and frequently with capitalism and science and other systems of power as well. Particular gendered discourses are generated, or at least practiced, by actors with local strategies and intentions, but as in the cases I discussed here, these ultimately feed into larger logics of domination. Hence, to return to the example given above, my enactment of both abstract masculinity and marked femininity function to legitimize images of objective information and knowledge and to solidify the implicit links between them and masculinity itself. At the same time, and contradictorily, my performance of explicit femininity also functions as a sign of alternative ways of knowing in the university context. This has consequences both for the experiences of young women and men as learners and for their capacity to grasp the situated character of social science itself. Thus, there is nothing obvious about what choices we should make, but bringing them into awareness makes it possible to discuss their consequences.

It takes work to make one's gendered self feel "unnatural," but it is work worth doing.[38] I am suggesting here that we engage in that project with a lens that heightens a particular aspect of gendered experience—the way that the meanings of femininity and masculinity vary across time and space in the service of idiosyncratic local strategies and intentions. This practice of noting differences across social arenas gives us each access to a traveler's—or better yet an ethnographer's—eye, as once-familiar situations appear new upon entry. This attention renders routine gendered practices strange, enabling us to choose more intentional and hopefully less constraining gendered selves.

It is no accident that the phrase "the personal is political" emerged from feminism, rather than from a non-gender-focused movement, as gendered meaning structures often provide the links between individual emotions and subjectivities and political and economic processes. That role is apparent not only in the example offered above, but on the maquila shop floors as well. Nonetheless, although gender makes these connections evident, it is not the only set of meanings which evokes politically consequential subjects. To the contrary, on the four shop floors examined here, we see subjects addressed through national and corporate as well as gendered discourses, and surely there are other meaning structures at work which are invisible through the lens I have constructed here. Thus, once we take seriously that gendered subjects shape and are shaped by economic processes, we find ourselves drawn to investigate the formation and effects of other axes of subjectivity as well. Capitalist production interpellates its inhabitants in a wide variety of structures of meaning. Studying gender we begin to notice the profound implications of those processes for both subjects and structures. Thus, beginning with gender, we end with subjectivity more generally. Feminism pushes us to recognize the pivotal role of subjects in generating economic life.

In popular discussions, the spread of global capital is often imagined as a natural process: "a great sucking sound"; a wave.[39] These images imply an impersonal process, out of human control. However, the fact that there is no planner, that indeed no one has decided that the contemporary world should look as it does, is no indication that the process is shaped outside the context of human subjectivity. Although human beings may not control global production's evolution, we certainly generate it, and as such it bears the imprints of the multiple locations and frameworks through which decisions are made. None of this is to say that there are no limits on economic choices or their consequences. In a political world committed to "free" trade, it would be difficult for a local manager to quadruple salaries without being fired or for an auto producer to pay all workers "manufacturing" wages and stay in business. Nonetheless, within these constraints, local beliefs, strategies, and intentions lead to a wide range of outcomes, and each one opens or closes possibilities for change. Remembering how ways of seeing, thinking, and feeling structure consequential decisions also keeps us from confusing the constraining effects of current structures with either their inherent "objectivity" or with the abstract necessity of their consequences.

Transnational managers, like state decision makers, are well placed to recognize the paradoxical relationship of subjectivity and structure. Under capitalism, transnational managers, more clearly than the rest of us, are located in positions from which their accumulated decisions operate as external forces. Thus, their choices constitute these forces even as they are subject to them. In consequence, in conversation, they shift back and forth between recognizing their power over and their subjection to this system. This description accurately captures a fundamental feature of contemporary global processes—their simultaneously objective and subjective nature. Thus, stopping for a moment to see the world from these managers' vantage points, we can see the vertiginous shifts from crystallized force to idiosyncratic decision and back again which make up the reality of contemporary transnational production. Structures are but a concatenation of common-sense understandings and decisions, seen from the perspective of those subject to their emergent consequences.[40] Insofar as we can get up close to these processes and delineate the logics of self and meaning through which they emerge, we can begin to question their inevitability and imagine other worlds.

Notes

Chapter 1. Ways of Seeing

1. All the names used here—for factories, corporations, company programs, and people alike—are fictitious.

2. See Burawoy (1998) for an extended discussion of this issue.

3. Haraway (1988).

4. *Maquilas* is the popular name for *maquiladoras*. These are export-processing factories located in Mexico, generally along the country's northern border, which assemble parts produced in the United States for sale on the U.S. market. Since 1965, they have operated under a system in which they are exempted from import taxes on both sides of the border. NAFTA has placed much of Mexican industry in the same situation, but in the early nineties, when I did my research, this was not the case.

5. The primary newspaper archives I used were assembled by the Centro de Orientación de la Mujer Obrera (COMO) in the late seventies and early eighties. For media coverage before and after the period covered by the COMO archives, a research assistant combed the archives of *El Fronterizo* for the years 1965–73 and of *El Diario de Juárez* for the years 1985–93. I also searched the archives of the local maquiladora association (AMAC).

6. I spent my days in the offices of three sets of labor lawyers and organizers and at the state labor board (Junta de Conciliación y Arbitraje).

7. See Burawoy (2000), Van Maanen (2001), Marcus (1998), and Comaroff and Comaroff (1992) for insightful discussions of the benefits and challenges of studying contemporary organizations and global structures ethnographically.

8. In addition to the four factories analyzed here, I toured seven shop floors and spent two and four weeks, respectively, in two others. I spent three months in the TV plant (Panoptimex), observing but not working in production. I

spent ten weeks in the Juárez harness plant (Anarchomex) and six weeks each in the "Santa María" harness (Particimex) and the Juárez scrub clothes (Andromex) plants, using less time as my analytic attention grew more focused over the course of the research. In each of these last three, I worked on the line for half of my period in the plant. In Santa María, I lived with one of my co-workers. In Juárez I lived alone. After leaving each of the three Juárez factories, I made several return visits to check my observations. In each of these plants, I also conducted a series of unstructured individual or small-group interviews in my home with ten of my co-workers.

9. "*Son muy liberales . . .*" In Juárez, describing U.S. women as promiscuous is a common aspect of constructing an appropriately modest "Mexican" femininity by contrast, both within and outside the maquilas (Vila 1994). Such tropes of "otherness" are a central element in structuring ethnography across borders.

10. These issues have been discussed extensively elsewhere. See Clifford (1998), Clifford and Marcus (1986), Behar and Gordon (1995), and Burawoy (1998). For an insightful and impassioned discussion of the challenges of writing what she calls "'good enough' ethnography" (28), see the first chapter of Nancy Scheper-Hughes's *Death without Weeping* (1992).

Chapter 2. Producing Women

1. Any description of the extreme gendering of contemporary transnational production runs the risk of making that process appear inevitable. Nonetheless, a quick glance at the logic of production's spread suggests precisely the opposite. In fact, as technical advances made it possible to produce over ever greater distances, one might have expected race and nationality to have taken gender's place in marking the paradigmatic exploitable worker. That this did not occur, and that gender continues to operate in tandem with these other categories, suggests the resilience of gendered categories, but not their necessity.

2. Ortner and Whitehead (1981), Scott (1988b).

3. I discuss "managers" rather than "capitalists" throughout the manuscript because, in the large corporations I deal with, owners are not involved in production decisions.

4. This inability to secure labor control externally is characteristic of capitalism and distinguishes it from other economic systems such as slavery and feudalism (Burawoy 1979).

5. Althusser (1971), p. 172.

6. What I'm calling here "the trope of productive femininity" emerged in my 1992–93 interviews and conversations with managers throughout the maquila industry—both in the plants described here and in others. Its repeated, unprompted, and practically verbatim citation was what first brought me to consider it as a trope, rather than as an empirical description. Evidence of the trope's extension, comprehensiveness, and ongoing importance in export-processing plants beyond the maquilas can be found throughout the literature

on transnational production. See Ong (1991) for a thorough review of these case studies and a discussion of the role of gender within them. For more recent examples in the maquilas, see Cravey (1998), De la O (1997), Reygadas (1992), Peña (1997), Tiano (1994), and Wright (1997, 2001). For recent examples outside Mexico, see Freeman (2000), Lee (1995, 1998), Lutz (1988), and Yelvington (1995).

7. I borrow this notion of "citation" from Judith Butler (1993b).

8. Pearson (1991) reports that Mexican officials went to Asia when designing the maquila program. Cravey (1998, p. 13) also discusses this self-conscious emulation of East Asian export factories on the part of maquila program designers.

9. Lutz (1988) has an elegant discussion of the selling of the docile image of Asian women by Asian governments and of the historical antecedents of the use of female labor. See also Carrillo and Hernández (1985), Iglesias (1985), Van Waas (1981, 1982), Tiano (1994), Cravey (1998), and Sklair (1993) for discussions of the centrality of "women" to the maquila development model.

10. I borrow this phrase from Sklair (1993, p. 177), who discusses a 1984 maquila industry seminar in which a speaker decried the scarcity of "maquiladora-grade females."

11. For instance, Harvey (1990) and Fröbel et al. (1980).

12. Kamel (1990), Fuentes and Ehrenreich (1983), Haraway (1983), Enloe (1989), Elson and Pearson (1981, 1986), Pearson (1986), Safa (1986), Standing (1989), Joekes (1985), Mies (1986), Iglesias (1985), Nash and Fernández-Kelly (1983), Tiano (1987a, 1987b), Benería and Roldán (1987).

13. See Fuentes and Ehrenreich (1983), Nash and Fernández-Kelly (1983), Frobel et al. (1980), Standing (1989), Enloe (1989), Elson and Pearson (1981, 1986), Pearson (1986), Safa (1986), Fernández-Kelly (1983), Sassen (1998a), Hossfeld (1990), Lim (1983), Barajas and Rodríguez (1990), Benería and Roldán (1987), Ong (1991), Gambrill (1981), Tiano (1987a, 1987b).

14. Frobel et al. (1980).

15. Scott (1988b), Baron (1991b, 1991c), Rose (1992).

16. Lee (1998), Freeman (2000), Cravey (1998), Wright (1997, 2001).

17. Grewal and Kaplan (1994), Sassen (1998b), Appadurai (1996).

18. See, for instance, Harvey (1990). Massey (1994) provides an elegant critique of Harvey around this issue in "Flexible Sexism."

19. The American Friends Service Committee and the Coalition for Justice in the Maquiladoras both work in this tradition. See AFSC's *Maquiladora Reader* (Kamel and Hoffman 1999) for a description of some of this activism.

20. I am indebted here to Haraway's (1988) argument that the visual is an important tool for thinking about the social, but that using it responsibly requires self-consciousness about the specific "technology" employed in looking.

21. Joan Scott's pathbreaking *Gender and the Politics of History* (1988b) came out five years after Fuentes and Ehrenreich's (1983) pamphlet.

22. Butler makes this critique in *Gender Trouble* (1990).

23. Fuentes and Ehrenreich (1983) and Standing (1989) are instances of these research strategies.

24. This managerial framework stands in stark contrast to the more recent fixation on creating malleable workforces through quality control and other

such techniques. Export-processing production would seem to be an exception to this trend; despite the current wave of "quality" rhetoric, global managers place inordinate emphasis on hiring in their public statements, for the most part omitting any discussion of internal labor control processes. This attitude is such a central element of transnational assembly that Melissa Wright (2001) describes a set of managerial claims about women workers' "untrainability" within a transnational plant ostensibly dedicated to "flexible production."

25. Taylor (1911, p. 33).

26. Braverman (1974, p. 51).

27. Braverman (1974, p. 27). In *The Politics of Production,* Burawoy (1985) provides an incisive analysis of Braverman's commitment to the "objective" rather than the "subjective" content of class.

28. Taylor (1911, p. 44), Braverman (1974, p. 104).

29. Butler (1990) describes this process in the first pages of *Gender Trouble.*

30. Taylor (1911, p. 44).

31. Foucault (1982), Althusser (1971).

32. In using the language of interpellation I am indebted to Burawoy (1979), who uses a version of this theoretical framework in analyzing the labor process. Like him, I take from Althusser the notion that subjects are constituted within social relations, and that what are often named "identities" take their meaning from these relations, and not from an inherent link to the selves so identified. On the other hand, I depart from the image that both authors present of a single discursive structure, in which each individual has but one place. To the contrary, I envision multiple interpellations here, with contradictions that make sea changes, ongoing fluctuation, and resistance comprehensible. For a similarly multiple use of the concept of interpellation, see de Lauretis (1987).

33. Leidner (1993), Edwards (1979), Kunda (1992), Hochschild (1997); also "When 'May I Help You' Is a Labor Issue: The Customer-Service Assembly Line," *New York Times,* August 12, 2000, p. C1.

34. Burawoy's analysis (1979) makes this process clear, although he slights the self in favor of analyzing what the self does. Collinson (1992) and Lee (1998) also illustrate this process in manufacturing.

35. Taylor (1911, p. 43).

36. Burawoy (1979) describes precisely such a set of practices in *Manufacturing Consent.*

37. Braverman (1974, p. 27).

38. This process of constituting docile and productive bodies through control of the most minute bodily gesture is of course a fundamental aspect of the disciplinary tactics identified by Foucault in *Discipline and Punish* (1979).

39. In Althusser's conceptualization, the subject is addressed by a single immanent discourse, and the content of the subjectivity so evoked is inherent in the relationship itself. Hence, workers emerge within class relations, believers within the church. The theory imagines no competing discourses—no pious workers, no productive churchgoers. Neither the multitude of potential actors nor the full content of emergent subjectivities can be fully grasped in this framework. Thus, we begin with Althusser, but in order to explain the consti-

tution of productive subjects, we need to rethink who speaks and what can be communicated.

40. Burawoy theorizes the interpellation of workers but not managers in *Manufacturing Consent* (1979). See Willmott (1987), Collinson and Hearn (1996), Collinson (1992), Smith (1990), and Morrill (1995) for analyses of managerial subjectivity.

41. In "The Extended Case Method," Burawoy (1998) discusses the inherent problem of "objectifying" external forces. In seeking to place managerial subjectivity within the purview of analysis, even if the analysis is by methodological necessity less thorough, I attempt to avoid this move.

42. Taylor (1911, p. 43).

43. Taylor (1911, p. 46).

44. For discussions of the constitution of national/ethnic identities through interpellatory processes, see Lie (2001, especially chap. 6) and Vila (2000, especially the appendix).

45. I use the term "identity" here and elsewhere in the manuscript to refer to the gestures by which people explicitly use categories to name themselves and others. Otherwise, following Althusser and Foucault, I use the terms "subject" and "subjectivity" to emphasize the process through which the self is externally evoked.

46. See, for instance, Rubin (1975).

47. See, for instance, Hartmann (1976, 1981).

48. See Chodorow (1978) for a classic example of this genre. See also Rubin (1975) and MacKinnon (1982) for pathbreaking arguments from the same period that attempted to explain domination and subjectivity together.

49. hooks (1984), Spelman (1988).

50. Riley (1988).

51. Butler (1990), especially chap. 2. See also Spelman (1988), hooks (1984), Scott (1988a, 1988b), Riley (1988).

52. de Lauretis (1987), Butler (1990), and Scott (1988b) all provide examples of this strategy. In this, they are following in a path trod initially by feminist anthropologists Ortner and Whitehead (1981).

53. Scott (1988b), Baron (1991b).

54. Foucault (1972).

55. Riley (1988) explicitly says she does not want to write an "intellectual history," but her actual empirical discussion fails to avoid the trap.

56. Riley (1988).

57. See, for instance, Riley (1988) and Butler (1990, 1993a).

58. This methodological focus in part reflects the legacy of early feminist anthropologists (e.g., Ortner and Whitehead 1981), whose work emphasized the varied content of gendered meaning systems, but took as a theoretical given that the relevant level of variation was that of a linguistic system or culture as a whole. Teresa de Lauretis's (1987) work is a notable exception here because of its conception of the notion of distinctive interpellatory structures that coexist in space and time. However, because de Lauretis's focus is film, her analysis does not extend to investigating this process empirically.

59. This is true even of the more materially grounded work of Joan Scott (see, for instance, 1988b, chap. 6) and more recent theorists of work (Baron 1991a, Rose 1992), whose focus on the cultural processes through which the meanings of gender and class are established in a particular period assumes that gendered meanings subsume, rather than are created within, individual work-places. Thus, their focus on public discussion leaves open the question of how gendered representations are specified and lived within particular sites.

60. I do not mean to imply here that only hands-on ethnography will do. Readings of historical materials with an ethnographic sensibility would achieve the same ends. What both these methodologies offer is a focus on the everyday, ground-level experience of gender.

61. For elegant discussions of the "fractal" nature of meaning making in general, as well as of its relationship to gender in particular, see chap. 3 of Gal and Kligman (2000) and Irvine and Gal (2000).

62. Although my focus was primarily impelled by my analysis of trans-national production, it also responded to my dismay at a long-standing popu-lar rhetoric about the intractability of Mexican gender roles in both the United States and Mexico itself. Octavio Paz's *El Laberinto de la Soledad* (1950) remains a classic statement of this set of attitudes. For a critique of this literature, see Gutmann (1994).

63. For an example of the opposite strategy, see Jennifer Pierce's *Gender Trials: Emotional Lives in Contemporary Law Firms* (1995). In a study of several workplaces, she emphasizes the way lawyers and paralegals across several law firms all enact a single set of culturally prescribed, externally generated gender roles such as "mother" or "Rambo."

64. Fuentes and Ehrenreich (1983).

65. This theoretical shift in focus is described by Scott (1988b). Cravey (1998) also describes this empirical move from masculine to feminine produc-tion "regimes."

66. For analyses of the importance of ethnography in studying globalization, see Burawoy (2000) and Marcus (1998).

67. Baudrillard (1988).

68. I am not the only scholar interested in showing these processes on the ground, of course. Ching Kwan Lee (1995, 1998) provides an elegant analysis of the centrality of gender to production and the varied gendered meanings which emerge on distinct shop floors. Unlike the argument I've made here, however, Lee focuses on the impact of the labor market and other external structures on shop-floor genders, rather than on causes within production. Aihwa Ong (1990) and Dorinne Kondo (1990) make similar arguments about the impact of exter-nal gendering on the shop floor.

69. For analyses of the masculinization of the category of breadwinner/ producer, see Kessler-Harris (1990), Collinson (1992), Willis (1979), and Halle (1984).

70. This lack of marking is typical of masculinity in general. Femininity is the marked category. Wittig (1992a, 1992b), de Beauvoir (1989).

71. See Lown (1990) for a historical analysis of the use of women as cheap labor in nineteenth-century silk manufacture in Britain. See Benería and Roldán (1987), Milkman (1987), Safa (1986), Enloe (1989, especially chap. 7), Pearson (1986), and Gordon et al. (1982) for more general discussions of the use of women as cheap labor in early industrialization.

72. Throughout the text I use the masculine pronoun when discussing maquila managers in the abstract. Most of these managers are men, and the job itself is masculinized. Using ungendered language would merely serve to obscure an empirically gendered reality.

Chapter 3. Trope Chasing

1. Fuentes and Ehrenreich (1983), p. 5.

2. The Border Industrialization Program (BIP).

3. This was at best disingenuous, since Mexican bureaucrats had already visited East Asian export-processing plants employing young female labor (Pearson 1991).

4. Baird and McCaughan (1979), Van Waas (1981).

5. INEGI (1990).

6. INEGI (1996).

7. Fernández-Kelly (1983), Carrillo and Hernández (1985).

8. The reasons for the maquilas' initial decision to hire women was the source of extensive discussion among researchers during the industry's early years. One group of analysts (Carrillo and Hernández 1985, Van Waas 1981, Tiano 1987a, 1987b) looked to the market, explaining the decision to hire women as a conscious attempt to create an industrial reserve army. This argument was made most strongly by Van Waas, who argued that these jobs were not traditionally women's jobs either in the United States or Mexico, and that therefore their feminization within the BIP was necessarily due to structural rather than "cultural" processes. Another group of analysts focusing on the gender of jobs took the opposite approach, comparing maquila jobs not to similar jobs in the United States and Mexico, but to similar industries based in Asia. They argued that Asian export-processing jobs were defined as "women's jobs," and that Mexican bureaucrats explicitly modeled themselves upon these projects (Fernández-Kelly 1983, Iglesias 1985, Gambrill 1981, Pearson 1991). Although there is no question that some maquila investors considered the benefits of increasing the pool of available labor (Carrillo and Hernández 1985, p. 88), I would argue, with the latter group, that maquila jobs were predicated upon a gendered configuration of labor power.

9. The reason for women's initial predominance in East Asian assembly work is the subject of an extensive literature. Analysts generally attribute it to women's "cheapness" and attribute this in turn to their position in the family (Safa 1986, Pearson 1991, Standing 1989). Lutz (1988) focuses instead on the circulation of images of women's docility. Although I am not attempting to ex-

plain this larger historical phenomenon here, the data suggest that such explanations are less distinct than they appear, and that women's disproportionate share of low-wage assembly is due to the way in which their familial situation is understood, used, and reconstructed by capitalist processes.

10. See Fernández-Kelly (1983), Carrillo and Hernández (1985), and Van Waas (1982) for discussion of the infamous Arthur D. Little report.

11. Baerresen (1971), p. 36.

12. Van Waas (1981), p. 346.

13. Sklair (1993) aptly terms this structure of meanings a "litany" which both describes and enforces its perspective (p. 172).

14. Interview with ex-worker. One of Iglesias's (1985) interviewees also discusses the maquilas as an alternative to working illegally on the other side of the border; she too comments on the significance of being paid in dollars. The practice of paying in dollars ended when the peso devaluation of the late seventies made the expediency of paying in pesos evident to maquila investors.

15. *El Fronterizo,* June 13, 1979. All newspaper articles dated between 1974 and 1985 come from the Centro de Orientacíon de la Mujer Obrero (COMO) archives, located on the premises of the Colegio de la Frontera Norte, Ciudad Juárez, in the early nineties.

16. Baird and McCaughan (1979), pp. 146–147.

17. Pablo Vila (2003) documents the pervasiveness of such discussions outside the formal media as well.

18. The actual number of people living in Ciudad Juárez is a matter of some dispute. The Mexican government—reputedly anxious to underestimate the population of a state controlled by the opposition—put it at roughly three-quarters of a million, whereas local business groups—interested in presenting a large, available workforce to prospective investors—put it at almost twice that number (Desarrollo Económico de Ciudad Juárez 1991). This issue is so well documented that in a handbook for prospective maquila investors, the author provided two population figures for Juárez, commenting, "There is a wide divergence between official census figures (shown first) and reliable estimates (shown in parentheses)." Baerresen (1971), p. 31.

19. For an excellent history of the establishment of the maquila program in Juárez, see Van Waas (1981) and Martínez (1978). Today, Juárez dominates the maquila industry and the industry dominates the city's economy. Although Tijuana has a larger number of maquila establishments, the Juárez industry has always been distinguished by the large size of its factories, which thus house the overwhelming bulk of Mexico's maquila employment. By the late eighties, maquilas employed 30 percent of Juárez's "economically active" population and 46 percent of its "economically active" women (Cruz Piñeiro 1990), and by 1990 its percentage of the overall EAP had risen to 35 percent (*El Diario de Juárez,* March 14, 1990). In the city, signs of maquila influence abound, from local government's obvious kowtowing to the industry, to private buses ferrying maquila workers to downtown bars on Friday afternoons, to coverage of the Señorita Maquiladora beauty contest in local newspapers' society pages.

20. Tiano (1987a, 1987b), Castellanos (1981).

21. *El Fronterizo,* June 5, 1965.

22. *El Fronterizo,* September 2, 1971.

23. Iglesias (1985), p. 70.

24. Fernández-Kelly (1983), pp. 133 and 139.

25. Martínez (1978), p. 134.

26. *Excélsior,* September 22 and 23, 1979.

27. *El Fronterizo,* October 10, 1972.

28. *El Fronterizo,* August 16, 1981, and September 12, 1981.

29. *El Correo,* June 24, 1974.

30. *El Correo,* August 27, 1977.

31. These work conditions were described by an ex-worker during a 1992 interview. They were also reported in *El Correo,* July 2, 1980. On December 17 and 18, 1980, *El Diario de Juárez* reported the story of a young male worker who was killed in the plant.

32. *El Fronterizo,* January 1, 1980.

33. *El Correo,* March 17, 1981.

34. Fernández-Kelly (1983), p. 133.

35. *El Correo,* April 22, 1974. In the same year, a series of articles refer to the large numbers of single mothers in the maquilas.

36. *El Mexicano,* August 5, 1981; *El Diario de Juárez,* August 11, 1981.

37. Unattributed clipping from the COMO archives, Ciudad Juárez, August 19, 1977.

38. *El Fronterizo,* April 17, 1978; *El Diario de Juárez,* June 30, 1978.

39. *El Correo,* May 22, 1980.

40. Reygadas (1992).

41. Although my fieldwork in Juárez did not focus on women's behavior outside the maquilas, I observed that young women workers, for the most part, controlled a good part of their salaries, and the disjuncture between the overall quiescence on shop floors and their increasing autonomy outside is difficult to miss.

42. See Wolf (1990) for an analysis of the variable impact of assembly work on women's community and familial roles. She reports divergent effects of factory work on young women's autonomy, dependent on the family structures and mores within which it takes place.

43. Carrillo (1985).

44. *El Diario de Juárez,* June 3, 1982.

45. Through the mid-eighties, the Juárez maquila industry was the scene of union conflicts over who would represent workers. Conflicts took place both between the two largest national unions, the CTM (Confederation of Mexican Workers) and the CROC (Regional Confederation of Workers and Peasants), and between them and the considerably smaller CRT (Revolutionary Confederation of Workers). The conflict at Andromex was between the CTM and one of its recently ousted leaders. He had established a local CRT branch and was attempting to reinsert himself into the Juárez union scene in this era by taking

over CTM contracts. Roughly a third of Juárez maquilas were unionized in 1987 (Carrillo and Ramírez 1990). In those that were unionized, workers generally saw little benefit, as all three Centrals operated as company unions.

46. For a detailed chronology of the conflict at Fashionmex as seen by COMO, see Beatríz Vera (n.d.). For an analysis of the "contract" see De la Rosa Hickerson (1979). Also see Carrillo and Hernández (1985), pp. 158–164.

47. For detailed histories of COMO, see Young and Vera (1984), Yudelman (1987), Kopinak (1989), and Peña (1997).

48. Fashionmex, for instance, did ultimately flee the city, leaving wages unpaid.

49. *El Correo,* November 17, 1980.

50. *El Fronterizo,* December 29, 1980.

51. *El Diario de Juárez,* July 29, 1981.

52. *El Mexicano,* August 5, 1981.

53. Jiménez (1989), p. 417.

54. Sklair (1993), p. 40.

55. INEGI (1991, 1996).

56. In the first decades of the maquiladora industry, workers seeking maquila jobs could go to the union hiring halls, from which they were sent to maquilas that requested workers. This system fell apart as the demand for workers outstripped supply. Until 1982, union complaints about insufficient employment were a fixture of Juárez public discussion, hence this headline's sarcastic tone.

57. *El Universal,* December 22, 1982.

58. *El Universal,* April 20, 1983.

59. *El Diario de Juárez,* May 24, 1983.

60. *El Universal,* April 6, 1983.

61. *El Universal,* April 20, 1983, and *El Fronterizo,* July 27, 1983. In fact, some companies did eventually seek out and hire women workers from nearby villages to avoid hiring men (see *El Universal,* June 18, 1983, and Chapter 4). As far as I can ascertain, however, no one traveled to the southern states to import migrant laborers.

62. Managerial interviews, 1992–93.

63. Jiménez (1989), pp. 422–423; Sklair (1993), p. 72.

64. Rosenbaum (1994), Santiago and Almada (1991).

65. Catanzarite and Strober (1993). *El Universal,* April 11 and February 17, 1984. Managerial interviews.

66. In the November 3, 1983, *El Universal,* AMAC (the maquiladora industry association) complained publicly that the state wouldn't permit the maquiladora industry to raise wages. Shaiken (1994, p. 58) reports similar pressures on the plants he studies. Nonetheless, industry complaints about this pressure are somewhat disingenuous. They have been the first to point out the possibilities of cheaper labor when it suits them. See Baird and McCaughan (1979, pp. 144–146) and Van Waas (1981) for an account of the tremendous (if unsuccessful) maquila campaign to lower the minimum wage in the inflationary mid-seventies, as minimum wages rose, and the multinationals' explicit references to the " 'loss

NOTES TO PAGES 42–45

of international competitiveness' of the BIP" (Van Waas, p. 245) in the service of this goal. Sklair (1993, p. 179) argues that the reasons for low maquila wages are less Byzantine than the industry argues, and that ultimately the maquilas have simply found turnover to be cheaper than wage increases.

67. In an industry conference in 1990, industry representatives claimed that they did not raise base salaries to avoid undercutting other economic sectors in the city (*El Diario de Juárez*, March 28, 1990).

68. Home offices generally insist that their third-world outposts pay "prevailing wages" (managerial interviews). Shaiken (1994, p. 58) also reports such pressures.

69. Jiménez (1989), p. 424.

70. *Twin Plant News* 3 (10), May 1988.

71. *El Diario de Juárez*, July 2, 1985, June 8, 1986.

72. *El Diario de Juárez*, April 20, 1988.

73. *Twin Plant News* 3 (10), May 1988, p. 8.

74. Shaiken (1990, p. 99) reports that although maquilas "would clearly like to reduce turnover, they have structured work in a way where transience in the production work force has a minimal negative impact." The highly fragmented labor process he refers to here pervades the industry. Just as complaints about labor shortages must be understood within the context of the decision not to raise wages, so complaints about turnover must be understood within the context of the decision not to introduce seniority systems.

75. *El Diario de Juárez*, February 5, 1984.

76. Panoptimex supervisor, 1992.

77. Managerial interviews, 1992–93.

78. *El Universal*, November 10, 1983.

79. *El Universal*, February 17, 1984.

80. *El Fronterizo*, August 31, 1983. Senior women workers in Andromex also told me they had teased new male workers during this period.

81. On September 5, 1983, amid the maquila "labor shortage," Banamex announced that unemployment was soaring in the city as a whole *(El Fronterizo)*.

82. *El Diario de Juárez*, June 11, 1983.

83. *El Diario de Juárez*, March 30, 1983.

84. *El Diario de Juárez*, August 23, 1983.

85. *El Diario de Juárez*, March 30, 1983.

86. Review of COMO archives.

87. By 1989, AMAC statistics were showing an average of a 144 percent turnover annually.

88. *El Diario de Juárez*, September 14, 1987, January 25, 1988, June 17, 1989, March 28, 1990, October 20, 1990.

89. *El Diario de Juárez*, April 1, 1989, November 29, 1989.

90. *El Diario de Juárez*, September 18, 1990.

91. *El Diario de Juárez*, October 11, 1990.

92. Not surprisingly, there is little evidence that either senior citizens or disabled workers were ever hired in large numbers.

93. *El Diario de Juárez*, May 27, 1989, November 29, 1989, August 27, 1990.

94. *El Diario de Juárez*, May 14, 1988.

95. *El Fronterizo*, May 31, 1983.

96. *El Diario de Juárez*, May 14, 1988.

97. Review of *El Diario de Juárez* archives.

98. INEGI (1991). These levels remained stable throughout the years of my fieldwork in the industry (INEGI 1996).

99. See, for example, De la O (1991, 1997), Quintero (1992), Jiménez (1989, p. 401–402), and Peña (1997), who focus on the gendering of work. They argue that low-level assembly work continues to be feminized, but that as the number of technical and other skilled jobs, traditionally understood as male, has increased, so has the number of men employed overall. Although they are undoubtedly correct about increases in the number of such jobs, the explanation cannot account for the surge in male workers in nontechnical, unskilled jobs throughout the industry (see Chapters 6 and 7). Brannon and Lucker (1989), Jiménez (1989), and Catanzarite and Strober (1993) emphasize market structure. Brannon and Lucker (1989) and Jiménez (1989, p. 403) argue that as the maquila boom demanded increasing numbers of workers, desperate employers became willing to hire previously unacceptable job applicants. Catanzarite and Strober (1993) argue that, following the economic crisis of 1982, as other, better paying possibilities disappeared, desperate male workers became willing to take previously unacceptably "feminine" maquila jobs. Here, I argue with Jiménez that gendered meanings structure and constitute the labor market; hence a complete explanation must include both types of analyses.

100. Catanzarite and Strober (1993) do in fact assert that, by the late eighties, maquila work was no longer feminized. My own research shows no support for this conclusion. In interviews, managers constantly referred to their preference for women workers, generally referencing their purportedly greater patience, tolerance for boredom, and shop-floor malleability.

101. See Chapter 2, note 10.

102. *El Diario de Juárez*, June 28, 1985.

103. A recession in the United States in 1991 halted industry expansion until the next peso devaluation in 1994, after I had finished my fieldwork.

104. *El Diario de Juárez*, July 2, 1985, June 8, 1986.

105. *El Diario de Juárez*, June 8, 1986, January 2, 1989.

106. *El Diario de Juárez*, June 7, 1989.

107. *El Diario de Juárez*, July 24, 1989.

108. *El Diario de Juárez*, December 20, 1989.

109. *El Diario de Juárez*, February 18, 1991.

110. *El Diario de Juárez*, January 2, 1989.

111. *El Diario de Juárez*, May 14, 1988.

112. *El Diario de Juárez*, February 18, 1991.

113. *El Diario de Juárez*, March 10, 1991.

114. This comment, made during a 1993 interview, is remarkably similar to Sklair's (1993) argument that "once the image of the 'ideal' maquila worker is institutionalized and accepted by the working-class along the border, the need

to employ women in preference to men diminishes, and job opportunities for docile, undemanding, nimble-fingered, nonunion and unmilitant men open up" (p. 173).

115. Managerial interviews, 1992–93.

Chapter 4. Bringing Fantasies to Life

1. Berger (1972), Mulvey (1975).

2. For an analysis focusing directly on the role of sexuality in Panoptimex, see Salzinger (2000). See Loe (1996), Rogers and Henson (1997), and Guiffre and Williams (1994) for ethnographic analyses in a similar vein. See Williams (1997) for a general theoretical discussion of the subject.

3. Lisa Rofel (1992) has an elegant discussion of the use of space in shop-floor control and its relationship to larger meanings.

4. In discussing Panoptimex, I will restrict myself to analyzing the dynamics in first shift. Second shift is often different from first; however, in this plant the differences are accentuated by the centrality of visual control, as the absence of top managers behind the shop-floor windows provides a very different context within which control is struggled over and (more tenuously) established.

5. The structure of production on any given shop floor is initially imagined and established by management. In the maquila industry, where capital faces a disorganized workforce and a captive state apparatus, this situation is particularly acute. These first decisions do not ensure managerial control, but they do set the context within which struggles over control will take place. Thus, in analyzing the role of gender in production, in each case study I turn first to the frameworks within which managerial "common sense" is established and to the strategies that emerge from this cluster of understandings.

6. Like most maquila managers in Ciudad Juárez, Panoptimex managers propose a budget to their U.S. superiors. Once the budget is accepted, their task is to spend no more than projected to assemble the promised quantity of goods. Spending more is considered a failure. But spending less is penalized as well, since the response is a smaller budget in the following fiscal year.

7. See Burawoy and Lukács (1992, especially chap. 3) for a discussion of the "inefficiencies" of production within large corporations and for an analysis of the similarity of these production systems to the dynamics of production under socialism.

8. In Panoptimex, Jones's refusal to let me work had the unexpected benefit of giving me extremely good access to management. In all the plants I studied, I interviewed the managers, sometimes quite casually, but only in Panoptimex was I able to observe managerial meetings. Once I had donned a worker's uniform in the other plants, even if my work on the line was relatively brief, attendance at managerial meetings felt inappropriate—not only to the managers, who didn't invite me, but to me as well.

9. The reasons for electronics maquilas' disproportionate capacity to attract

women are complex (Tiano 1994, Cravey 1998). The work is done sitting and is relatively "clean," both attributes which are understood and framed as feminine by managers and workers throughout the industry. These characteristics also make it possible to work in high heels and delicate fabrics, and this reinforces the initial attribution of femininity. In addition, electronics plants paid somewhat better than other maquilas in the industry's early years (Fernández-Kelly 1983), and this has left them with an image that makes recruitment easier overall. Nonetheless, throughout the eighties, hiring anyone, male or female, was difficult for all branches of the industry, and most electronics plants hired a far higher proportion of male workers than did Panoptimex.

10. The current plant manager is a notable and not terribly credible exception to this pattern. Having decided upon first meeting me that as an American woman I am an advocate of "gender blindness," he eschews any consciousness of gender in conversation with me, repeating that nothing matters but the will to work. After one of our interviews, he is so concerned to prove this that he begins badgering Jones to hire a blind man. Jones later complains to me that Carlos came to him with some "tomfool" idea. An older American man heading for retirement and not looking to please, Jones does not seriously consider the request. The head of personnel is more tactful about her boss, but makes her skepticism obvious when I mention his ostensibly gender-blind stance. Her response comes as no surprise, as Carlos's clear and not exactly disinterested preference for young women makes up an ongoing thread of personnel office gossip.

11. See Rosenbaum's *Market Basket Survey* (1994) for an analysis of the gap between maquila salaries in general and the cost of living in Mexico's border cities. Young and Vera (1992) argue that maquila workers earn less than service workers with similar backgrounds.

12. Wages are supplemented by a variety of coupons (for lunch and transportation, for instance), as well as by yearly bonuses. This brings the real value closer to US$50 weekly. Even with these additions, however, pay remains low for Juárez. Some workers supplement their income by selling candy, jewelry, makeup, and other items illicitly on the shop floor. This is difficult in chassis, but relatively easy for group leaders and those in certain positions in final. Management doesn't interfere unless the informal trading becomes too blatant. As a wage subsidy, it has its advantages for them too.

13. Since the collapse of the peso in 1994, the dollar value of maquila wages has fallen still further. Here and elsewhere in the narrative, I discuss wages as they were during the period I was doing fieldwork in Juárez.

14. There is one female supervisor, but she is on second shift.

15. Group leaders in turn are aided by assistants—relatively experienced women workers who cover for workers who need to take a bathroom break. Although they have no official supervisory authority at all, they can easily make workers' lives miserable by refusing to cover for them, so they are generally treated with some care on the line.

16. During my first conversation with the American head of production, he commented blandly, "What they call a union here, we have no problem with."

17. This term is used by Burawoy in his pathbreaking *Manufacturing Con-*

sent (1979, p. 150) in his contention that places, not their occupants, matter in labor control.

18. Butler (1990, 1993a).

19. This incident is so egregious from this young man's perspective because normally, in Spanish, if just one man is present, the whole group is referred to in the masculine.

20. See Auslander (1996, chap. 6) for a subtle analysis of the way in which men's commitment to a particular mode of masculinity can undercut their capacity to advocate for themselves as producers.

21. This gendered focus also emerges in the plant news sheet, where the joke of the week virtually always deals with gender, from cuckolding women to an employer looking for married men "because they know how to obey."

22. Critiques of the physical objectification of women have been a staple of feminist theory since its inception (MacKinnon 1982; Mulvey 1975). Feminist analysis of its troubling pleasures have been less developed. Two authors who do discuss this are Chancer (1998) and Steele (1985).

23. Baudrillard (1988).

Chapter 5. Re-forming the "Traditional Mexican Woman"

1. Santa María is a fictitious name for a small agricultural city near Chihuahua.

2. Here, obviously, the fact that I am American rather than Mexican mattered. In interviews with managers throughout the industry, my North American interviewees explicitly addressed me as one of "us," comfortable discussing "them."

3. See Vila (2000) for an extended discussion of the relationship of region and identity along the border.

4. Scott (1988b).

5. Gutmann (1994).

6. Although all the maquilas work within large corporations and therefore operate within "soft" budget constraints (for a more general analysis of these dynamics see Burawoy 1992 and Lukács, chap. 3), this structure is particularly accentuated in Particimex because of the Juárez-based layer of management that intervenes between the local plant manager and corporate headquarters in the United States.

7. Even in the majority of plants which have American plant managers, personnel departments are generally headed by Mexicans.

8. For two excellent reviews of new production systems, see Smith (1997) and Applebaum and Batt (1994). For a critique of the impact of "team work" on workers, see Parker and Slaughter (1988). For reviews of new production models in the maquilas and discussions of their local logic, see Carrillo and Ramírez (1992), Wilson (1990), and Shaiken (1994).

9. I of course made clear to Gianini that I would not provide more than very general impressions, and that I would not communicate anything to him that I had not communicated to managers in the plants themselves. Perhaps the most interesting aspect of this deal was how entirely uninterested he ultimately proved to be in my feedback. This turned out to be a common theme. Although I spent a good deal of time watching production, and was always worried managers would ask questions I would have to refuse to answer, in fact, they never really asked anything. Managerial questions were invariably an excuse to provide me with their own accounts, not to hear mine. I expect that this is not an uncommon fieldwork experience.

10. For other descriptions of systems of labor control based on a reconfiguration of the self, see Leidner (1993), Kunda (1992), Kondo (1990), Burawoy (1979), and Edwards (1979). For a more general discussion of such systems of social control, see Foucault (1977).

11. In making these complaints, managers reinstate and instantiate their basic, internal "Mexican-ness."

12. Supervisors are particularly vocal about the challenges of involving people in participatory management without direct economic compensations. See Biewener (n.d.) for a fuller theoretical discussion of this issue.

13. *Quinceañeras* are elaborate coming-out parties for fifteen-year-old girls.

14. As elsewhere in the text, in discussing turnover, I am referring here not to managerially determined layoffs, but to worker-initiated departures.

15. This also reflects a more general Autoworld practice. The transnational has strict policies regarding sexual harassment throughout its Mexican operations. At Autoworld, unlike most other maquilas, supervisors are actually fired if they are discovered having affairs with their workers and refuse to call them off. Supervisors in Particimex tell the story of a supervisor who was fired from a plant in a city nearby because he refused to end an affair with a worker.

16. Maquilas routinely and openly test women for pregnancy prior to hiring. The practice violates Mexican law and has been hard fought by local and international labor organizations.

17. I have focused here on the way in which community and family life affects women's experiences on the shop floor. Given the still-new experience of factory life, the impact of assembly work on women's roles in the community is still unclear. Most seem to keep substantial control of their wages, suggesting that over time, external gender relationships may well shift. See Wolf (1990) for discussion of how the impact of assembly work on young women workers' role outside the factory varies depending on prevailing cultural norms regarding their economic responsibilities to their parents.

18. The apparent contradiction between the relatively large proportion of coordinators and supports who are women and the comparatively low chance that women will be chosen to fill these positions when men are available is explained by the fact that their overwhelming numerical superiority means that many production teams have no male members at all. In these teams, women indeed take on those roles.

Chapter 6. Manufacturing "Workers"

1. Sklair (1993) argues convincingly that once the feminization of maquila work is sufficiently established, men can be brought in to the plants under "feminized" conditions. I am taking this further and arguing that, since gender differences always operate through contrasts, once work is truly feminized, it becomes possible to identify production in a particular plant as "men's work" (this being a relative category) without ceding much control or spending much money.

2. In previous analyses (see Salzinger 1997, 1998), I argued that this shop floor was ungendered because it was organized around the explicitly ungendered category of "worker." After going back through the data and rethinking the history of the category of worker itself, I am convinced that this analysis was incorrect. Although gender indeed operates quite differently in this plant than it does in the other plants I studied, it is gendered nonetheless. That masculinity is not actually cited is less a function of its unimportance than it is symptomatic of differences in the operation of masculinity and femininity. In my previous analyses, I took the category of "worker" too much at face value. However, given the long history of masculinization of the categories of breadwinner and producer, being interpellated as a "worker" in this context is itself a process of masculinization. Although I would still argue that an ungendered shop floor is theoretically conceivable, the historical relationship of masculinity and paid work (see Kessler-Harris 1990) would make its emergence even more difficult than I originally theorized.

3. See Wittig for a discussion of the masculine "appropriation of the universal" (1992a, p. 80) and conflation with the general (1992b, p. 60) and of the corollary injunction to mark the feminine. It is no accident that feminization is overt and masculinization implicit in these plants.

4. The notion of a "hegemonic regime" comes from Burawoy's *Manufacturing Consent* (1979). However, Burawoy focuses on the constitution of workers (class members) as individuals through the organization of the labor process as a game. Like Burawoy (1979), I find a system in which productive subjects are evoked through struggle over details within a framework set by management. However, in Andromex, fighting is so stylized and so highly prized that the emergent subject is fundamentally masculinized. This might in fact be true in Burawoy's case as well, but evaluating this would require not simply a new analysis, but data not available to a reader given the focus of his ethnographic attention in the field.

5. Even the current plant manager says salaries were "a pittance."

6. COMO, the local grassroots organization of women workers, was particularly scathing about the bad faith of both parties (*El Diario de Juárez*, September 25, 1980).

7. This was one of several lengthy strikes that occurred in this period (see Peña 1997 and Vera n.d.). See Chapter 3, note 45, for a discussion of the unions involved. See Van Waas (1981) for a full discussion of the strike itself.

8. The narrative that follows is based on local newspaper accounts archived in the COMO collection, Colegio de la Frontera Norte, Ciudad Juárez.

9. Andromex's hegemonic regime is particularly striking because it has been established outside the context of the state structures, such as social insurance and labor regulation (Burawoy 1985, p. 126), that were supposed to make such a regime possible. Its emergence here suggests that regimes of labor control may be less subject to strictly material conditions than was originally theorized, and that individual managers may have an array of internal logics that would lead them to create such a system, even in the absence of external pressures.

10. *El Diario de Juárez,* September 19, 1980.

11. The understanding of these jobs as "women's jobs" was as tenacious among workers as it was among managers. During the first years after men began working, management encountered so much resistance and discomfort on the shop floor that they had to keep men and women in separate lines. A woman who worked in the plant at the time recounted that she and her co-workers would go and stand staring at the men working. She explained, "When I first began working with men, it was very hard. This was . . . light work, for women. It seemed very weird to all of us." The union head recalls, "At first, the men showed up really shy and the women shouted *piropos* [flattering and flirtatious remarks, generally yelled by men at women] at them." A group chief told me she had saved the first payroll with men on it, it had struck her as so strange and historic an occasion.

12. *El Fronterizo,* December 29, 1980.

13. "Burn" (*quemar*) is slang for being marked or discredited. In this context, it simultaneously refers to being embarrassed and ridiculed in the community as women, and to being marked as bad workers among industry employers.

14. *El Conversador,* November 1985.

15. Gómez argues that this distinction can be seen in the structure of the corporation. In the large auto manufacturers, the vice president of manufacturing is the most important of the VPs, whereas in Pharmaworld, the vice president of sales holds that status.

16. Edwards (1979) and Milkman (1987) both argue that low capital-intensive industries—such as sewing—tend to employ piecework as a mode of labor control because they lack machines capable of enforcing production speed unilaterally. Whether or not the situation is this overdetermined, the initial level of capital intensivity often sets a pattern of labor control, and this history goes on to have profound effects on what seems reasonable and possible to later managerial strategists. This seems to be the case in sewing.

17. Willis (1979) provides an incisive description of this form of shop-floor masculinity. See also Collinson (1992) and Halle (1984). Knights (1990) and Davies (1990) both suggest that this is what Burawoy sees at work in *Manufacturing Consent,* but that he ignores its gendered dimensions.

18. This of course is not simply an idiosyncrasy of Andromex; it is typical of garment factories overall.

19. Although I remain convinced, Gómez adamantly disagrees that these structural factors affect his clout in plant headquarters, attributing his unusual autonomy to his own capacity to negotiate work relationships.

20. NAFTA was already much discussed in the period during which I did my fieldwork, and managers were already planning to shift production to Juárez as soon as they were legally able to.

21. *Guey* is a slang form of the word *buey*, meaning "ox" (beast of burden), and is used in conversation the way "man" is in English. *Jale* marks masculinized work. *Lana* means cash or "dough." All are used widely in informal conversation, but are particularly typical of working-class men's speech in the area.

22. A friend of mine from an elite family in Juárez laughs when I mention Gómez's surprising ascent, saying that their families socialized together when she was a girl and that they'd been friends during his initial stint in TVA.

23. *Güero* generally means "blondie." It can also, less commonly, refer to skin color. Gómez has dark hair and somewhat fair skin. In this context, use of this term, although obviously not interpreted as such by him, marks him as elite on the basis of his skin color.

24. Burawoy (1979) explores how the experience of doing piecework can "manufacture consent." He does not ask if the process is gendered.

25. Company newsletter, *El Conversador,* November 1985.

26. With my own eye for gender markings, I find myself coveting a "feminine" white cap within weeks of my arrival. I never manage to get one.

27. The impact of the disjuncture between uniformed and ununiformed bodies was brought quite literally home to me during an (ununiformed) afternoon interview with a male co-worker from Andromex when he suddenly tried to kiss me. I had interviewed male co-workers from the other maquilas with no similar incidents or even tensions.

28. This of course is not entirely true. Group chiefs do request particular genders. Nonetheless, because these preferences are so idiosyncratic, they are not reflected in an overall job gendering in the plant.

29. Simone de Beauvoir put this elegantly when she wrote half a century ago, "Man represents both the positive and the neutral, as is indicated by the common use of *man* to designate human beings in general; whereas woman represents only the negative, defined by limiting criteria" (1989, xxi). See also Wittig (1992b, 1992a) and Kimmel (1994, p. 126).

30. Cravey (1998) points out that in the Mexican heartland, the model of production is similar to that in the United States.

31. See Burawoy (1979), Willis (1979), Collinson (1992), Kessler-Harris (1990), Halle (1984).

32. See Chapter 2, note 61.

Chapter 7. Gendered Meanings in Contention

1. See Burawoy (1979) for a full description of the sort of production regime to which Smith had become accustomed.

2. This is one of several incidents in which the costs of Smith's weak Spanish become evident.

3. In Anarchomex, everyone goes to get paid as a group, and not surprisingly, my salary immediately becomes raw material for the fundamental shop-floor business of teasing. "At least it pays for gas," my co-workers comment acidly, making explicit note of the differential importance the money plays in their lives and mine.

4. Smith is not alone in these attitudes in Autoworld as a whole. The corporation runs a language institute in the United States for American managers, staffed by old army trainers. Along with language, they teach "cultural literacy." When explaining this aspect of the training, Gianini gives handling bribes as a prime example of teaching about Mexican culture.

5. This belief that women are the answer to shop-floor problems is pervasive in Juárez's Autoworld plants overall. After a wildcat strike in a nearby Autoworld harness plant, managers' first solution is to hire more women workers.

6. Fernández-Kelly (1983), Iglesias (1985), Tiano (1994).

7. Karen Hossfeld (1990, p. 163) came across a similar ideological framework in her interviews with employers in high-tech Silicon Valley factories. "Employers repeatedly asserted that they believed the low-level jobs were filled only by women because men could not afford to or would not work for such low wages."

8. Milkman (1987) uses the term "idioms" to describe the gendered language through which managers describe decisions around job gendering. This formulation implies that categories such as the trope of productive femininity are merely post hoc rationalizations, and thus that they always fit by definition. I am arguing here that such descriptions are constitutive as well as opportunistic, and therefore can misportray as well as justify job gendering.

9. Although the plants don't formally coordinate wages, big corporations make an effort to be in a top range. Hence, despite differences in the way in which various aspects of the wage packet are calculated, plants like Panoptimex and Anarchomex pay almost identically in total.

10. See Chapter 4, note 11.

11. Gianini explains this policy: "Personnel wants to hire bombshells, gorgeous women. You get a supervisor with a concubine, three to four girls on the line and they find out about each other . . . it could shut down the whole line."

12. Farnsworth-Alvear (1997, p. 171) describes another factory where worker interaction is ultimately about each other and not about production. She suggests that this is not "resistance," but that it nonetheless "combated the very basis of industrial discipline." I am trying to capture a similar situation here.

13. See Foucault (1979) for a discussion of the differential efficacy of "punitive" versus "disciplinary" modes of control.

14. Gottfried and Graham (1993) describe a Japanese transplant in which managerial attempts to refashion production inadvertently undercut the work's masculine texture. The language used by male workers to respond to this situation is remarkably similar to that which I report here.

15. This is one of the many conversations where I play as the symbolic "feminist." This is due not only to my own comments, but to the general linkage made along the Mexican side of the border between American women and dogmatic claims about gender equality.

Chapter 8. Why Femininity(ies)?

1. For a discussion of the various ways in which feminists have theorized this structure, see Butler (1990, chap. 1).

2. Ortner (1989) makes this point in an elegant discussion of a set of classic anthropological studies.

3. Foucault (1977).

4. See Chapter 2, note 71.

5. See for, instance, Gordon et al. (1982) and Milkman (1987). Enloe (1989, p. 160) also notes the slippage between references to women and "cheap labor." Pearson (1986, p. 449) felicitously describes the process of creating women as cheap labor within export processing as "the greening of women's labor."

6. Lutz (1988) makes a similar argument in a compelling analysis of the creation of Asian women as cheap labor.

7. See Chapter 2, note 6.

8. Frobel et al. (1980).

9. See Frobel et al. (1980), Pearson (1991), Fuentes and Ehrenreich (1983), and Lutz (1988) for examples.

10. Kessler-Harris (1990).

11. The centrality of structures of "heteronormativity" for understanding gender has been much discussed in recent years (see for instance Butler 1990, 1993a). For a discussion of the importance of this recognition in sociology see Ingraham (1994).

12. In a meticulous case study, Judy Lown (1990) documents these links as they emerged over the course of early industrialization.

13. Both Wittig (1992b, 1992a) and de Beauvoir (1989) present this duality as an inherent aspect of gender. Riley (1988) and Nicholson's (1995) more historical accounts both illustrate that these are contingent, if long-standing, social productions, and argue that they emerged in western thought over the course of the last three centuries.

14. See Gal and Kligman (2000), especially chap. 6, for a similar discussion of "differential rates of change within the realm of gender relations" (p. 112).

15. The stability (or instability, for that matter) of gendered meaning struc-

tures may also be a consequence of factors other than extension, such as their fit with other reigning structures.

16. Foucault (1972).

17. In all industries, managers play a crucial role in structuring the shop floor, but in some contexts they share this role with labor and/or the state. In the maquila industry, where state mechanisms are at the disposal of the transnationals and worker organizations are weak or nonexistent, managers frame the context within which production takes place. In another industry, one might need to focus as well on the subjectivity of bureaucrats or union leaders.

18. This tendency to focus exclusively either on structure or agency is visible in the literature as well. See Piore and Sabel (1984) for an example of the former problem and Applebaum and Batt (1994) for an instance of the latter. Collinson (1992), Fligstein (1990, p. 4), Knights (1990), and Smith (1990, pp. 91–93) note this problem as well.

19. An important body of empirical work has begun to emerge in this area. The work of British sociologists is particularly well developed in the analysis of subjectivity at work generally (see Knights 1990, Knights and Willmott 1989), although their framework is somewhat more psychological and less focused on the social than what I offer here. Their analyses of management, seen through this lens, are particularly strong. See Willmott (1987), Collinson (1992), and Collinson and Hearn (1996). In the United States, Smith (1990) provides an insightful analysis of the constitution of managerial interests, although she is more concerned with what managers do than how they see, while Morrill (1995) offers a powerful analysis of cultural meanings while ignoring questions of managerial location. The present analysis builds on these emerging literatures.

20. Sayer and Walker (1992) move in this direction at a more general level when they argue that managers have differently located interests than do capitalists, placing more emphasis on control and less on profits.

21. Wright (2001) provides an insightful discussion of managerial subjectivity in an article on maquila supervision practices.

22. It might make more sense to say "masculinity" rather than "gender," when discussing managerial subjectivity. In the maquila sector, the historically developed links between masculinity and management operate at full force. See Collinson and Hearn (1996), especially chaps. 1–5, for a discussion of this issue. Nonetheless, I use the term "gender" in order to leave open the theoretical possibility of something different.

23. Fifty percent of Andromex's workforce and 60 percent of Anarchomex's workforce are men, although the central production area in Andromex, where I located myself, was 70 percent men.

24. Panoptimex's few male workers are similarly feminized, evoking a desperate determination to convince management of their essential masculinity. Here a comparison with Anarchomex is also fruitful. Whereas Anarchomex workers are primarily left to their own devices, Panoptimex workers are actively addressed on the shop floor. Hence, managerial disrespect produces resistance in the former context and desperate attempts at repair in the latter.

25. Haraway (1988).

26. Nader (1999 [1969]).

27. The most famous of these was Esther Boserup (1970), whose *Woman's Role in Economic Development* became a foil for much of the later literature.

28. Catherine MacKinnon's (1982) "Feminism, Marxism, Method and the State" is an explicit instance of a feminist theory inspired by Marx's form, not content, but there are many other versions.

29. Freire (1971).

30. Peña (1997) provides an extensive, in-depth discussion of COMO's methodology.

31. For a description of some of these efforts, see the American Friends Service Committee's *The Maquiladora Reader* (Kamel and Hoffman 1999).

32. For examples of these organizing innovations outside the maquilas, see Bronfenbrenner et al. (1998).

33. The problems that emerge from such frameworks are predictable. For instance, a cross-border delegation of union activists from the United States was deeply disturbed by the frivolous dress, high heels, and elaborate makeup used by women in the plant they toured. A deeper understanding of the way in which such femininities come to be would have made discussion and reflection both more possible and more fruitful.

34. See Salzinger (2000) for a fuller discussion of the issue of "sexual harassment" in Panoptimex.

35. See Kamel and Hoffman (1999) for examples of this work.

36. Personal conversations with a CFO organizer about her experiences as a worker in the industry's early years (summer 1993).

37. I was struck by this similarity in watching Frente Auténtico de Trabajo (FAT) organizing efforts during the summer of 1993.

38. This of course was the work demanded by consciousness-raising in the seventies.

39. Although their analyses tend to be more sophisticated than those implicit in the popular "nature" metaphors, globalization theorists also tend to neglect the role of subjectivities when they move from discussing culture or identities to analyzing production (see Harvey 1990, Arrighi 1994, Frobel et al. 1980).

40. See Burawoy (1998) for an insightful discussion of the way in which ethnography, in focusing on a particular site, necessarily reproduces this social process by "objectifying" social "forces." See Marcus (1998) for a discussion of ways to study globalization which attempt to avoid this pitfall.

References

Acker, Joan. 1990. "Hierarchies, Jobs, Bodies: A Theory of Gendered Organizations." *Gender and Society* 4 (2): 139–158.

Althusser, Louis. 1971. "Ideology and Ideological State Apparatuses (Notes towards an Investigation)." In *Lenin and Philosophy and Other Essays*, 127–186. New York: Monthly Review Press.

Appadurai, Arjun. 1996. *Modernity at Large: Cultural Dimensions of Globalization*. Minneapolis: University of Minnesota Press.

Applebaum, Eileen, and Rosemary Batt. 1994. *The New American Workplace: Transforming Work Systems in the United States*. Ithaca: ILR Press.

Arrighi, Giovanni. 1994. *The Long Twentieth Century: Money, Power and the Origins of Our Times*. London: Verso.

Asociación de Maquiladoras A.C. (AMAC). 1989. "Analysis [of] Turnover." Internal document.

Auslander, Leora. 1996. *Taste and Power: Furnishing Modern France*. Berkeley: University of California Press.

Baerresen, Donald. 1971. *The Border Industrialization Program of Mexico*. Lexington, Mass.: Heath Lexington Books.

Baird, Peter, and Ed McCaughan. 1979. *Beyond the Border*. New York: North American Congress on Latin America.

Barajas Escamilla, Rocío, and Carmen Rodríguez Carrillo. 1990. "La mujer ante la reconversión productiva: El caso de la maquiladora electrónica." Paper presented at "Los empresarios y la apertura comercial," seminar, Fundación Freidrich Ebert, Nuevo León.

Baron, Ava. 1991a. "An 'Other' Side of Gender Antagonism at Work." In *Work Engendered: Toward a New History of American Labor*, edited by Ava Baron, 47–69. Ithaca: Cornell University Press.

———. 1991b. "Gender and Labor History: Learning from the Past, Looking to the Future." In *Work Engendered: Toward a New History of American Labor*, edited by Ava Baron, 1–46. Ithaca: Cornell University Press.

————, ed. 1991c. *Work Engendered: Toward a New History of American Labor.* Ithaca: Cornell University Press.

Baudrillard, Jean. 1988. "Simulacra and Simulations." In *Jean Baudrillard: Selected Writings,* edited by Mark Poster, 166–184. Stanford: Stanford University Press.

Beauvoir, Simone de. 1989 [1949]. *The Second Sex.* New York: Vintage Books.

Behar, Ruth, and Deborah Gordon, eds. 1995. *Women Writing Culture.* Berkeley: University of California Press.

Benería, Lourdes, and Martha Roldán. 1987. *The Crossroads of Class and Gender.* Chicago: University of Chicago Press.

Berger, John. 1972. *Ways of Seeing.* Middlesex: British Broadcasting Corporation.

Biewener, Judith. n.d. "Worker Participation in the United States." Unpublished manuscript. Berkeley Roundtable on the International Economy, Berkeley.

Boserup, Esther. 1970. *Woman's Role in Economic Development.* New York: St. Martin's.

Brannon, Jeffery, and William Lucker. 1989. "The Impact of Mexico's Economic Crisis on the Demographic Composition of the Maquiladora Labor Force." *Journal of Borderlands Studies* 4 (1): 39–70.

Braverman, Harry. 1974. *Labor and Monopoly Capital: The Degradation of Work in the Twentieth Century.* New York: Monthly Review Press.

Bronfenbrenner, Kate, et al., eds. 1998. *Organizing to Win: New Research on Union Strategies.* Ithaca: Cornell University Press.

Burawoy, Michael. 1979. *Manufacturing Consent.* Chicago: University of Chicago Press.

————. 1985. *The Politics of Production: Factory Regimes under Capitalism and Socialism.* London: Verso.

————. 1998. "The Extended Case Method." *Sociological Theory* 16 (1): 4–33.

————. 2000. "Introduction: Reaching for the Global." In *Global Ethnography: Forces, Connections and Imaginations in a Postmodern World,* edited by Michael Burawoy et al., 1–40. Berkeley: University of California Press.

Burawoy, Michael, and János Lukács. 1992. *The Radiant Past: Ideology and Reality in Hungary's Road to Capitalism.* Chicago: University of Chicago Press.

Butler, Judith. 1990. *Gender Trouble: Feminism and the Subversion of Identity.* New York: Routledge.

————. 1993a. *Bodies that Matter: On the Discursive Limits of "Sex."* New York: Routledge.

————. 1993b. "Introduction." In *Bodies that Matter: On the Discursive Limits of "Sex."* New York: Routledge.

Carrillo, Jorge. 1985. *Conflictos laborales en la industria maquiladora.* Tijuana: Centro de Estudios Fronterizos del Norte de México.

Carrillo, Jorge, and Alberto Hernández. 1985. *Mujeres fronterizas en la industria maquiladora.* Tijuana: Centro de Estudios Fronterizos del Norte de México.

Carrillo, Jorge, and Miguel Angel Ramírez. 1990. "Maquiladoras en la frontera norte: Opinión sobre los sindicatos." *Frontera Norte* 2 (4): 121–152.

———. 1992. "Nuevas tecnologías en la industria maquiladora: Una aproximación empírica a sus efectos laborales." Paper presented at the Association of Borderland Scholars, El Paso.

Carrillo, Jorge, and Jorge Santibáñez. 1992. "Determinantes de la rotación de personal en las maquiladoras de Tijuana." Paper presented at COLEF II, Tijuana, Mexico.

Castellanos Guerrero, Alicia. 1981. *Ciudad Juárez: La vida fronteriza*. Mexico City: Nuestro Tiempo.

Catanzarite, Lisa, and Myra Strober. 1993. "The Gender Recomposition of the Maquiladora Labor Force." *Industrial Relations* 32 (1): 133–147.

Centro de Orientación de la Mujer Obrero, A.C. (COMO). n.d. *Manual de la mujer obrera*. Ciudad Juárez: COMO.

Chancer, Lynn. 1998. "The Beauty Context: Looks, Social Theory and Feminism." In *Reconcilable Differences: Confronting Beauty, Pornography and the Future of Feminism*, 82–172. Berkeley: University of California Press.

Chodorow, Nancy. 1978. *The Reproduction of Mothering: Psychoanalysis and the Sociology of Gender*. Berkeley: University of California Press.

Clifford, James. 1988. *The Predicament of Culture: Twentieth-Century Ethnography, Literature and Art*. Cambridge: Harvard University Press.

Clifford, James, and George Marcus. 1986. *Writing Culture: The Poetics and Politics of Ethnography*. Berkeley: University of California Press.

Collinson, David. 1992. *Managing the Shopfloor: Subjectivity, Masculinity and Workplace Culture*. New York: Walter de Gruyter.

Collinson, David, and Jeff Hearn, eds. 1996. *Men as Managers, Managers as Men: Critical Perspectives on Men, Masculinities and Management*. London: Sage.

Comaroff, John, and Jean Comaroff. 1992. "Ethnography and the Historical Imagination." In *Ethnography and the Historical Imagination*, 3–48. Boulder: Westview.

Cravey, Altha. 1998. *Women and Work in Mexico's Maquiladoras*. Lanham, Md.: Rowman and Littlefield.

Cruz Piñeiro, Rudolfo. 1990. "Mercados de trabajo y migración en la frontera: Tijuana, Ciudad Juárez, Nuevo Laredo." *Frontera Norte* 2 (4): 61–93.

Davies, Scott. 1990. "Inserting Gender into Burawoy's Theory of the Labor Process." *Work, Employment and Society* 4 (3): 391–406.

De la O Martínez, María Eugenia. 1991. "Reconversión industrial en la industria maquiladora electrónica: Cuatro estudios de caso participación femenina en Ciudad Juárez, Chihuahua." Unpublished manuscript, Tijuana.

———. 1997. "Y Por eso Se Llaman Maquilas . . . La configuración de las relaciones laborales en la modernización: Cuatro estudios de plantas electrónicas en Ciudad Juárez." Ph.D. dissertation, Colegio de México, Mexico City.

De la Rosa Hickerson, Gustavo. 1979. "La contratación colectiva en las maquiladoras: Analisis de un caso de sobreexplotación." Professional thesis, Universidad Autónoma, Escuela de Derecho, Ciudad Juárez.

Desarrollo Económico de Ciudad Juárez. 1991. *Ciudad Juárez en cifras.* Ciudad Juárez: Desarrollo Económico.

Edwards, Richard. 1979. *Contested Terrain: The Transformation of the Workplace in the Twentieth Century.* New York: Basic Books.

Elson, Diane, and Ruth Pearson. 1981. "The Subordination of Women and the Internationalization of Factory Production." In *Of Marriage and the Market: Women's Subordination in International Perspective,* edited by Kate Young, Carol Wolkowitz, and Roslyn McCullagh, 144–166. London: CSE Books.

———. 1986. "Third World Manufacturing." In *Waged Work: A Reader,* edited by Feminist Review, 67–92. London: Virago.

Enloe, Cynthia. 1989. *Bananas, Beaches and Bases: Making Feminist Sense of International Politics.* Berkeley: University of California Press.

Farnsworth-Alvear, Ann. 1997. "Talking, Fighting, Flirting: Workers' Sociability in Medellín Textile Mills, 1935–1950." In *The Gendered Worlds of Latin American Women Workers: From Household and Factory to the Union Hall and Ballot Box,* edited by John French and Daniel James, 147–175. Durham: Duke University Press.

Fernández-Kelly, María Patricia. 1983. *For We Are Sold, I and My People: Women and Industry in Mexico's Frontier.* Albany: State University of New York Press.

Fligstein, Neil. 1990. *The Transformation of Corporate Control.* Cambridge: Harvard University Press.

Foucault, Michel. 1972. *The Archaeology of Knowledge.* New York: Pantheon.

———. 1977. "Nietzsche, Genealogy, History." In *Language, Counter-Memory and Practice: Selected Essays and Interviews,* edited by Donald Bouchard, 139–164. Ithaca: Cornell University Press.

———. 1979. *Discipline and Punish: The Birth of the Prison.* New York: Vintage Books.

———. 1982. "The Subject and Power." In *Michel Foucault: Beyond Structuralism and Hermeneutics,* edited by Hubert Dreyfus and Paul Rabinow, 208–226. Chicago: University of Chicago Press.

Fraser, Nancy. 1992. "The Uses and Abuses of French Discourse Theory for Feminist Politics." In *Revaluing French Feminism,* edited by Nancy Fraser and Sandra Lee Bartky, 177–194. Cambridge: Cambridge University Press.

Freeman, Carla. 2000. *High Tech and High Heels in the Global Economy.* Durham: Duke University Press.

Freire, Paolo. 1971. *Pedagogy of the Oppressed.* London: Herder and Herder.

Fröbel, Folker, Jurgen Heinrichs, and Otto Kreye. 1980. *The New International Division of Labor: Structural Unemployment in Industrialized Countries and Industrialization in Developing Countries.* Cambridge: Cambridge University Press.

Fuentes, Annette, and Barbara Ehrenreich. 1983. *Women in the Global Factory.* Boston: South End Press.

Gal, Susan, and Gail Kligman. 2000. *The Politics of Gender after Socialism: A Comparative Historical Essay.* Princeton: Princeton University Press.

Gambrill, Mónica. 1981. "Composición y conciencia de la fuerza de trabajo en las maquiladoras: Resultados de una encuesta y algunas hipótesis interpretivas." In *La frontera del norte*, edited by Roque González Salazar, 106–124. Mexico City: Colegio de México.

———. 1986. "Sindicalismo en las maquiladoras de Tijuana: Regresión en las prestaciones sociales." In *Reestructuración industrial: Maquiladoras en la frontera México-Estados Unidos*, edited by Jorge Carrillo, 183–220. Mexico City: Consejo Nacional de Fomento Educativo.

———. 1988. "Las maquiladoras: Política salarial." In *Viejos desafíos, nuevas perspectivas: México, Estados Unidos y América*, edited by Raúl Benítez Manaut, 131–156. Mexico City: UNAM, Coordinación de Humanidades.

Gordon, David, Richard Edwards, and Michael Reich. 1982. *Segmented Work, Divided Workers: The Historical Transformation of Labor in the United States*. Cambridge: Cambridge University Press.

Gottfried, Heidi, and Laurie Graham. 1993. "Constructing Difference: The Making of Gendered Subcultures in a Japanese Automobile Assembly Plant." *Sociology* 27 (4): 611–628.

Grewal, Inderpal, and Caren Kaplan. 1994. *Scattered Hegemonies: Postmodernity and Transnational Feminist Practices*. Minneapolis: University of Minnesota Press.

Guiffre, Patty, and Christine Williams. 1994. "Boundary Lines: Labeling Sexual Harassment in Restaurants." *Gender and Society* 8 (3): 378–401.

Gutmann, Matthew. 1994. "The Meanings of Macho: Changing Mexican Male Identities." *Masculinities* 2 (1): 21–33.

———. 1996. *The Meanings of Macho: Being a Man in Mexico City*. Berkeley: University of California Press.

Halle, David. 1984. *America's Working Man: Work, Home, and Politics among Blue-Collar Property Owners*. Chicago: University of Chicago Press.

Haraway, Donna. 1983. "A Manifesto for Cyborgs: Science, Technology, and Socialist Feminism in the 1980's." *Socialist Review* 80: 65–107.

———. 1988. "Situated Knowledges: The Science Question in Feminism as a Site of Discourse on the Privilege of Partial Perspective." *Feminist Studies* 14 (3): 575–599.

Hartmann, Heidi. 1976. "Capitalism, Patriarchy and Job Segregation by Sex." *Signs* 1 (3/2): 137–169.

———. 1981. "The Unhappy Marriage of Marxism and Feminism." In *Women and Revolution*, edited by Lydia Sargent, 1–41. Boston: South End Press.

Harvey, David. 1990. *The Condition of Postmodernity*. Cambridge: Blackwell.

Hochschild, Arlie. 1997. *The Time Bind: When Work Becomes Home and Home Becomes Work*. New York: Metropolitan Books.

hooks, bell. 1984. *Feminist Theory: From Margin to Center*. Boston: South End Press.

Hossfeld, Karen. 1990. "'Their Logic against Them': Contradictions in Sex, Race and Class in Silicon Valley." In *Women Workers and Global Restructuring*, edited by Kathryn Ward, 149–178. Ithaca: ILR Press.

Iglesias Prieto, Norma. 1985. *La flor más bella de la maquiladora*. Mexico City: Secretaría de Educación Pública and Centro de Estudios Fronterizos del Norte de México.

Ingraham, Chrys. 1994. "The Heterosexual Imaginary: Feminist Sociology and Theories of Gender." *Sociological Theory* 12 (2): 203–219.

Instituto Nacional de Estadística, Geografía e Informática (INEGI). 1990. *Estadística de la industria maquiladora de exportación, 1975–1988*. Mexico City: INEGI.

———. 1991. *Estadística de la industria maquiladora de exportación, 1979–1989*. Mexico City: INEGI.

———. 1996. *Estadística de la industria maquiladora de exportación, 1990–1995*. Mexico City: INEGI.

Irvine, Judith, and Susan Gal. 2000. "Language Ideology and Linguistic Differentiation." In *Regimes of Language: Ideologies, Politics, and Identities*, edited by Paul Kroskrity, 35–83. Santa Fe: School of American Research Press.

Jiménez Betancourt, Rubí. 1989. "Participación femenina en la industria maquiladora: Cambios recientes." In *Fuerza de trabajo femenina urbana en México*, 2d ed., edited by Jennifer Cooper, Teresita de Barbarieri, Teresa Rendón, Estela Juárez, and Esperanza Tuñon, 393–424. Mexico City: UNAM.

Joekes, Susan. 1985. "Working for Lipstick? Male and Female Labor in the Clothing Industry in Morocco." In *Women, Work and Ideology in the Third World*, edited by Haleh Afshar, 183–213. London: Tavistock.

Kamel, Rachel. 1990. *The Global Factory: Analysis and Action for a New Economic Era*. Philadelphia: American Friends Service Committee.

Kamel, Rachel, and Anya Hoffman. 1999. *The Maquiladora Reader: Cross-Border Organizing since NAFTA*. Philadelphia: American Friends Service Committee.

Kessler-Harris, Alice. 1990. *A Woman's Wage: Historical Meanings and Social Consequences*. Lexington: University Press of Kentucky.

Kimmel, Michael. 1994. "Masculinity as Homophobia: Fear, Shame, and Silence in the Construction of Gender Identity." In *Theorizing Masculinities*, edited by Harry Brod and Michael Kaufman, 119–141. Thousand Oaks: Sage.

Knights, David. 1990. "Subjectivity, Power and the Labor Process." In *Labor Process Theory*, edited by David Knights and Hugh Willmott, 297–335. London: Macmillan.

Knights, David, and Hugh Willmott. 1989. "Power and Subjectivity at Work: From Degradation to Subjugation in Social Relations." *Sociology* 23 (4): 535–558.

Kondo, Dorinne. 1990. *Crafting Selves: Power, Gender, and Discourses of Identity in a Japanese Workplace*. Chicago: University of Chicago Press.

Kopinak, Kathryn. 1989. "Living the Gospel through Service to the Poor: The Convergence of Political and Religious Motivations in Organizing Maquiladora Workers in Juárez, Mexico." *Socialist Studies: A Canadian Annual* 5: 217–245.

————. 1995. "Gender as a Vehicle for the Subordination of Mexican Women Maquiladora Workers in Mexico." *Latin American Perspectives* 22 (1): 30–48.

Kunda, Gideon. 1992. *Engineering Culture: Control and Commitment in a High-Tech Corporation*. Philadelphia: Temple University Press.

Lauretis, Teresa de. 1987. "The Technology of Gender." In *Technologies of Gender: Essays on Theory, Film and Fiction*, edited by Teresa de Lauretis, 1–30. Bloomington: Indiana University Press.

Lee, Ching Kwan. 1995. "Engendering the Worlds of Labor: Women Workers, Labor Markets, and Production in the South China Economic Miracle." *American Sociological Review* 60: 378–397.

————. 1998. *Gender and the South China Miracle: Two Worlds of Factory Women*. Berkeley: University of California Press.

Leidner, Robin. 1993. *Fast Food, Fast Talk: Service Work and the Routinization of Everyday Life*. Berkeley: University of California Press.

Lie, John. 2001. *Multiethnic Japan*. Cambridge: Harvard University Press.

Lim, Linda. 1983. "Capitalism, Imperialism, and Patriarchy: The Dilemma of Third-World Women Workers in Multinational Factories." In *Women, Men and the International Division of Labor*, edited by June Nash and María Patricia Fernández-Kelly, 70–91. Albany: State University of New York Press.

Loe, Meika. 1996. "Working for Men—At the Intersection of Power, Gender, and Sexuality," *Sociological Inquiry* 66 (4): 399–421.

Lown, Judy. 1990. *Women and Industrialization: Gender at Work in Nineteenth-Century England*. Minneapolis: University of Minnesota Press.

Lugo, Alejandro. 1990. "Cultural Production and Reproduction in Ciudad Juárez, Mexico: Tropes at Play among Maquiladora Workers." *Cultural Anthropology* 5 (2): 173–196.

Lutz, Nancy Melissa. 1988. "Images of Docility: Asian Women and the World Economy." In *Racism, Sexism and the World-System*, edited by Joan Smith et al., 57–73. New York: Greenwood.

MacKinnon, Catherine. 1982. "Feminism, Marxism, Method and the State: An Agenda for Theory," *Signs* 7 (3): 515–544.

Marcus, George. 1998. *Ethnography through Thick and Thin*. Princeton: Princeton University Press.

Martínez, Oscar. 1978. *Border Boom Town: Ciudad Juárez since 1848*. Austin: University of Texas Press.

Massey, Doreen. 1994. "Flexible Sexism." In *Space, Place and Gender*, 212–248. Minneapolis: University of Minnesota Press.

Mies, Maria. 1986. *Patriarchy and Accumulation on a World Scale: Women in the International Division of Labor*. London: Zed Books.

Milkman, Ruth. 1987. *Gender at Work: The Dynamics of Job Segregation by Sex during World War II*. Urbana: University of Illinois Press.

Morrill, Calvin. 1995. *The Executive Way: Conflict Management in Corporations*. Chicago: University of Chicago Press.

Mulvey, Laura. 1975. "Visual Pleasure and Narrative Cinema." *Screen* 16 (3): 6–18.

Nader, Laura. 1999 [1969]. "Up the Anthropologist—Perspectives Gained from Studying Up." In *Reinventing Anthropology,* edited by Dell Hymes, 284–311. Ann Arbor: University of Michigan Press.

Nash, June, and Maria Patricia Fernández-Kelly. 1983. *Women, Men and the International Division of Labor.* Albany: State University of New York.

Nicholson, Linda. 1995. "Interpreting Gender." In *Social Postmodernism: Beyond Identity Politics,* edited by Linda Nicholson and Steven Seidman, 39–67. Cambridge: Cambridge University Press.

Ong, Aihwa. 1987. *Spirits of Resistance and Capitalist Discipline.* Albany: State University of New York Press.

———. 1990. "Japanese Factories, Malay Workers: Class and Sexual Metaphors in West Malaysia." In *Power and Difference: Gender in Island Southeast Asia,* edited by Jane Monnig Atkinson and Shelly Errington, 385–422. Stanford: Stanford University Press.

———. 1991. "The Gender and Labor Politics of Postmodernity." *Annual Review of Anthropology* 20: 279–309.

Ortner, Sherry. 1989. "Gender Hegemonies." *Cultural Critique* 14: 35–80.

Ortner, Sherry, and Harriet Whitehead. 1981. *Sexual Meanings: The Cultural Construction of Gender and Sexuality.* Cambridge: Cambridge University Press.

Parker, Mike, and Jane Slaughter. 1988. *Choosing Sides: Unions and the Team Concept.* Boston: South End Press.

Paz, Octavio. 1950. *El laberinto de la soledad.* Mexico City: Fondo de Cultura Económica.

Pearson, Ruth. 1986. "Female Workers in the First and Third Worlds: The Greening of Women's Labor." In *The Changing Experience of Employment,* edited by K. Purcell et al., 449–466. London: Macmillan and the British Sociological Association.

———. 1991. "Male Bias and Women's Work in Mexico's Border Industries." In *Male Bias in the Development Process,* edited by Diane Elson, 133–163. Manchester: Manchester University Press.

Peña, Devon. 1997. *The Terror of the Machine: Technology, Work, Gender, and Ecology on the US-Mexican Border.* Austin: University of Texas Press.

Pierce, Jennifer. 1995. *Gender Trials: Emotional Lives in Contemporary Law Firms.* Berkeley: University of California Press.

Piore, Michael, and Charles Sabel. 1984. *The Second Industrial Divide: Possibilities for Prosperity.* New York: Basic Books, 1984.

Quintero Ramírez, Cirila. 1990. *La sindicalizacíon en las maquiladoras tijuanenses, 1970–1988.* Mexico City: Consejo Nacional para la Cultura y las Artes.

———. 1992. "Reestructuración sindical y mujer trabajadora en las maquiladoras fronterizas." Paper presented at the II Semana de la Mujer, Matamoros, Mexico.

Reygadas, Luis. 1992. *Un rostro moderno de la pobreza: Problemática social de las*

trabajadoras de las maquiladoras de Chihuahua. Chihuahua: Ediciones Go-
bierno de Estado de Chihuahua.

Riley, Denise. 1988. *"Am I that Name?" Feminism and the Category of "Women"
in History*. Minneapolis: University of Minnesota.

Rofel, Lisa. 1992. "Rethinking Modernity: Space and Factory Discipline in
China." *Cultural Anthropology* 7 (1): 93–114.

Rogers, Jackie, and Kevin Henson. 1997. "'Hey, Why Don't You Wear a Shorter
Skirt?' Structural Vulnerability and the Organization of Sexual Harassment
in Temporary Clerical Employment." *Gender and Society* 11 (2): 215–237.

Rose, Sonya. 1992. *Limited Livelihoods: Gender and Class in Nineteenth-Century
England*. Berkeley: University of California Press.

Rosenbaum, Ruth. 1994. *Market Basket Survey: A Comparison of the Buying
Power of Maquiladora Workers in Mexico and UAW Assembly Workers in GM
Plants in the US*. San Antonio: Coalition for Justice in the Maquiladoras.

Rubin, Gayle. 1975. "The Traffic in Women: Notes on the 'Political Economy'
of Sex." In *Toward an Anthropology of Women*, edited by Rayna Reiter, 157–
210. New York: Monthly Review Press.

Safa, Helen. 1986. "Runaway Shops and Female Employment: The Search for
Cheap Labor." In *Women's Work: Development and the Division of Labor by
Gender*, edited by Eleanor Leacock and Helen Safa, 58–71. South Hadley,
Mass.: Bergin and Garvey.

Salzinger, Leslie. 1997. "From High Heels to Swathed Bodies: Gendered Meanings under Production in Mexico's Export-Processing Industry." *Feminist
Studies* 43 (3): 549–574.

———. 1998. "Gender under Production: Constituting Subjects in Mexico's
Global Factories." Ph.D. Dissertation, University of California, Berkeley.

———. 2000. "Manufacturing Sexual Subjects: 'Harassment,' Desire and Discipline on a Maquiladora Shopfloor." *Ethnography* 1 (1): 67–92.

Santiago, Guadalupe, and Hugo Almada Mireles. 1991. *Condiciones actuales de
trabajo en la industria maquiladora de Ciudad Juárez*. Ciudad Juárez: Centro de Estudios Regionales y Comunicación Alternativa (CERCA).

Sassen, Saskia. 1988. *The Mobility of Labor and Capital*. Cambridge: Cambridge
University Press.

———. 1991. *The Global City*. Princeton: Princeton University Press.

———. 1998a. "Notes on the Incorporation of Third World Women into Wage
Labor through Immigration and Offshore Production." In *Globalization
and Its Discontents*, 111–131. New York: New Press.

———. 1998b. "Toward a Feminist Analytics of the Global Economy." In *Globalization and Its Discontents*, 81–110. New York: New Press.

Sayer, Andrew, and Richard Walker. 1992. *The New Social Economy: Reworking
the Division of Labor*. Oxford: Basil Blackwell.

Scheper-Hughes, Nancy. 1992. *Death without Weeping: The Violence of Everyday
Life in Brazil*. Berkeley: University of California Press.

Scott, Joan. 1988a. "Deconstructing Equality-Versus-Difference: Or, The Uses
of Poststructuralist Theory for Feminism," *Feminist Studies* 14 (1): 33–50.

———. 1988b. *Gender and the Politics of History*. New York: Columbia University Press.

Sewell, William H. Jr. 1996. "The Concept(s) of Culture." In *Beyond the Cultural Turn: New Directions in the Study of Society and Culture,* edited by Victoria Bonnell and Lynn Hunt, 35–61. Berkeley: University of California Press.

Shaiken, Harley. 1990. *Mexico in the Global Economy: High Technology and Work Organization in Export Industries.* San Diego: Center for U.S.-Mexican Studies, UCSD.

———. 1994. "Advanced Manufacturing and Mexico: A New International Division of Labor." *Latin American Research Review* 29 (3): 39–71.

Shaiken, Harley, and Stephen Herzenberg. 1987. *Automation and Global Production: Automobile Engine Production in Mexico, the United States, and Canada.* San Diego: Center for U.S.-Mexican Studies, UCSD.

Sklair, Leslie. 1993. *Assembling for Development: The Maquila Industry in Mexico and the United States.* San Diego: Center for U.S.-Mexican Studies, UCSD.

Smith, Vicki. 1990. *Managing in the Corporate Interest: Control and Resistance in an American Bank.* Berkeley: University of California Press.

———. 1997. "New Forms of Work Organization." *Annual Review of Sociology* 23: 315–339.

Spelman, Elizabeth. 1988. *Inessential Woman: Problems of Exclusion in Feminist Thought.* Boston: Beacon Press.

Standing, Guy. 1989. "Global Feminization through Flexible Labor." *World Development* 17 (7): 1077–1095.

Steedman, Carolyn. 1987. *Landscape for a Good Woman.* New Brunswick: Rutgers University Press.

Steele, Valerie. 1985. *Fashion and Eroticism: Ideals of Feminine Beauty from the Victorian Era to the Jazz Age.* New York: Oxford University Press.

Stevens, Evelyn. 1973. "Marianismo: The Other Face of Machismo in Latin America." In *Male and Female in Latin America,* edited by Ann Pescatello, 89–101. Pittsburgh: University of Pittsburgh Press.

Taylor, Frederick. 1911. *The Principles of Scientific Management.* New York: Harper and Brothers.

Tiano, Susan. 1987a. "Maquiladoras in Mexicali: Integration or Exploitation?" In *Women on the US-Mexico Border: Responses to Change,* edited by Vicki Ruiz and Susan Tiano, 77–102. Boston: Allen and Unwin.

———. 1987b. "Women's Work and Unemployment in Northern Mexico." In *Women on the US-Mexico Border: Responses to Change,* edited by Vicki Ruiz and Susan Tiano, 17–39. Boston: Allen and Unwin.

———. 1994. *Patriarchy on the Line: Labor, Gender and Ideology in the Mexican Maquila Industry.* Philadelphia: Temple University Press.

Van Maanen, John. 2001. "Natives 'R' Us: Some Notes on the Ethnography of Organizations." In *Inside Organizations: Anthropologists at Work,* edited by David Gellner and Eric Hirsch, 233–261. Oxford and New York: Berg.

Van Waas, Michael. 1981. "The Multinational's Strategy for Labor: Foreign Assembly Plants in Mexico's Border Industrialization Program." PhD. dissertation, Stanford University.

———. 1982. "Multinational Corporations and the Politics of Labor Supply." *The Insurgent Sociologist* 11 (3): 49–57.

Vera, Beatríz. n.d. "Informe preliminar." Unpublished manuscript, Ciudad Juárez.

Vila, Pablo. 2000. *Crossing Borders, Reinforcing Borders: Social Categories, Metaphors and Narrative Identities on the U.S.-Mexico Frontier.* Austin: University of Texas Press.

———. 2003. "Gender and the Overlapping of Region, Nation and Ethnicity on the U.S.-Mexico Border." In *Border Ethnographies*, edited by Pablo Vila. Minneapolis: University of Minnesota Press.

Williams, Christine. 1997. "Sexual Harassment in Organizations: A Critique of Current Research and Policy." *Sexuality and Culture* 1: 19–43.

Willis, Paul. 1979. "Shop Floor Culture, Masculinity and the Wage Form." In *Working Class Culture*, edited by J. Clarke, C. Critcher, and R. Johnson, 185–198. London: Hutchinson.

Willmott, Hugh. 1987. "Studying Managerial Work: A Critique and a Proposal." *Journal of Management Studies* 24 (3): 249–270.

Wilson, Patricia Ann. 1990. "The New Maquiladoras: Flexible Production in Low-wage Regions." In *The Maquiladora Industry: Economic Solution or Problem?* edited by Khosrow Fatemi, 135–158. New York: Praeger.

Wittig, Monique. 1992a. "The Mark of Gender." In *The Straight Mind*, 76–89. Boston: Beacon Press.

———. 1992b. "The Point of View: Universal or Particular." In *The Straight Mind*, 59–67. Boston: Beacon Press.

Wolf, Diane. 1990. "Daughters, Decisions and Domination: An Empirical and Conceptual Critique of Household Strategies." *Development and Change* 21: 43–74.

Wright, Melissa. 1997. "Crossing the Factory Frontier: Gender, Place and Power in a Mexican Maquiladora." *Antipode* 29 (3): 278–296.

———. 2001. "Desire and the Prosthetics of Supervision: A Case of Maquiladora Flexibility." *Cultural Anthropology* 16 (3): 354–374.

Yelvington, Kevin. 1995. *Producing Power: Ethnicity, Gender, and Class in a Caribbean Workplace.* Philadelphia: Temple University Press.

Young, Gay, and Beatriz Vera. 1984. "Extensive Evaluation of Centro de Orientación de la Mujer Obrera, A.C. in Ciudad Juárez." Unpublished manuscript, Inter-American Foundation, Ciudad Juárez.

———. 1992. "Women, Work and Households in Ciudad Juárez." Unpublished manuscript, Asociación de Maquiladoras, A.C., Ciudad Juárez.

Yudelman, Sally. 1987. *Hopeful Openings: A Study of Five Women's Development Organizations in Latin America and the Caribbean.* West Hartford: Kumarian Press.

Index

advertisements: for female workers, 37, 45, 49, 133–34, 143; for male workers, 45–46; by third-world states, 154

agricultural workers, 36, 90. *See also* rural areas

Althusser, Louis, 176n31, 176–77n38, 177n44

AMAC (maquiladora industry association), 43, 183n87

American Friends Service Committee (AFSC), 175n19, 195n31

Anarchomex (pseud., auto parts plant): Andromex compared to, 122, 151, 161–62, 194n23; distant type of manager at, 129–36, 139–40; failure of, 128–29; fieldwork at, 6, 130, 138, 173–74n8, 193n15; gay male workers at, 37; gender contentions at, 49, 142–51; hiring at, 132–35, 192n5, 192n11; masculinity defined at, 135–36; overview of, 32–33; Particimex compared to, 130–31, 137, 159–61; physical structure of, 132, 136–37; possible organizing at, 167; production as meaningless at, 136–42; products of, 128; promotions at, 130, 139; sexualization at, 146–51; wages at, 130, 135, 138–39, 192n3; work defined as manly at, 143–46; work rhythm in, 140–41

Andromex (pseud., hospital garments plant): Anarchomex compared to, 122, 151, 161–62, 194n23; costs of,

108–9; description of, 111–12; fieldwork at, 7, 112, 173–74n8, 191nn26–27; fighting as stylized and prized in, 189n4; gender obscured at, 121–25; hegemonic regime in, 102, 103–4, 189n4, 190n9; male workers hired at, 44–45; masculinization at, 49, 101–11, 122, 124–27; mastering work at, 111–13; material shortages at, 113–16; overview of, 31–32, 100–101; Panoptimex compared to, 106; promotions at, 107; respect at, 118–21; standards at, 116–18; strike at, 102–5; unions' conflict at, 41, 181–82n45; wages at, 106–7, 189n5; women's teasing of male workers at, 183n80

appearance: at Anarchomex, 145, 148; at Andromex, 101, 104, 111, 122–23; local understandings of, 123; of Mexican managers, 109; objectification and, 1–2, 70–73; at Panoptimex, 5–6, 30, 51, 53–59, 64, 70–73, 74; at Particimex, 82, 85

Arthur D. Little report, 36

assembly work: feminization of, 11, 100–101, 155–57, 184nn98–99, 189n1; gender distinctions downplayed in, 137; manufacturing vs., 26, 100–101, 125–26; as meaningless, 136–42; monitoring of, 140–42; quality control and, 175–76n24; teamwork in, 31, 83–88, 188n18; as women's

209

Indexer: Margie Towery
Compositor: G&S Typesetters, Inc.
Text: 10/13 Galliard
Display: Galliard
Printer and Binder: Malloy Lithographing, Inc.